RAPID
TESTING

ISBN 0-13-091294-8

90000

9 780130 912947

Software Quality Institute Series

The Software Quality Institute Series is a partnership between the Software Quality Institute (SQI) at The University of Texas at Austin and Prentice Hall Professional Technical Reference (PHPTR). The books discuss real-life problems and offer strategies for improving software quality and software business practices.

Each publication is written by highly skilled, experienced practitioners who understand and can help solve the problems facing software professionals. SQI series topic areas include software development practices and technologies, management of software organizations, integration of high-quality software into other industries, business issues with reference to software quality, and related areas of interest.

TITLES IN THE SOFTWARE QUALITY INSTITUTE SERIES

RAPID
TESTING

Robert Culbertson

Chris Brown

Gary Cobb

Prentice Hall PTR
Upper Saddle River, NJ 07458
www.phptr.com

A CIP catalogue record for this book can be obtained from the Library of Congress.

Editorial/Production Supervision: *Jessica Balch (Pine Tree Composition)*
Project Coordinator: *Anne R. Garcia*
Acquisitions Editor: *Paul Petralia*
Marketing Manager: *Debby Van Dijk*
Manufacturing Manager: *Alexis Heydt-Long*
Editorial Assistant: *Richard Winkler*
Cover Design: *Nina Scuderi*
Interior Design: *Wee Design Group*

 © 2002 by Prentice Hall PTR
Prentice-Hall, Inc.
Upper Saddle River, NJ 07458

For permission to use copyrighted material, grateful acknowledgment is made to copyright holders on p. 384, which is hereby made part of this copyright page.

Prentice Hall books are widely used by corporations and government
agencies for training, marketing, and resale.

The publisher offers discounts on this book when ordered in bulk quantities.
For more information, contact: Corporate Sales Department, Phone: 800-382-3419;
Fax: 201-236-7141; E-mail: corpsales@prenhall.com; or write: Prentice Hall PTR,
Corp. Sales Dept., One Lake Street, Upper Saddle River, NJ 07458.

Printed in the United States of America

10 9 8 7 6 5 4 3 2 1

ISBN 0-13-091294-8

Pearson Education LTD.
Pearson Education Australia PTY, Limited
Pearson Education Singapore, Pte. Ltd.
Pearson Education North Asia Ltd.
Pearson Education Canada, Ltd.
Pearson Educación de Mexico, S.A. de C.V.
Pearson Education—Japan
Pearson Education Malaysia, Pte. Ltd.

Contents

Chapter 10

Dynamic Testing Techniques and Tips   *207*

Preface

This book presents a practical approach to software testing, placing emphasis on a test process that is geared to today's aggressive pace of software development. It is designed for use by practicing test engineers and test managers, and includes tips, techniques, and examples that can be used to improve the efficiency and speed of software testing. The book should also be suitable for people who are beginning a career in software testing. It includes an extensive set of references that are intended to support established test professionals as well as those just starting out.

The speed and efficiency of software testing depends how well the test process integrates with the overall development life cycle and upon the efficiency of the test techniques used. This book shows how to improve the speed and efficiency of your testing effort by focusing on three areas:

- Beginning the testing life cycle simultaneously with the project's requirements phase, so that bugs can be caught as early as possible and so test planning and test case development can start as soon as possible.
- Presenting efficient static testing techniques such as inspections and walkthroughs that can be used to test work products that are generated during the development life cycle.
- Presenting efficient dynamic testing techniques that can be used to find bugs during integration, system, and acceptance test phases.

Key Features

The following features of this book are intended to help you improve your software testing efficiency:

- An emphasis is placed on tailoring the test processes to meet aggressive time-to-market goals without sacrificing product quality.

- Software testing is placed in the context of the overall software development life cycle. The development life cycle is viewed from the vantage point of the test engineer. Development models such as evolutionary prototyping and spiral development models are considered, as well as the traditional waterfall.

- Static testing techniques are presented that can be used to get the test team involved early in the development life cycle. Static testing will find bugs early in the life of the product and will allow you to define test plans and test cases as soon as possible.

- Includes examples of key work products of the test process.

How the Book is Organized

This book consists of three parts that are organized as follows:

Part I.   The Rapid Testing Process—This part defines the basic concepts and terms related to software testing. It describes rapid testing processes that are closely integrated with the overall software development life cycle. The traditional waterfall development model is considered, as well as life cycles based on incremental delivery and evolutionary prototyping. Each phase of the software development process is examined from the viewpoint of the software test engineer, and methods of bug detection and prevention are described as means of improving test efficiency.

Part II.   Rapid Testing Techniques and Tips—This part describes in detail the tips and techniques that can be used to develop a rapid test process. Methods are presented for eliciting and analyzing requirements, estimating and scheduling the test effort, conducting inspections and reviews, designing black box tests, and reporting test results. A variety of dynamic testing methodologies are discussed, including functional analysis, equivalence partitioning, boundary value analysis, testing for memory leaks, use-case testing, and performance tests.

Part III.   Rapid Testing Examples—Part III contains a set of examples for the process and techniques discussed in the first two parts of the book. The examples are based on the Test Management Toolkit (TMT), which is a pedagogical application that allows test managers and engineers to manage test plans, bug reports, test results, and other information related to software testing. It is a web-based application that permits several users, even when geographically dispersed, to support one or more test projects simultaneously.

There are examples of four key work products related to the test process:

- Requirements Definition
- Test Plan
- Test Procedure Specification
- Test Summary Report

About the Authors

Robert Culbertson has over 25 years of experience in engineering, software development, software testing, and project management. In work at Cisco Systems, Texas Instruments, IBM, the University of Texas, and DSC Communications, he has experienced first hand the subjects presented in Rapid Testing. Robert has B.S.E.E. and M.S.E.E. degrees from the University of Texas at Austin, and a Ph.D. in electrical and electronic engineering from the University of Birmingham in England.

Gary Cobb has pursued a dual career of teaching and working in industry in the Austin area over the last 25 years. He has taught in the University of Texas at Austin Departments of Mathematics, Computer Science, and Electrical and Computer Engineering. He has also taught multimedia courses for the Department of Computer Science at Southwest Texas State University, where he was the Director of the Multimedia Laboratory. His industrial experience includes full-time employment at Texas Instruments Inc., Lockheed Martin, and Dell Computer Corporation. He teaches short courses for the University of Texas' Software Quality Institute, which also sponsored his development of the Software Criteria for the Greater Austin Quality Award. Gary has a Ph.D. in mathematics from the University of Texas in Austin.

Chris Brown has over 20 years experience in the software and computer industry. He has worked in various testing roles at Advanced Micro Devices, Cisco Systems, Compaq Computer Corporation, and IBM. At AMD he was responsible for systems level silicon validation and compatibility testing of all available hardware and software configurations. At Compaq he was responsible for scripting and testing of prototype and pilot computer systems for the Portable Products Computing Division. Chris was the team lead for OS/2 Database Manager, Communications Manager, LAN Transport and LAN Manager defect support while at IBM. He was President/CEO of Computer Security Corporation, a company that sold virus protection software to the United States Air Force, Prudential, Boeing, and other major companies and labs. He also served as a Regional Manager and Vice President at Dataserv Computer Maintenance/BellSouth, where he was responsible for field maintenance of over 40,000 computers. Chris has a Bachelor of Science degree in Electrical Engineering and an MBA.

Acknowledgments

The authors are indebted to Al Dale, founder of the Software Quality Institute (SQI), for his support of this book and the entire SQI book series. We also wish to thank Paul Petralia for his encouragement and support throughout the writing and production process. Thanks also go to the capable members of the SQI and Prentice Hall teams for their constant support and professional help. Jessica Balch and the production team at Pine Tree Composition did an excellent job of bringing the book to life, and it was a pleasure working with them.

Robert Culbertson wishes to acknowledge his family—Terri, Shelley, and Michael—who encouraged Dad and who gave up countless hours of family time in support of this project. Robert thanks his mom, Lorene, and brother, Lawrence, for their unfailing support. Robert is also grateful to all the managers, engineers, and teachers who have served as mentors and colleagues throughout the years. In particular, thanks go to Bob Marinconz, Mark Sherwood, Mark Schnucker, Karen Boyd, Mark Scafidi, Loy Dossman, John Whitworth, Arthur Holly, Orhan Berktay, Tom Muir, and David Blackstock.

Gary Cobb thanks his wife, Marilyn, for her patience and support during the long hours dedicated to writing his portion of this book. He also thanks their children, Glen Cobb, Molly Pierson, Stephen Cobb, and Meredith McLarty for their support. For the people who have had significant impact on Gary's career, he wants to thank his parents, J. D. and Mary Louise Cobb and the following teachers and professionals: Dr. W. T. Guy, Dr. H. S. Wall, Dr. Herbert Woodson, Dr. Roger Bate, L. C. Craig, Joanne Click, Ed Martin, Jim Nelson, and Mike Crosby.

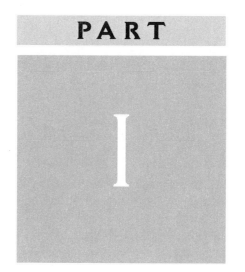

PART

I

The Rapid Testing Process

Introduction to Rapid Testing

Topics Covered in the Chapter

- Basic Definitions for Software Testing
- What is Rapid Testing?
- Developing a Rapid Testing Strategy
- The Software Development Process
- A Waterfall Test Process
- Tying Testing and Development Together
- What's Next
- References

Over the past two decades, computer systems and the software that runs them have made their way into all aspects of life. Software is present in our cars, ovens, cell phones, games, and workplaces. It drives billing systems, communications systems, and Internet connections. The proliferation of software systems has reached the point that corporate and national economies are increasingly dependent on the successful development and delivery of software.

As the stakes grow higher in the software marketplace, pressure grows to develop more products at a faster pace. This places increasing demands on software developers and on software testers not only to produce faster, but also to make products that are of good enough quality that the customer will be satisfied with them.

There are therefore two major demands placed on today's software test engineer:

- We need to test quickly to meet aggressive product delivery schedules.
- We need to test well enough that damaging defects don't escape to our customers.

The challenge is to satisfy each of these needs without sacrificing the other. The purpose of this book is to define an efficient test process and to present practical techniques that satisfy both demands. We begin by examining the fundamentals of software development and software testing.

Basic Definitions for Software Testing

Before launching into a discussion of the software development process, let's define some basic terms and concepts. The logical place to start is with software testing.

Software testing is a process of analyzing or operating software for the purpose of finding bugs.

Simple as this definition is, it contains a few points that are worth elaboration. The word *process* is used to emphasize that testing involves planned, orderly activities. This point is important if we're concerned with rapid development, as a well thought-out, systematic approach is likely to find bugs faster than poorly planned testing done in a rush.

According to the definition, testing can involve either "analyzing" or "operating" software. Test activities that are associated with analyzing the products of software development are called *static testing*. Static testing includes code inspections, walkthroughs, and desk checks. In contrast, test activities that involve operating the software are called *dynamic testing*. Static and dynamic testing complement one another, and each type has a unique approach to detecting bugs.

The final point to consider in the definition of software testing is the meaning of "bugs." In simple terms, a *bug* is a flaw in the development of the software that causes a discrepancy between the expected result of an operation and the actual result. The bug could be a coding problem, a problem in the requirements or the design, or it could be a configuration or data problem. It could also be something that is at variance with the customer's expectation, which may or may not be in the product specifications. More details about the terminology of bugs is given in Sidebar 1.1.

SIDEBAR 1.1

THE LIFE OF A BUG

The life of a software bug may be described as follows. A bug is born when a person makes an *error* in some activity that relates to software development, such as defining a requirement, designing a program, or writing code. This error gets embedded in that person's work product (requirement document, design document, or code) as a *fault*.

As long as this fault (also known as a *bug* or *defect*) remains in the work product, it can give rise to other bugs. For example, if a fault in a requirements document goes undetected, it is likely to lead to related bugs in the system design, program design, code, and even in the user documentation.

A bug can go undetected until a *failure* occurs, which is when a user or tester perceives that the system is not delivering the expected service. In the system test phase, the goal of the test engineer is to induce failures through testing and thereby uncover and document the associated bugs so they can be removed from the system. Ideally the life of a bug ends when it is uncovered in static or dynamic testing and fixed.

One practical consequence of the definition of testing is that test engineers and development engineers need to take fundamentally different approaches to their jobs. The goal of the developer is to create bug-free code that satisfies the software design and meets the customer's requirements. The developer is trying to "make" code. The goal of the tester is to analyze or operate the code to expose the bugs that are latent in the code as it is integrated, configured, and run in different environments. The tester is trying to "break" the code. In this context, a good result of a software test for a developer is a pass, but for that same test a successful outcome for the test engineer is a fail. Ultimately, of course, both the developer and tester want the same thing: a product that works well enough to satisfy their customers.

There are two basic functions of software testing: one is verification and the other is validation. Schulmeyer and Mackenzie (2000) define verification and validation (V&V) as follows:

Verification is the assurance that the products of a particular phase in the development process are consistent with the requirements of that phase and the preceding phase.

Validation is the assurance that the final product satisfies the system requirements.

The purpose of validation is to ensure that the system has implemented all requirements, so that each function can be traced back to a particular customer requirement. In other words, validation makes sure that the right product is being built.

Verification is focused more on the activities of a particular phase of the development process. For example, one of the purposes of system testing is to give assurance that the system design is consistent with the requirements that were used as an input to the system design phase. Unit and integration testing can be used to verify that the program design is consistent with the system design. In simple terms, verification makes sure that the product is being built right. We'll see examples of both verification and validation activities as we examine each phase of the development process in later chapters.

One additional concept that needs to be defined is quality. Like beauty, quality is subjective and can be difficult to define. We will define software quality in terms of three factors: failures in the field, reliability, and customer satisfaction. A software product is said to have good *quality* if:

- It has few failures when used by the customer, indicating that few bugs have escaped to the field.
- It is reliable, meaning that it seldom crashes or demonstrates unexpected behavior when used in the customer environment.
- It satisfies a majority of users.

One implication of this definition of quality is that the test group must not only take measures to prevent and detect defects during product development, but also needs to be concerned with the reliability and usability of the product.

What is Rapid Testing?

We use the term "rapid testing" in this book as a complement to the notion of "rapid development." As Steve McConnell has pointed out, rapid development means different things to different people. To some people, it's rapid prototyping. To others, it's a combination of CASE tools, intensive user involvement, and tight time boxes. Rather than identify rapid development with a specific tool or method, McConnell (1996, p. 2) makes the following definition:

> Rapid development is a generic term that means the same thing as "speedy development" or "shorter schedules." It means developing

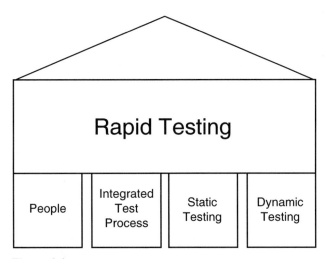

Figure 1.1
Essential components of rapid testing.

software faster than you do now. A "rapid development project," then, is any project that needs to emphasize development speed.

In a similar vein, *rapid testing* means testing software faster than you do now, while maintaining or improving your standards of quality. Unfortunately, there is no simple way to achieve rapid testing. Figure 1.1 shows a somewhat simplistic sketch that represents rapid testing as a structure that is built on a foundation of four components. If any of these components is weak, the effectiveness of testing will be greatly impaired. As illustrated in the figure, the four components that must be optimized for rapid testing are people, integrated test process, static testing, and dynamic testing. We'll briefly examine each of the four components.

People

As every test manager knows, the right people are an essential ingredient to rapid testing. There are several studies that show productivity differences of 10:1 or more in software developers. The same is true with test engineers—not everyone has the skills, experience, or temperament to be a good test engineer. Rapid testing particularly needs people who are disciplined, flexible, who can handle the pressure of an aggressive schedule, and who are able to be productive contributors through the early phases of the development life cycle. While the main focus of this book is on test process and technique, some ideas about the "people side" of testing will be included in Chapter 6.

Integrated Test Process

No matter how good your people may be, if they do not have a systematic, disciplined process for testing, they will not operate at maximum efficiency. The test process needs to be based on sound, fundamental principles, and must be well integrated with the overall software development process. We will spend a good portion of Part I of this book describing ways to improve the test process, with a more detailed discussion of practical techniques and implementation tips presented in Part II. The focus of our discussion will be to explore ways of better integrating the development and test activities.

Static Testing

In the previous section we defined static testing as test activities associated with analyzing the products of software development. Static testing is done for the purpose of *validating* that a work product such as a design specification properly implements all the system requirements, and *verifying* the quality of the design. Static testing is one of the most effective means of catching bugs at an early stage of development, thereby saving substantial time and cost to the development. It involves inspections, walkthroughs, and peer reviews of designs, code, and other work products, as well as static analysis to uncover defects in syntax, data structure, and other code components. Static testing is basically anything that can be done to uncover defects without running the code. In the experience of the authors, it is an often-neglected tool. Static testing will be discussed throughout Parts I and II of this book.

Dynamic Testing

Often when engineers think of testing, they are thinking of dynamic testing, which involves operating the system with the purpose of finding bugs. Whereas static testing does not involve running the software, dynamic testing does. Generally speaking, dynamic testing consists of running a program and comparing its actual behavior to what is expected. If the actual behavior differs from the expected behavior, a defect has been found. As we'll see in later chapters, dynamic testing will be used to perform a variety of types of tests such as functional tests, performance tests, and stress tests. Dynamic testing lies at the heart of the software testing process, and if the planning, design, development, and execution of dynamic tests are not performed well, the testing process will be very inefficient. Dynamic testing is not only performed by the test team; it should be a part of the development team's unit and integration testing as well.

Developing a Rapid Testing Strategy

If you were to analyze your current software development process for ways to improve testing efficiency, where in the process would you look? Would you start by looking at the way you conduct test planning? At the means and contents of your automation? What about your defect tracking system?

Our approach in this book will be to look at every phase of the software process from the viewpoint of the test engineer to see if there is a way to speed up testing while maintaining or improving quality. The image we have in mind is one of you sitting in the "test engineer's swivel chair," turning to look at every aspect of the development process to see if you can prevent defects from escaping that phase of the process, or to see if you can extract information from that phase that will speed up your test effort.

Before we can take a detailed look at each phase of the software development process from the testing perspective, we need to lay some groundwork. In this chapter we define basic terms and concepts of software testing, and provide an overview of the software development process. Then we examine each phase of a typical development process to see how the efficiency and speed of testing can be improved. When examining each development phase, we bear the following questions in mind.

- Is there any action that the test team can take during this phase that will prevent defects from escaping?
- Is there any action that the test team can take during this phase that will help manage risk to the development schedule?
- Is there any information that can be extracted from this phase that will allow the test team to speed up planning, test case development, or test execution?

If a test process is designed around the answers to these questions, both the speed of testing and the quality of the final product should be enhanced.

The Software Development Process

So far we have talked about examining the software development process without defining exactly what it entails. One reason for not being specific is that there is no one development process that is best suited for all rapid development projects. You might want to develop an embedded controller for a heart pacemaker as "rapidly as possible," but you are not likely to use the same process that a friend down the street is using to develop an online dictionary.

Shari Pfleeger (2001) defines a *process* as "a series of steps involving activities, constraints, and resources that produce an intended output of some kind." The following is adapted from Pfleeger's list of the attributes of a process:

- The process prescribes all of the major process activities.

- The process uses resources, subject to a set of constraints (such as a schedule), and provides intermediate and final products.

- The process may be composed of subprocesses that are linked in some way. The process may be defined as a hierarchy of processes, organized so that each subprocess has its own process model.

- Each process activity has entry and exit criteria, so that we know when the activity begins and ends.

- The activities are organized in a sequence or in parallel to other independent subprocesses, so that it is clear when one activity is performed relative to the other activities.

- Every process has a set of guiding principles that explains the goals of each activity.

- Constraints or controls may apply to an activity, resource, or product. For example, the budget or schedule may constrain the length of time an activity may take or a tool may limit the way in which a resource may be used.

When a process relates to the building of a product, it is often called a life cycle. The development of a software product is therefore called a *software life cycle*. A software life cycle can be described in a variety of ways, but often a model is used that represents key features of the process with some combination of text and illustrations.

One of the first software life cycle models used was the waterfall, shown in Figure 1.2. A main characteristic of the waterfall model is that each phase or component of the model is completed before the next stage begins. The process begins with a definition of the requirements for the system, and in the waterfall model the requirements are elicited, analyzed, and written into one or more requirements documents before any design work begins. The system design, program design, coding, and testing activities are all self-contained and thoroughly documented phases of the process. It should be noted that different names are commonly used for some of the phases; for

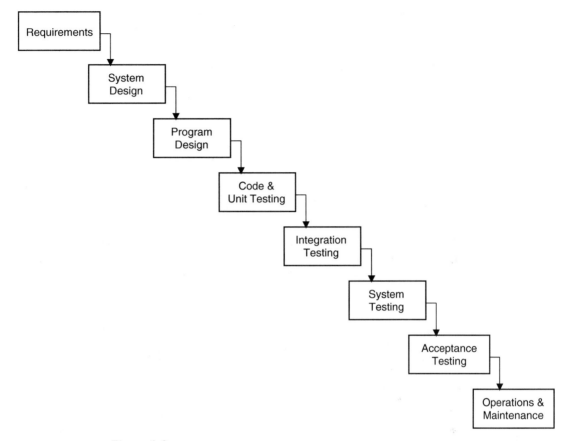

Figure 1.2
Waterfall life cycle model.

example, the system design phase is often called "preliminary design," and the program design phase is often called "detailed design."

The waterfall model has a number of critics. One criticism questions the possibility of capturing all the requirements at the front-end of a project. Suppose you are asked to state all the requirements for a new car before it is designed and built. It would be impossible as a customer to conceive of all the detailed requirements that would be needed to design and build a car from scratch. Yet, this is the kind of demand that the waterfall model places upon customers and analysts at the front-end of a waterfall process.

Curtis, Krasner, Shen, and Iscoe (1987, cited in Pfleeger, 2000) state that the major shortcoming of the waterfall model is that it fails to treat software as a problem-solving process. The waterfall was adapted from the world of hardware development, and represents a manufacturing or assembly-line view of software development in which a component is developed and then replicated many times over. But software is a creation process rather than a manufacturing process. Software evolves iteratively as the understanding of a problem grows. There are a lot of back and forth activities that involve trying various things to determine what works best. It is not possible, in other words, to accurately model the software development process as a set of self-contained phases as the waterfall attempts to do. Other models such as the spiral, staged delivery and evolutionary prototype models are better suited to the iterative nature of software development. Iterative models are discussed further in Chapter 2.

If you have worked as a test engineer in a waterfall environment, you may have direct experience with another problem that is all too common with the waterfall. Unless certain precautions are taken, all the errors made in defining the requirements, designing the system, and writing the code flow downhill to the test organization. If the waterfall is used, the test team may find a lot of bugs near the end of development—bugs that have to be sent back upstream to be fixed in the requirements, design, or coding of the product. Going back upstream in a waterfall process is difficult, expensive, and time-consuming because all the work products that came from the supposedly "completed" phases now must be revised.

In spite of its problems, the waterfall model is worth understanding because it contains the basic components that are necessary for software development. Regardless of the model used, software development should begin with an understanding of what needs to be built; in other words, an elicitation and analysis of the requirements. The development process should include design, coding, and testing activities, whether they are done in a linear sequence as in the waterfall, or in an iterative sequence as in the evolutionary prototyping or staged delivery models. We use the waterfall as a context for discussing process improvement, but the basic principles of rapid testing should be applicable to whatever life cycle model is used.

A Waterfall Test Process

In the traditional waterfall model shown in Figure 1.2, the role of the test organization is not made explicit until the system testing and acceptance testing phases. Most of the activity of the earlier phases, such as design, coding, and unit testing, are associated primarily with the software development team. For this reason it is useful to derive a corresponding life cycle model for the test process. Since the development of dynamic tests is a very similar process to that of developing software, it follows that a waterfall life cycle model for dynamic testing will closely resemble the model discussed in the previous section. An example of a waterfall test process life cycle model is shown in Figure 1.3. Note that the model describes dynamic testing but does not show static testing activities.

A summary of the inputs and outputs for each phase of the waterfall test process is presented in Table 1.1. A brief description will now be given of the activities, inputs, and outputs for each phase of the waterfall test process. More detail will come in the remaining chapters of Part I.

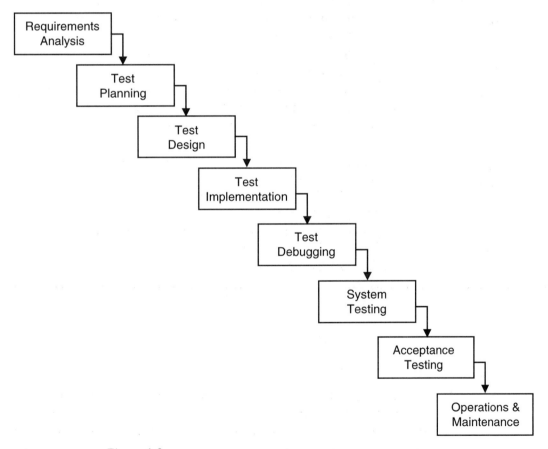

Figure 1.3
Waterfall test process.

Table 1.1
Inputs and Outputs for the Waterfall Test Process

Activity	Inputs	Outputs
Requirements analysis	Requirements definition, requirements specification	Requirements traceability matrix
Test planning	Requirements specification, requirements trace matrix	Test plan—test strategy, test system, effort estimate and schedule
Test design	Requirements specification, requirements trace matrix, test plan	Test designs—test objectives, test input specification, test configurations
Test implementation	Software functional specification, requirements trace matrix, test plan, test designs	Test cases—test procedures and automated tests
Test debugging	"Early look" build of code, test cases, working test system	Final test cases
System testing	System test plan, requirements trace matrix, "test-ready" code build, final test cases, working test system	Test results—bug reports, test status reports, test results summary report
Acceptance testing	Acceptance test plan, requirements trace matrix, beta code build, acceptance test cases, working test system	Test results
Operations and maintenance	Repaired code, test cases to verify bugs, regression test cases, working test system	Verified bug fixes

Requirements Analysis

When analyzing software requirements, the goals of the test team and the development team are somewhat different. Both teams need a clear, unambiguous requirements specification as input to their jobs. The development team wants a complete set of requirements that can be used to generate a system functional specification, and that will allow them to design and code the software. The test team, on the other hand, needs a set of requirements that will allow them to write a test plan, develop test cases, and run their system and acceptance tests.

A very useful output of the requirement analysis phase for both development and test teams is a requirements traceability matrix. A *requirements traceability matrix* is a document that maps each requirement to other work products in the development process such as design components, software modules, test cases, and test results. It can be implemented in a spreadsheet, word processor table, database, or Web page. The requirements trace matrix and its role in "gluing together" the various activities of the development and test processes will be discussed in more detail in Chapter 2.

Test Planning

By test planning we mean determining the scope, approach, resources, and schedule of the intended testing activities. Efficient testing requires a substantial investment in planning, and a willingness to revise the plan dynamically to account for changes in requirements, designs, or code as bugs are uncovered. It is important that all requirements be tested or, if the requirements have been prioritized, that the highest priority requirements are tested. The requirements traceability matrix is a useful tool in the test planning phase because it can be used to estimate the scope of testing needed to cover the essential requirements.

Ideally, test planning should take into account static as well as dynamic testing, but since the waterfall test process described in Figure 1.3 and Table 1.1 is focused on dynamic testing, we'll exclude static testing for now. The activities of the test planning phase should prepare for the system test and acceptance test phases that come near the end of the waterfall, and should include:

- Definition of what will be tested and the approach that will be used.
- Mapping of tests to the requirements.
- Definition of the entry and exit criteria for each phase of testing.
- Assessment, by skill set and availability, of the people needed for the test effort.
- Estimation of the time needed for the test effort.
- Schedule of major milestones.
- Definition of the test system (hardware and software) needed for testing.
- Definition of the work products for each phase of testing.
- An assessment of test-related risks and a plan for their mitigation.

The work products or outputs that result from these activities can be combined in a test plan, which might consist of one or more documents. Test planning will be discussed in more detail in Chapter 3 and an example test plan will be provided in Part III.

Test Design, Implementation, and Debugging

Dynamic testing relies on running a defined set of operations on a software build and comparing the actual results to the expected results. If the expected results are obtained, the test counts as a pass; if anomalous behavior is observed, the test counts as a fail, but it may have succeeded in finding a bug. The defined set of operations that are run constitute a test case, and test cases need to be designed, written, and debugged before they can be used.

A test design consists of two components: test architecture and detailed test designs. The test architecture organizes the tests into groups such as functional tests, performance tests, security tests, and so on. It also describes the structure and naming conventions for a test repository. The detailed test designs describe the objective of each test, the equipment and data needed to conduct the test, the expected result for each test, and traces the test back to the requirement being validated by the test. There should be at least a one-to-one relationship between requirements and test designs.

Detailed test procedures can be developed from the test designs. The level of detail needed for a written test procedure depends on the skill and knowledge of the people that run the tests. There is a tradeoff between the time that it takes to write a detailed, step-by-step procedure, and the time that it takes for a person to learn to properly run the test. Even if the test is to be automated, it usually pays to spend time up front writing a detailed test procedure so that the automation engineer has an unambiguous statement of the automation task.

Once a test procedure is written, it needs to be tested against a build of the product software. Since this test is likely to be run against "buggy" code, some care will be needed when analyzing test failures to determine if the problem lies with the code or with the test.

System Test

A set of finished, debugged tests can be used in the next phase of the waterfall test process, system test. The purpose of system testing is to ensure that the software does what the customer expects it to do. There are two main types of system tests: function tests and performance tests.

Functional testing requires no knowledge of the internal workings of the software, but it does require knowledge of the system's functional requirements. It consists of a set of tests that determines if the system does what it is supposed to do from the user's perspective.

Once the basic functionality of a system is ensured, testing can turn to how well the system performs its functions. *Performance testing* consists of such things as stress tests, volume tests, timing tests, and recovery tests. Reliability, availability, and maintenance testing may also be included in performance testing.

In addition to function and performance tests, there are a variety of additional tests that may need to be performed during the system test phase; these include security tests, installability tests, compatibility tests, usability tests, and upgrade tests. More details on system testing will be given in Chapter 5 and in Part II.

Acceptance Test

When system testing is completed, the product can be sent to users for acceptance testing. If the users are internal to the company, the testing is usually called *alpha* testing. If the users are customers who are willing to work with the product before it is finished, the testing is *beta* testing. Both alpha and beta tests are a form of *pilot* tests in which the system is installed on an experimental basis for the purpose of finding bugs.

Another form of acceptance test is a *benchmark* test in which the customer runs a predefined set of test cases that represent typical conditions under which the system is expected to perform when placed into service. The benchmark test may consist of test cases that are written and debugged by your test organization, but which the customer has reviewed and approved. When pilot and benchmark testing is complete, the customer should tell you which requirements are not satisfied or need to be changed in order to proceed to final testing.

The final type of acceptance test is the *installation* test, which involves installing a completed version of the product at user sites for the purpose of obtaining customer agreement that the product meets all requirements and is ready for delivery.

Maintenance

Maintenance of a product is an often challenging task for the development team and the test team. Maintenance for the developer consists of fixing bugs that are found during customer operation and adding enhancements to product functionality to meet evolving customer requirements. For the test organization, maintenance means verifying bug fixes, testing enhanced functionality, and running *regression* tests on new releases of the product to ensure that previously working functionality has not been broken by the new changes.

Even though the acceptance test and maintenance activities are important, they will not be discussed in detail in this book. The basic principles of regression testing and bug verification apply well to these phases of the life cycle. For a detailed treatment of software maintenance from a testing perspective, Lewis (2000) offers a great deal of information.

Tying Testing and Development Together

The previous few sections have described waterfall models for the software development process and for the test process. The two models have common starting and ending points, but the test and development teams are involved in separate and different activities all along the way. This section presents two models that tie the two sets of activities together.

One way of seeing how test and development activities are related is shown with the V diagram, which is illustrated in Figure 1.4. In this model, also called the hinged waterfall, the analysis and design activities form the left side of the V. Coding is the lowest point of the V, and the testing activities form the right side. Maintenance activities are omitted for simplicity.

The double-headed, dashed arrows in the figure highlight the relationships between the test activities on the right side of the diagram and the requirements and design activities on the left. The top dashed arrow shows that the purpose of acceptance testing is to validate requirements, and that the acceptance tests are based upon the requirements. Similarly, system testing serves to verify the system design, and the system tests are derived from the system design. One purpose of the V diagram, therefore, is to show the purpose of the test activities in terms of verification or validation of earlier development activities.

Although the V diagram helps illustrate the relationship between development and testing, it does not show the two parallel threads of activities that the two teams perform during the course of development. One way to show the separate activities that are associated with development and testing is illustrated by the parallel waterfall model in Figure 1.5. This figure is a little more complex than the previous models, but it has several key features that make the extra complexity worthwhile.

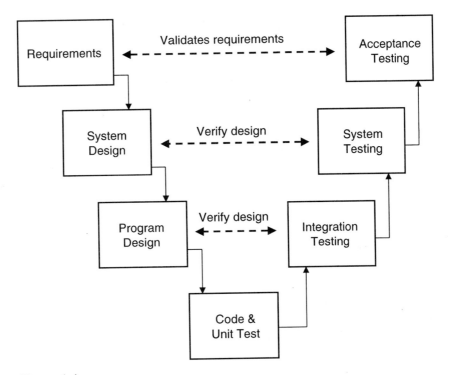

Figure 1.4
The V diagram or hinged waterfall.

- The parallel development and test threads are clearly shown.
- The arrow connecting system test to system design shows that the purpose of the system test phase is to verify the system design.
- The arrow connecting acceptance test to requirements shows that the purpose of the acceptance test is to validate the requirements.
- Similar arrows show that the purpose of the unit and integration test is to verify the program design and the purpose of test debugging is to verify the test design.
- Each remaining phase of the development and test threads have "feedback loops" whose purpose is to verify that the work products of system design, program design, test planning, and so on meet the requirements placed upon them at the beginning of the phase. This check is done using static testing.

A little reflection on Figure 1.5 shows why software testing is such a demanding and difficult job. Even while working in the traditional waterfall

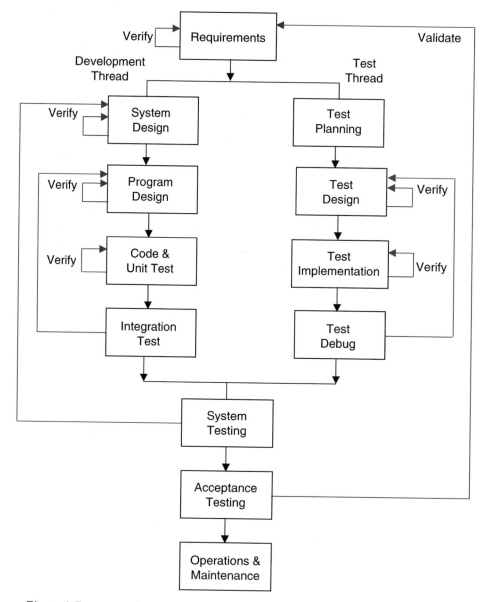

Figure 1.5
Parallel waterfall model.

environment, the test team must perform a range of activities, each of which is dependent on output from the development team. Good communication must be maintained between the development and test threads of the process, and each team needs to participate in some of the other team's verification activities. For example, the test team should participate in verifying the system design, and the development team should participate in verifying the test plan.

What's Next

In this chapter we defined the basic concepts of software testing. We introduced the idea of rapid testing as being a way to test faster without sacrificing quality, and discussed the critical roles of people, process, static testing, and dynamic testing in building an efficient rapid testing process. We examined the waterfall software development process and the dynamic testing process, and noted that they need to be closely integrated if the test effort is to be more efficient. Finally, we looked at the V diagram and the integrated waterfall model as tools for tying together the development and test processes.

We have begun to integrate the test and development processes by means of the parallel waterfall model, but there is a great deal of work remaining before a rapid test process is defined. Each phase of the test process needs to be analyzed to see how it can be optimized for speed and efficiency. We begin this work in the next chapter.

References

Curtis, Bill, Herb Krasner, Vincent Shen, and Neil Iscoe. (1987). "On building software process models under the lamppost." *Proceedings of the 9th International Conference on Software Engineering* (pp. 96–103). Monterey, CA: IEEE Computer Press Society.

Lewis, William E. (2000). *Software Testing and Continuous Quality Improvement.* Boca Raton, FL: Auerbach.

McConnell, Steve. (1996). *Rapid Development: Taming Wild Software Schedules.* Redmond, WA: Microsoft Press.

Pfleeger, Shari Lawrence. (2001). *Software Engineering: Theory and Practice* (2nd ed.). Upper Saddle River, NJ: Prentice Hall.

Schulmeyer, G. Gordon and Garth R. Mackenzie. (2000). *Verification and Validation of Modern Software-Intensive Systems.* Upper Saddle River, NJ: Prentice Hall.

Requirements Analysis and Testing

Topics Covered in the Chapter

- ▶ The Requirements Process
- ▶ Requirements Testing
- ▶ What's Next
- ▶ References

In the previous chapter we stated that development and test activities need to be closely integrated if product development is to be done fast. This integration of development and test activities needs to begin at the front-end of the development process, when requirements are elicited from the user. The development team needs a clear set of requirements in order to design the software system, and the test team needs requirements that are clear, unambiguous, and testable in order to develop a test plan and test designs. If both teams are involved at the front-end of the process, they are much more likely to get a set of requirements that meet their needs early in the schedule.

A second reason for involving the test team when requirements are elicited and analyzed is to perform static testing on the requirements. In a Standish Group survey of more than 350 companies in 1994, it was found that only 9% of the 8,000+ software projects were delivered on time and within budget (Standish, 1994). Thirty-one percent of the projects were cancelled before completion. A follow-up study (Standish, 1995) was conducted to identify the causes of the failed projects. By examining the list of the top factors that contributed to project overrun or failure, it can be seen that over 50% of the top contributors relate to some aspect of the requirements process. The top factors that relate to requirements are listed below, along with the percent of projects for which the problem was the top factor:

- Incomplete requirements (13.1%)
- Lack of user involvement (12.4%)
- Unrealistic expectations (9.9%)
- Changing requirements and specifications (8.7%)
- System no longer needed (7.5%)

One implication of the survey results is that large numbers of defects can be introduced during the requirements phase. When defects are introduced into the requirements, there is a rippling effect throughout the development process that is expensive and time-consuming. Boehm and Papaccio (1988, cited in Pfleeger, 2001) report that if it costs $1 to find and fix a defect in the requirements phase, it may cost $5 during design, $10 during coding, $20 during unit testing, and up to $200 after delivery to find and fix the same problem. A plot of the cost to fix a defect by phase is shown in Figure 2.1. A large part of this cost escalation is associated with the rework required in each stage preceding the one in which the defect is discovered and fixed.

In considering the Standish Group data on reasons for project failure, and in reviewing the expense of fixing defects late in the development cycle rather than at the front-end, it is pretty clear that static testing needs to be used in the requirements phase to prevent defects from migrating downstream.

The two reasons for involving the test team early in the requirements phase can therefore be summarized as follows:

- The test team needs early and accurate requirements specifications on which to base a test plan and test designs. This is a key to getting a head start on testing.
- The test team needs to apply static testing to the requirements specifications to prevent defects from escaping to later phases. Successful static testing in the requirements phase saves time and cost.

In this chapter we discuss the requirements process from the point of view of the test engineer. We begin by looking at the requirements elicitation and analysis tasks, identifying specific work products and points in the process where static testing can be applied. We consider the types of requirements that are needed for completeness, and suggest ways in which requirements can be tested. The use of prototypes in requirements analysis is discussed, as well as the role of testing in a prototype-based life cycle.

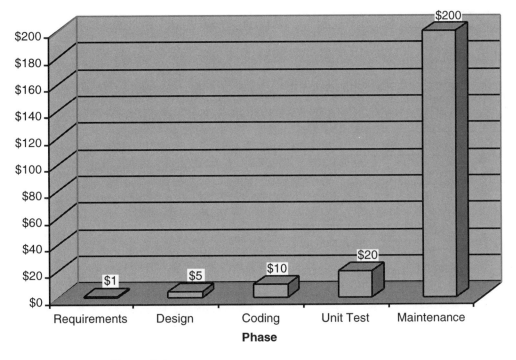

Figure 2.1
Cost to fix a defect by development phase. *From Boehm (1981).*

The Requirements Process

Software projects begin their life cycle when a customer needs to replace an existing system or needs something that is completely new. The customer may be a department within your company, a separate company or agency that is contracting work from you, or a mass market that is looking for a shrink-wrap product. The customer's needs may be described by a set of requirements, where a *requirement* is a description of something the system is capable of doing or some operating condition that the system requires in order to fulfill its purpose. A requirement focuses on *what* the system will do rather than *how* it will be done. This means that a requirement is focused on the customer's problem and business rather than on an implementation solution.

The process of determining requirements for a software system is illustrated in Figure 2.2. We examine this process from the viewpoint of the test

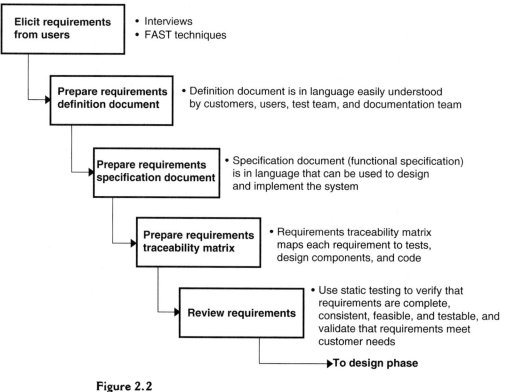

Figure 2.2
The requirements process.

engineer, trying to extract information that will support early test planning, and trying to detect defects early in the requirements so they won't lead to an avalanche of errors in later phases of development.

The first step shown in Figure 2.2 is eliciting customer requirements. This is done by asking customers questions and suggesting concepts to them using slides, mockups, or prototypes. Communication with the customer might occur through a series of interviews or by using facilitated application specification techniques (FAST), which are structured meetings that promote good requirements elicitation.

As requirements are obtained from the customer, they need to be captured in a *requirements definition* document. This document should be a list of all requirements captured in the elicitation meetings. It represents an agreement between the customer and the development organization of what will be developed. The requirements definition document is written in natural language that can be easily understood by the customer and by teams that will develop and maintain the system.

While the requirements definition document may be easy to understand, it can lack the precision and technical detail that is needed to design and implement the product. For this reason a second document, called the *requirements specification* or *functional specification,* is prepared for use by the development team. Good introductions to the concepts and terminology used in requirements specification can be found in Sommerville (1992), Pressman (1997), and Pfleeger (2001). A more detailed discussion can be found in Robertson and Robertson (1999).

Once the requirements have been defined and specified, preparation of a *requirements traceability matrix* should begin. The purpose of the matrix is to map each requirement to tests, design components, and code. Ideally the development and test teams would participate in this work so that over time there are associated design components, unit tests, integration tests, system tests, and acceptance tests. If used properly, the requirements traceability matrix is a tool that will help each participant in the development process to perform work that directly relates to the customer's needs and not waste time on tasks that are not needed. From the test team's perspective, it is a tool that can be used in test planning and design to ensure good test coverage.

In the next few sections, we examine the activities and work products of the requirements process in more detail from the test perspective.

Eliciting Requirements

The communication between customer and developer while defining a product is so important to the success of a project that a great deal of effort needs to be spent in making the communication effective. One factor that can limit effective communication is the amount of knowledge that the customer has regarding how a product is developed. Often a customer will not have enough background knowledge of the development process to be able to state their requirements in a way that will be understood by the system designer.

The process of defining a software system has been compared to that of designing a custom home: you may not know enough about building a house to tell your builder exactly what is needed, so communication will probably include looking at existing homes, examining house plans to select desired features, and finally reviewing a set of custom plans and drawings. For a software system it is often useful to demonstrate existing software, look at paper or software prototypes, and discuss the business environment in which the product will be used. The results of this communication is of immediate interest to the test team, who needs to know how the customer plans to use the software so that realistic system and acceptance tests can be designed.

One class of methods that can be used to elicit requirements is called *fast application specification techniques* (FAST). One of the most popular approaches to FAST is *Joint Application Development (JAD)*, which was developed by IBM (Pressman, 1997). Another method, *Joint Application Requirements (JAR)*, was developed by Gary Cobb and is described in Chapter 8.

FAST sessions typically apply some variation of the following guidelines (Pressman, 1997):

- Both customers and developers attend a meeting that is dedicated to defining requirements.

- Rules for preparation and participation are established and followed. An atmosphere must be maintained that is conducive to the success of the task.

- A facilitator controls the meeting. The facilitator may be a customer, a developer, or someone from outside who is agreeable to both parties.

- A mechanism such as flip charts, wallboard, or paper taped to the wall is used to capture requirements.

- The goal of the meeting is to define the customer's problem or need, propose a solution, negotiate different approaches, and specify a set of requirements.

It is very useful to have a test engineer participate in or even facilitate a FAST meeting so that static testing can be built into the meeting. The JAR technique defined in Chapter 8 is especially conducive to built-in static testing, which is called "perfective maintenance" in JAR terminology.

One type of information that can be extracted from requirements elicitation is an agreement between customer and developer as to the priority of the requirements. For example, each requirement could be placed into one of the following categories:

- Requirements that are essential.

- Requirements that are highly desirable.

- Requirements that would be nice to have.

If the requirements are prioritized in this way, it makes it easier to manage the development schedule. For example, a schedule can be made that delivers all essential requirements in a first release, desirable requirements in a second release, and the rest in a third release. Similarly, the test team can develop tests for the highest priority requirements first. This type of incremental or versioned delivery is a common solution when the project schedule is of critical concern.

There is a special case to be considered where the test engineer is asked to test products for which there are no requirements, or where the requirements are incomplete. Unfortunately this is a fairly common problem; you'll recall that the Standish data cited at the beginning of this chapter listed incomplete requirements as the top reason for projects being late or failing. One of this book's authors recalls an extreme situation where a test engineer was given a CD containing a program and told to test it—there was no documentation at all, much less a written set of requirements!

In a situation where there is no requirements specification, you may have no choice other than to write your own requirements definition document. Depending on how much time you have for the complete test effort, your requirements definition may not be as thorough as you would like, but it is essential to have key requirements defined. It is impossible to test a software system without having some definition of its intended functionality. If you are stuck defining the requirements, you may wish to conduct a JAR session with key developers and preferably with marketing or customer representatives. At least you'll want to interview the development and marketing teams and write as complete a requirements definition document as time permits.

SIDEBAR 2.1

ELICITING REQUIREMENTS FOR AN OBJECT-ORIENTED DEVELOPMENT

In an object-oriented development approach, requirements are often defined with use cases. A *use case* describes how a function is to be performed from the viewpoint of an external user or system. A collection of all possible use cases describes the total functionality of the system.

Each use case is typically formatted as a diagram showing the objects involved plus a textual description, called a scenario script, of how the function is performed. It is usually very easy to define a system test from a use case, because the use case does not provide any visibility as to how the system performs the function, but clearly defines what functionality is to take place. System test design can therefore be based directly on use cases, with one or more tests being developed for each use case.

For information on use case testing, see Chapter 10.

Requirements Definition

The requirements definition document captures all the system requirements in natural language so that it is easy to understand by customers and by those involved in product development. From a test perspective, we're interested in gleaning enough information from this document to begin planning and designing tests. For our purposes, the requirements definitions should have the following characteristics.

- Each requirement should be uniquely identified so that we can refer to it unambiguously when we plan for test coverage, design test cases, and report test results.

- The requirements should be presented from a system user's viewpoint. System and acceptance tests will need to be designed based on the requirement definitions, so the definitions must be stated from a system-level perspective. This explicitly precludes requirements that deal with system internal details, which would require detailed knowledge of the code in order to perform testing. Such requirements should be derived in later phases of development, and should be covered by unit and integration testing.

- Both *functional* and *nonfunctional* requirements should be included. Functional requirements are those that describe the services or features that the system is to perform. Nonfunctional requirements describe constraints that apply to system operation, such as the number of concurrent users and standards with which the system must comply. We need to test both types of requirements.

- The requirements definition document needs to be placed under configuration management. This means at a minimum that the document should be under version control, and that all versions of the document should be placed in a safe repository such as a directory that is routinely backed up. As the requirements change, we need to be able to track the changes and make corresponding changes to the systems and acceptance test cases.

One possible outline for the requirements definition document is shown in Figure 2.3. The contents shown in the figure are based on IEEE Standard 830: *The IEEE Guide to Software Requirements Specifications* (IEEE, 1984). An example for the requirements definition document corresponding to Figure 2.3 is presented in Part III. You may find the example useful if you are in a situation where you have to generate your own requirements definition document, or it may help you in static-testing an existing requirements document.

Requirements Definition Document
Table of Contents

Figure 2.3
Example outline for requirements definition document. Adapted from IEEE Std. 830: *The IEEE Guide to Software Requirements Specifications.* Copyright 1984 IEEE. All rights reserved.

The requirements definition document outlined in Figure 2.3 includes a general description that places the product into perspective with other related products and provides an overview of the functionality of the product. It summarizes key features and describes the skill set of the intended users, but does not include a detailed definition of the functionality. The section on specific requirements includes definitions of functional, performance, interface, and other requirements. The document should also include definitions of acronyms and technical terminology used to describe the product.

Once it is written, the requirements definition document needs to be static-tested to verify that the requirements are complete, consistent, feasible, testable, unambiguous, and relevant.

Types of Requirements   We earlier defined a requirement as being a description of something the system is capable of doing or some operating condition that the system requires in order to fulfill its purpose. This covers a wide range of information, and it is useful to partition requirements into categories. An example set of categories is given in the following list.

- **Functionality.** This is a set of requirements that defines what the product is supposed to do at a system or user level. If needed for clarity, these requirements might also include what the product will *not* do.

- **Interfaces.** This describes the inputs from external systems and the outputs to external systems. Are there constraints on the data format or media that apply to these interfaces?

- **Data.** These requirements describe the input and output data to the system. What formats are required? What data needs to be stored? How much data will flow to and from the system and at what rate? What accuracy is required for data computations?

- **Performance.** These requirements describe scaling and timing issues such as how well the system must perform in terms of number of simultaneous users, number of transactions per time unit, and how long a user must wait for a response to a request. Care should be taken to quantify these requirements so they can be validated.

- **Users and human factors.** These requirements describe the people who will use the system in terms of their skills and training. They also relate to the usability of the product; for example, how many discrete actions are required to perform a common operation on the system? How clear is the feedback for each action?

- **Physical environment.** This specifies where the equipment is to function. Is there more than one location? Are there temperature, humidity, or other environmental constraints?

- **Security.** This describes how access to the system and its data will be controlled. This is also a good place to describe how system data will be backed up. How often will the backups be made? What media will store the backed-up data?

- **Documentation.** This defines the documentation that will be required, specifies if it is to be printed or online, and describes the audience for the documentation.

- **Fault handling.** These requirements describe how the system will respond to failures. Will the system detect faults and issue alarms? What is the required mean time between failures? Is there a maximum downtime?

- **Maintenance.** These requirements relate to how problems found in the system will be fixed, how upgrades to the system software will be delivered to the customer, and how users will convert to the upgraded system.

- **Release schedule.** If the requirements are prioritized, you may want to define a release schedule that shows what requirements will be addressed in each of a series of incremental releases.

While performing static testing on requirements documents, you may want to refer to the list above when testing for completeness. As you build a history of static testing over several projects, you can expand the list into a requirements checklist that is suitable for your product line. If you are in the position of having to test with an incomplete set of requirements, you might want to consider the above list to stimulate ideas on what tests are needed beyond coverage of the documented requirements.

Examples of Requirements   An example of some functional requirements is shown in Figure 2.4. The example is for a fictitious product that we "develop" throughout the course of this book. This example product, called the Test Management Toolkit (TMT), is an application targeted toward test teams who need an automated tool to support their test planning, test case development, and test execution. A requirements definition for the Test Management Toolkit is presented in Part III.

The requirements in Figure 2.4 relate to some of the key features of the product.

Requirements Specification

The requirements specification describes the same needs as the requirements definition document, but the specification is written from the system designer's perspective and in a language or notation that benefits the development team. The requirements specification is often called a system functional specification, even though it deals with more than just the functional requirements of the system.

The requirements specification, or functional specification, is more than a simple translation of the requirements definition document into technical

---

**Test Management Toolkit
Requirements**

2.2.1 The application shall provide a means for creating, modifying, viewing, storing, and retrieving test plan documents.

2.2.2 The application shall provide a means for creating, modifying, viewing, storing, and retrieving a list of tests to be executed. This list will be referred to in this document as the "run list."

2.2.3 The application shall provide a means for creating, modifying, viewing, storing, and retrieving individual tests, which may consist of components such as setup procedures, equipment lists, test procedures, test data, and test cleanup procedures.

2.2.4 The application shall provide a means for executing tests from the run list in such a way that test results and log files can be created for each test.

2.2.5 The application shall provide a means for creating, modifying, viewing, sorting, storing, and retrieving bug reports.

2.2.6 The application shall provide a means for producing reports that summarize testing status, test results, and bug reports.

Figure 2.4
Example requirement definitions.

language. The specification may further partition the requirements, adding more detail by formulating a set of derived requirements. For example, the original requirements definition may state that the system must operate over some specified range of temperature, but the specification may detail different operating characteristics for various subranges of temperature. To some degree the requirements definition is a statement of what the customer wants and needs, and the specification is a response from the engineering team as to what the system will be able to do.

The writers of the requirements specification may use natural language, or may choose from a wide variety of languages and notations that have been developed to support the specification process. Because terms in natural language can be interpreted in a variety of ways, its use can widen the gap of understanding between customer and designer unless extreme care is taken to nail down definitions of words such as "performance," "usability," "reliable," and the like. For an introduction to methods other than natural language that may be used to express requirements, see Pfleeger (2001).

If a formal requirements specification is prepared, it needs to be static-tested to verify that every requirement captured in the requirements definition is treated in the requirements specification, and that every requirement can be traced or mapped from one document to the other. The final requirements specification needs to be static-tested to verify that the requirements are complete, consistent, feasible, testable, unambiguous, and relevant.

Requirements Traceability Matrix

The purpose of the requirements traceability matrix is to map each requirement to design components, code, and test cases. An example of a requirements traceability matrix is shown in Figure 2.5. In the example, each requirement in the requirements definition document is mapped to one or more requirements in the requirements specification, the design, the code, and unit, integration, system, and acceptance test cases. A "Dewey decimal" notation is used in numbering the requirements. This notation allows the original requirements in the requirements definition document to be related to the derived requirements and various tests in a one-to-many relationship

These identifiers map the requirements
between definition and specification documents.

These identifiers map all testing back to the requirements.

Requirement Definition ID	Requirement Specification ID	Design Component ID	Code Component ID	Unit Test Case ID	Integration Test Case ID	System Test Case ID	Acceptance Test Case ID
RD2.2.4	RS2.2.4.1	D2.2.4.1	CC2.2.4.1	UT2.2.4.1	IT2.2.4	ST2.2.4	AT2.2.4
RD2.2.4	RS2.2.4.2	D2.2.4.2	CC2.2.4.2	UT2.2.4.2	IT2.2.4	ST2.2.4	AT2.2.4
RD2.2.4	RS2.2.4.3	D2.2.4.3	CC2.2.4.3	UT2.2.4.3	IT2.2.4	ST2.2.4	AT2.2.4
RD2.2.4	RS2.2.4.4	D2.2.4.4	CC2.2.4.4	UT2.2.4.4	IT2.2.4	ST2.2.4	AT2.2.4

These identifiers trace the design and code
components back to the requirements.

Figure 2.5
Example format of requirements traceability matrix.

(for example, one requirement to many system tests). Even if the design and coding information is not included in the matrix, it is useful to maintain a reduced matrix that relates system and acceptance tests to the requirements. A more detailed example of requirements traceability is shown in Part III.

Requirements Testing

The final activity in the requirements process is to perform static testing on the requirements documents. One purpose of the static testing is to verify that the requirements are complete, consistent, feasible, and that they can be tested (statically or dynamically) when implemented. An additional purpose of this static testing is to validate that the requirements as documented in their final form meet the customer needs as captured in the requirements elicitation. If properly done, static testing of requirements gives very good return on investment in terms of time and cost. Recall from the Standish data discussed at the beginning of the chapter that problems with requirements have been found to relate to more than 50% of project failures and cost overruns. Static testing of requirements is the most effective way to detect these defects before they impact schedule or cost.

There are a variety of ways to perform static testing, but three of the most popular are inspections, walkthroughs, and peer reviews. Sometimes the names of these methods vary; inspections are also known as technical reviews, and peer reviews are also called "buddy checks." The characteristics of each of these static test types are summarized in Table 2.1. More information on static testing methods can be found in Sidebar 2.2 and in Chapter 9.

Table 2.1
Characteristics of Selected Static Testing Methods [adapted from Kit (1995)]

	Inspections	Walkthroughs	Peer Reviews
Presenter	Not author	Anyone	None
Participants	1–6 people	Can be 5 or more	1 or 2
Preparation	Yes	Presenter only	None
Data collected	Yes	Optional	None
Output report	Yes	Optional	Verbal or email comments
Advantages	Most effective	More participants	Least expensive
Disadvantages	Most expensive	Finds fewer bugs	Finds fewest bugs

SIDEBAR 2.2

STATIC TESTING METHODS

Three popular methods for static testing are inspections, walkthroughs, and peer reviews. The basic characteristics of each method are summarized here.

Inspections

The key component of an inspection is a meeting in which a work product is reviewed for defects. Each participant in the meeting prepares before the meeting, and the meeting is conducted in accordance with a set of rules. Defects are recorded and a meeting report is published. Inspections have proven to be very effective at finding defects. Data reported by Boehm (1981) indicates that if about 20% of the programming effort is devoted to inspections, then about 80% of unit-level errors can be removed from the inspected code. The original guidelines for inspections were formulated by Fagan (1976) at IBM, but over the years other organizations have adopted them as standard or recommended practice.

Walkthroughs

Walkthroughs are less formal than inspections in that no preparation is required on the part of anyone other than the presenter, no data must be collected, and no output report is prepared. Because there is less formality, walkthroughs can cover more material than inspections, but they are not as efficient at finding and documenting defects.

Peer Reviews

Peer reviews involve little more than passing the work product to a coworker and asking for comments. The review might be done face-to-face or can be done through email. There are no formal procedures, and the effectiveness in finding and documenting defects is lowest of the three methods.

It can be seen in Table 2.1 that, while inspections cost more than the other methods, they are also the most effective at finding defects in the work product being inspected. Due to the importance of finding as many defects as possible during the requirements stage, inspections are the recommended method for reviewing the requirements.

What to Look For When Testing Requirements

There are six basic criteria that should be used in the static testing of requirements specifications. The criteria ask that each requirement be complete, unambiguous, consistent, traceable, feasible, and testable.

Complete. A set of requirements is complete if all of its component parts are present and each part is fully developed. Here are some things to watch for when testing for completeness:

- A requirement should not contain a "TBD," "etc.," "and so on," or similar term.

- A requirement should not refer to a nonexistent reference, such as a specification that does not exist.

- A requirement should not refer to functionality that is not defined.

Unambiguous. Each requirement should be precise and clear; it should lend itself to no more than a single interpretation. The requirement should also be easy to read and understand. If there is excessive complexity, collateral material such as a diagram or chart may be needed for clarification. If persuasive terms like "it is obvious" or "clearly" are used, the author of the requirement may be trying to persuade you to overlook an ambiguous statement.

Consistent. Requirements should not conflict with one another or with governing standards. If requirements are in conflict, they need to be prioritized so that the conflict can be resolved. Being able to identify consistency defects requires good knowledge of the entire requirements document and familiarity with existing standards or other external specifications.

Traceable. Each requirement should have a unique identifier that allows the progress of its development to be traced throughout the life cycle. In work products that come later in the life cycle, such as a test plan, each reference to a system feature should be traceable back to the requirements definition and specification. The requirements traceability matrix, discussed earlier in the chapter, is a great tool for ensuring traceability.

Feasible. Each requirement should ask the system to provide a feature that is practical to develop and maintain. If the customer is making an unrealistic request in terms of the time and cost needed to develop the feature, or is requesting a feature that will be unreliable or unsafe in operation, the risks need to be identified and addressed. In general the system must be economically feasible, maintainable, reliable, and usable.

Testable. We must be able to write economically feasible and operationally practical tests for each requirement to demonstrate that the functionality, performance, or compliance to standards is achieved by the product under test. This means that each requirement must be measurable or quantifiable, and that the testing can be performed under reasonable conditions.

The Use of Prototypes

In addition to using static testing methods to verify and validate require-ments, it is also very effective to use prototyping. A *prototype*, whether it is a paper mockup or a software simulation, allows you to present options to the customer and get feedback that allows the requirements to be more ac-curately defined. A prototype will often expose defects in the completeness, consistency, or feasibility of the requirements specification, and therefore can serve as a good complement to static testing.

There are two approaches to the use of prototypes. In one approach a *throwaway prototype* is constructed that is used solely to define requirements; it is not delivered to the customer as a product. A second approach is to de-velop an *evolutionary prototype* that is used on the front-end of the process to elicit and analyze requirements, but is also iteratively refined into a product that can be delivered to the customer. Testing an evolutionary prototype is discussed in the next section.

One way to incorporate a prototype in the development life cycle is shown in Figure 2.6 (Pfleeger, 2001). In this approach, prototypes can be constructed during the requirements and design phases of the development cycle. The prototype is used during requirements analysis to clarify and test requirements. During the system and program design phases, developers can use a prototype to assess alternative design strategies. The code devel-oped for the prototype may be reused or thrown away in this development model.

The test team can use prototypes developed during requirements analy-sis to get a head start on testing. Preliminary tests can be developed and run against the prototype to validate key requirements. These tests can be re-fined later in the process to form a core set of tests for the system and accep-tance test phases. Just as the prototype can make the requirements "more real" to the customer and developer, so too will the prototype allow the test team to "see" how to define a set of tests for the system. Even if the proto-type is a paper mockup or set of storyboards, it can go a long way toward helping the test team understand how to devise a good set of tests.

In addition to helping the test team get an early start, prototyping supports static or dynamic testing during the requirements phase. The pro-totype can be used to help determine the completeness, consistency, feasibil-ity, and relevance of requirements.

Prototyping is used in life cycle models other than the waterfall; in fact, in the case of the evolutionary prototype, it can form the basis of the devel-opment process. One of the most sophisticated life cycle models is the spiral

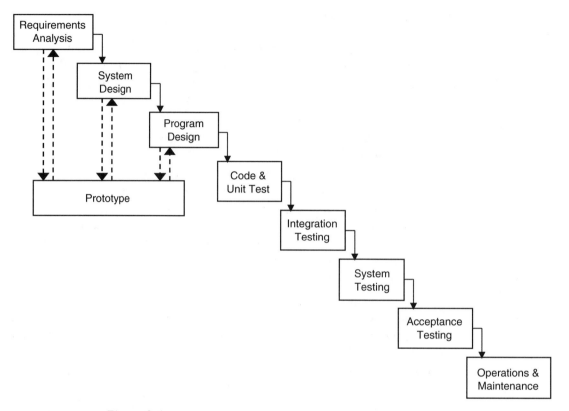

Figure 2.6
Prototyping added to the waterfall life cycle. *From Pfleeger (2001); adapted by permission of Prentice Hall.*

model, which was developed by Boehm (1988). The spiral model is a risk-oriented approach that partitions the project into a series of "miniprojects," each of which addresses a major risk. After all major risks have been addressed, the model ends with a conventional waterfall development of the final product.

Testing in an Evolutionary Prototyping Life Cycle

Evolutionary prototyping is a method of developing a system in evolving stages, with each stage being driven by customer feedback and test results. It is particularly useful if you cannot determine solid requirements at the beginning of a project, but are able to work with the customer to iteratively define the needs. Both static testing and dynamic testing need to be involved during each iteration of the development. An example development life cycle is shown in Figure 2.7.

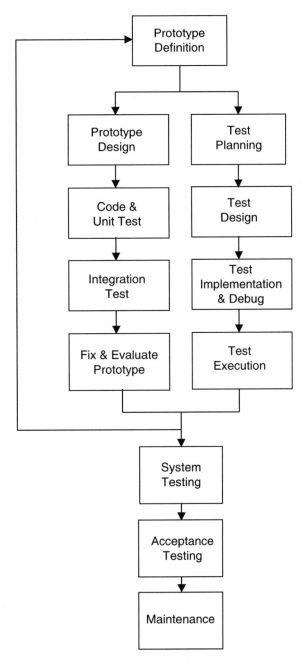

Figure 2.7
Testing in an evolutionary prototyping life cycle.

Development begins in the evolutionary model by defining the initial prototype. If development is following the spiral model, the focus of the initial prototype may be to assess a major risk to the project. In other cases the initial prototype may be a mockup of the user interface so that users can provide feedback on the functionality and usability of the system. Static testing should be applied to the development of the initial prototype by means of a review or a joint working session such as a JAR.

Once the prototype is defined, the development team designs, codes, and tests the prototype while the test team in parallel works in test planning, test development, and test execution. This model requires close communication between the development and test teams to ensure that each prototype is sufficiently tested before demonstration to the customer. If the functionality of the system is being expanded with each iteration, the test team needs to perform regression testing for each cycle through the development cycle; in other words, tests should be run to verify that old functionality is not broken or "regressed" when the new functionality is added. Automation can be very beneficial in regression testing. If a growing number of manual tests are run during each development cycle, the test effort can become large and time-consuming.

When enough development cycles have been completed, a final system and acceptance test can be performed before releasing the final product to the customer. It can be seen from the example in Figure 2.7 that the basic functions of dynamic testing (test planning, design, implementation, and execution) are all performed in an evolutionary prototyping life cycle, but they are done iteratively, and there is a need for solid regression testing.

What's Next

In this chapter we examined the requirements phase of the development process from the viewpoint of the systems test engineer. We identified two reasons for involving the test team early in the requirements phase:

- To obtain specifications on which to base a test plan and test designs.
- To apply static testing to the requirements specifications in order to prevent defects from escaping to later phases.

We identified three work products that are produced in the requirements phase:

- The requirements definition document, which is a presentation of the customer's requirements in natural language.

SIDEBAR 2.3

TOOLS FOR REQUIREMENTS MANAGEMENT

There are several commercially available software tools that can be used in the requirements phase. Software tools are particularly useful in capturing requirements and managing traceability throughout the development process. Two examples of requirements management tools are DOORS and Requisite Pro. DOORS is a requirements traceability tool available from Quality Systems and Software (QSS) Ltd. Another tool is Requisite Pro, which is available from Rational Software. The Atlantic Systems Guild, Inc. maintains an independent survey of requirements tools at their Web site, *http://www.systemsguild.com*.

- The requirements specification, also called a functional specification, which is an engineering statement of the requirements in notation that can be used to design the products.
- The requirements traceability document, which is used to map testing back to the requirements and thereby assure testing for all requirements.

We described the contents of each of these documents and presented some ideas on how to verify them. More information on static testing during the requirements phase, including a description of how to conduct a Joint Application Requirements (JAR) session, may be found in Chapter 8. Finally, we discussed the role of prototyping during the requirements phase and looked at how testing is performed in an evolutionary prototype life cycle.

In the next chapter we take a more detailed look at what happens after the requirements have been captured. The focus will be on test planning and test effort estimation.

References

Boehm, Barry W. (1981). *Software engineering economics.* Englewood Cliffs, NJ: Prentice-Hall, Inc.

Boehm, Barry W. (1988). "A spiral model for software development and enhancement." *IEEE Computer*, 21(5) (May): 61–72.

Fagan, M.E. (1976). "Design and code inspections to reduce errors in program development." *IBM Systems Journal*, 15(3): 182–210.

IEEE. (1984). *IEEE Standard 830: The IEEE Guide to Software Requirements Specifications.* Los Alamitos, CA: IEEE Computer Society Press.

Jones, Capers. (1997). *Software Quality: Analysis and Guidelines for Success*. Boston: International Thompson Computer Press.

Kit, Edward. (1995). *Software Testing in the Real World: Improving the Process*. Reading, MA: Addison-Wesley.

Pfleeger, Shari Lawrence. (2001). *Software Engineering: Theory and Practice* (2nd ed.). Upper Saddle River, NJ: Prentice Hall.

Pressman, Roger. (1997). *Software Engineering: A Practitioner's Approach* (4th ed.). New York: McGraw-Hill.

Robertson, Suzanne, and James Robertson. (1999). *Mastering the Requirements Process*. Reading, MA: Addison-Wesley.

Sommerville, Ian. (1992). *Software Engineering* (4th ed.). Reading, MA: Addison-Wesley.

The Standish Group. (1994). *The CHAOS Report*. Dennis, MA: The Standish Group.

The Standish Group. (1995). *The Scope of Software Development Project Failures*. Dennis, MA: The Standish Group.

Test Planning 3

As we have emphasized from the beginning, a key principle of rapid testing is to integrate the test process as closely with development as possible throughout the life cycle of the product. During requirements elicitation and analysis this integration is achieved using static testing techniques such as reviews to detect defects in the requirements and by participation in the requirements process to gather specifications as early as possible for use in test planning. The principle of integrating the development and test activities needs to continue during the planning and effort estimation process. Software testing is an expensive, resource-intensive job that can consume as much as half the total cost of a project. The effectiveness of test planning and effort estimation can make or break the success of the overall test effort in terms of meeting the project budget and schedule.

A diagram of test planning activities is shown in Figure 3.1. The inputs to the planning process are the requirements documents described in Chapter 2. As mentioned in Chapter 2, if you do not have requirements documents available, you will have to generate at least an abbreviated version of them yourself—it is impossible to properly test a software product without knowing the functionality and customer expectations.

The output of the test planning activities is a test plan, a document or set of documents that should be reviewed by the test team, the development team, and program management. The test plan identifies the resources that will be needed to test the product, defines what will be tested, how the testing will be done, and what outputs or deliverables will result from testing. The contents and format of the test plan are discussed in this chapter.

The core activities that make up the test planning process are:

- Define the test strategy
- Define the test system (hardware and software)
- Estimate the test effort (resources and schedule)
- Assess risks to the schedule and prepare mitigation plans
- Prepare and review the test plan documents

Each of these activities will be discussed in this chapter. Effort estimation techniques are covered in more detail in Chapter 12. An example of a test

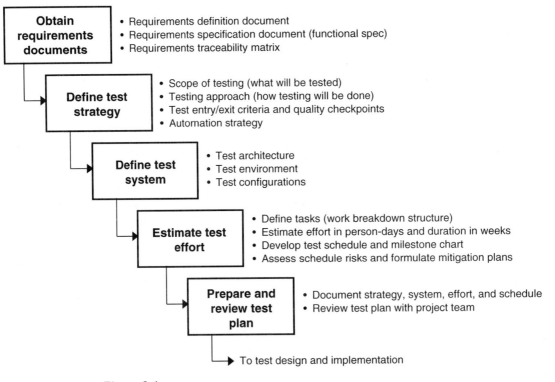

Figure 3.1
Test planning activities.

plan for the Test Management Toolkit application is provided in Part III. Although Figure 3.1 shows a linear sequence of the core activities, they are often done in parallel or in an iterative order. While the order of the activities may vary, it is important that all of them be done as part of test planning.

Test planning is like peeling an onion—it is a layered process. Planning begins by defining a high-level test strategy, and then more layers of detail are added that describe the test architecture, test environment, and the test cases themselves until a complete test plan has been developed. Once the test plan has been documented and approved, planning still does not stop, because there are likely to be changes to requirements, changes in schedule, or other changes that call for the test plan to be updated. The test plan should be maintained throughout the product development as a living document. It should be stored in a safe repository under version control.

Test Strategy

The first step in test planning is to construct a high-level test strategy. In general a test strategy should include the overall scope of testing, the types of testing methodologies that are to be used to find bugs, the procedures that will be used to report and fix bugs, and the entry/exit criteria that will govern the test activities. In keeping with the principle of closely integrating test and development activities to optimize the development schedule, the test strategy should map the test activities to the development life cycle. Both static and dynamic testing should be considered when formulating the overall strategy.

If automation is going to be used to support any of the test activities, the automation strategy needs to be considered as part of the overall test strategy. Automation requires an independent, parallel development effort that must be carefully planned and executed if it is to be effective.

We suggest the following approach to formulating a test strategy:

1. Define the scope of testing by evaluating the product requirements documents to identify what needs to be tested. Consider testing that may not be explicitly called out in the requirements documents, such as tests for installing or upgrading the software, usability, and interoperability with other equipment in the customer environment.

2. Define the testing approach by outlining the static and dynamic tests that will be associated with each phase of development. Include a

description of all work products that need to be produced by the test team.

3. Define the entry and exit criteria for each phase of testing as well as all quality checkpoints that require participation by the test team.

4. Define an automation strategy if automation is going to be used to support any of the test activities. Automation requires an independent, parallel development effort that must be carefully planned and executed if it is to be effective.

Define the Scope of Testing

An important question to consider when defining the scope of testing is how much of this product can be tested. It is a well-known fact in software testing that any program that delivers significant functionality cannot be completely tested. This fact is explored in Sidebar 3.1, "Can You Completely Test a Program?" The answer derived in the sidebar is a resounding "no!" You may be able to exhaustively test an old-fashioned "hello, world" type of program that consists of a few lines of code with no branching and no GUI, but a real-world program will always have some specific input values, some combination of input sequences, or some branches of the code that go untested.

SIDEBAR 3.1

CAN YOU COMPLETELY TEST A PROGRAM?

An important point to resolve before starting test design deals with the overall scope of testing. Should we try to test the software completely, or are we fundamentally limited in what we can expect from the test effort? In this sidebar we analyze an example software component with this question in mind.

Consider a software component that computes the cost to ship a product of known weight when given the destination zip code. The program has a GUI that can be used to enter the zip code (along with other data relevant to the transaction). In this case the shipping cost is an intermediate computation that is not displayed to the user; you have to query a database to see the result of the calculation.

The basic idea is shown as a block diagram in Figure 3.2. The diagram shows the relationship between input and output without bothering you with the details of the GUI or the database.

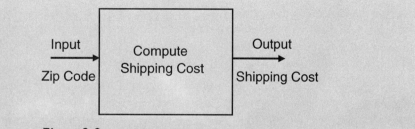

Figure 3.2
Functionality of software under test.

For simplicity assume that any five-digit, positive integer may be used as a valid zip code. In other words, the range of input values is 00000 to 99999. Each input produces a corresponding shipping cost that ranges in value from $5 to $20. The mapping of input to output is many-to-one, meaning that several zip codes can result in the same shipping cost.

Now that we have an idea of what this part of the software does, we want to return to the question regarding our ability to completely test a program. In this case, we specifically want to know if it's possible to test this program for all possible values of input.

There are two classes of input: valid and invalid. Five-digit, positive integers are valid inputs, but negative integers, decimal numbers, letters of the alphabet, control keys, and blanks may be considered invalid.

A simple count of the number of allowed zip codes tells us that there are 100,000 valid inputs (here the five-digit numbers not allowed by the post office are ignored). Assume that no automation is involved—the program will be tested manually. The test procedure calls for the tester to manually enter a valid input, query the database for the shipping cost, compare the resulting shipping cost, and record the result. You could easily spend 3 minutes per input, so checking all valid inputs would consume 5,000 hours, or over 2 working years! Not only this, but during the course of testing a release, the same test may have to be repeated half a dozen times.

Practically speaking, there is no way that you will test all these inputs. The story changes if you automate the test, but even then you would not want to waste time automating and testing each possible input. In Chapters 4 and 11 we'll see how to reduce the range of test inputs to a smaller, manageable set of equivalent values using the technique of equivalence partitioning.

If you additionally consider all the invalid inputs, the range of possibilities becomes much larger. Any negative integers, decimal numbers, or non-numeric values that can be entered via the GUI may be tried as invalid inputs. This leads to an even larger set of possible inputs, and there is no way to try them all. Based on these considerations we arrive at a fundamental limit of testing:

Testing Limitation: You cannot completely test a computer program.

In a related analysis, Pressman (1997) describes a 100-line C program with two nested loops that execute from 1 to 20 times each. Inside the interior loop are four if-then-else constructs. Pressman concludes that automated testing of this program, if executing each of the 10^{14} possible paths in one millisecond, would take 3,170 years.

Our example with the zip codes showed that exhaustive input testing is impossible, and Pressman's example demonstrates that, even with automation, exhaustive logical testing is unfeasible. Clearly one of the keys to rapid testing is going to be intelligent selection of what tests to run.

Since everything can't be tested, the importance of deciding what to test becomes clear. If you "overtest," meaning there is too much redundancy in the test coverage, it will take too long to test the product and the project schedule is at risk. If you "undertest," meaning that the test coverage is incomplete, you run the risk of missing bugs that will be costly to repair once the product is released. Striking the right balance is a matter of experience and of measuring the success of the testing.

Here are some suggestions for developing a testing strategy that provides reasonable test coverage.

Test the highest priority requirements first. Assuming that you have a requirements definition document with prioritized requirements, select the requirements that are most important to the customer or that will cause the customer most concern in case of failure. If your schedule and resources permit, you should of course test all requirements thoroughly, but in the event of a crunch, you need to have the highest priority requirements well tested before shipping the product, perhaps obtaining customer agreement that the partially tested or untested requirements will not be supported until a later release.

Test new functionality and code that has been modified to fix or improve old functionality. The rule of thumb is: If the code has been touched, test it. For an initial release of a product everything will be new, but if the release is an upgrade or maintenance release, there should be special focus on new code. Be aware, however, that any changes in code can break parts of a program that are supposedly "untouched" by the change. It is best to run regression tests as often as possible on all functionality of a program whenever changes are made.

Use equivalence partitioning and boundary value analysis techniques to reduce the test effort. These techniques are described in Chapters 4 and 10; both techniques may be used to maximize test coverage by choosing a subset of input values when testing input/output components.

Test areas that are most likely to have problems. There is an old saying that "bugs congregate together." Whenever a bug is found, there are often several other bugs waiting to be discovered. If during the requirements analysis some areas were particularly troublesome, or if you learn from the developers that particular components had a lot of problems during unit and integration testing, you should identify these components as good candidates for careful examination during system test.

Focus on functions and configurations that will most often be used by the end-users. If the requirements specification employed use cases or if you have access to the end-users' operational profile (a description of how often each function is expected to be used), then you have an additional means of prioritizing the testing. Most of your test time should deal with the most-used configurations and operations. Testing multiple configurations will be discussed in more detail in the section "Test Configurations" later in this chapter.

One additional approach to make system testing more effective is to get the development team to perform thorough unit and integration testing before delivering code to the test team. All too often a build is delivered to the test team, only to find that the code cannot be installed, or that if it installs, will not function. A good deal of system test time can be saved if there are entry criteria in place that prevent unusable code from being delivered to the test team.

The scope of testing should be defined in the test plan documents. A sample format for a test plan is described later in this chapter. An example test plan is presented in Part III.

Define the Testing Approach

The second part of formulating the test strategy is to define the testing approach. Building a testing approach begins by examining each phase of the development life cycle to identify the static and dynamic tests that can be used in that phase. It doesn't matter if the development life cycle model being followed is a waterfall, spiral development, or iterative release life cycle model—the phases of any life cycle model can be examined with the intent of identifying effective tests. As an example we examine the phases for a waterfall model to see what types of testing might be used.

Requirements phase: Identify all requirements documents that are produced in this phase and all inspection results that are generated as a result of static testing. If you are working on the test plan during the requirements phase, this step may help you plan and schedule the necessary inspections. Identify the test team members that will take part in the inspections. Identify a repository where the inspection results will be stored.

System design phase: Identify all design documents that will be produced in this phase and plan for test team participation in the associated inspections. The requirements documents will tell you *what* needs to be tested; the high-level design documents will allow you to begin to understand *how* to do the testing.

Program design, code, unit test, and integration test phases: If the test team is involved in static or dynamic testing for any of these activities, corresponding test plans will be needed. Sometimes the test team will run memory leak tests or cyclomatic complexity testing during the unit or integration test phase; if so, the plan for these tests needs to be included in the overall test planning. If the development team will be solely responsible for these phases, state their role as an assumption.

System test: Describe the types of testing that you plan: functional, stress, load, security, upgrade, usability, and so on. State the high-level objectives of these tests and how they will be tied back to requirements or functional specs. If some types of tests are going to be omitted, state the rationale for the omission and evaluate the risk of the omission.

Acceptance test: Describe plans for acceptance testing, including alpha, beta, or other acceptance tests. It is often useful to produce a standalone acceptance test plan that describes the scope and constraints of the testing, entry and exit criteria, and the test environment. Since the purpose of the acceptance test is often as much to demonstrate functionality to customers as to find bugs, it is often a good idea to consider the acceptance test plan as an externally directed document.

Regression test: Describe plans for any regression testing, whether it is for ongoing maintenance releases or as part of an iterative release strategy. Describe how regression tests will be chosen and developed, what equipment will be used, and the strategy for automating the regression tests. Assuming that not all functionality will be covered, describe the scope of the regression tests and identify the risks associated with not covering the areas that are omitted.

The test approach needs to be captured in the test plan documentation. One way to do this is shown in the template described later in this chapter. An example test plan for the Test Management Toolkit application is provided in Part III.

Define Testing Criteria and Quality Checkpoints

The purpose of defining testing criteria is to set rules in place to govern the flow of testing. It is important to define testing criteria before testing starts. Once you've started executing your test plan, it's too late to announce the criteria that you will use to start or stop testing. For example, if you are counting on the software passing a set of unit and integration tests before it comes to the test team for system testing, you need to say so up front in your test plan, and have the test plan reviewed and approved by the people who will be running the unit and integration tests. Setting and adhering to testing criteria can help a project stay on schedule by avoiding the waste of time associated with testing software that is not ready to be tested, or by continuing to test software that needs to be fixed.

Since testing criteria affect other teams, they should not be unilaterally imposed by the test group, but should be derived from a discussion with all the affected teams. Criteria may be established for unit and integration testing, but these are usually set by the development organization. The testing criteria discussed here mainly apply to system testing.

Here are five types of criteria that can be defined before the start of system testing.

Entry criteria explain what needs to be done before you begin testing. For example, you might want to have requirements and specification documents finalized. You might require that the build be packaged in the same way that it will be delivered to the customer. There may be utilities, configuration files, or data that will be used by the customer that you need during testing. If you're responsible for verifying product documentation, it will need to be available in time for testing. One way to ensure that the entry criteria are met is to conduct a system test readiness review. This review can involve a checklist of action items that other teams have agreed to provide as an input to testing.

Exit criteria describe what you consider to be necessary in order to conclude testing. While test groups often try to make their exit criteria a condition on shipping the product, this is unrealistic. The decision to ship is and should be made by higher-level management. The exit criteria should be something like: "All planned tests have been run, all fixed bugs have been verified, and all new bugs found have been reported. Exceptions to the plan, such as not running a set of tests because of equipment problems, have been documented." As was done with the entry criteria, a readiness review can be conducted to ensure that all testing has been completed, and to assess the readiness of the product for shipment based upon the test results.

Suspension/resumption criteria describe what will happen if testing is blocked by bugs. In other words, if things are so bad that you can't run the planned tests, then you need to suspend testing until they are fixed.

Test pass/fail criteria. Each test that is run should have a defined expected result. If the expected result is obtained, the test passes; otherwise it fails. However, there may be a group of tests that are not run because they are broken, because they are blocked by bugs, or because sufficient resources were not available to run them. It is a good idea to specify up front how you are going to deal with tests that are not run. Perhaps you plan to log each test not run with an "N" in the results report and explain in a comments field what happened and what was done if anything to get around the problem. Or perhaps your plan is to substitute *ad hoc* testing for tests that are broken and log the results in the test report.

Other criteria determined by process or standards. If your product must comply with a standard, or if your company places requirements on your process, you may have additional test criteria to consider. For example, there may be particular means defined by your local process for reporting bugs or for reporting test results.

In addition to the above criteria, it is also useful to define testing criteria and provide checklists for the readiness in the test plan documents. This is illustrated in the description of the test plan later in the chapter, and in the example test plan in Part III.

Define Automation Strategy

With proper planning and reasonable expectations, the use of automated tools and automated test cases is an excellent way to reduce the time required to test a product. Any task that is done repetitively is a candidate for automation. However, it usually takes much more time to automate a task than to perform it, so for each task that might be automated, it is worth carefully analyzing the benefits to be achieved with automation. In performing a benefits analysis, it should be remembered that automation has a complete and separate life cycle of its own. Effective automation requires training, development, debugging, and verification just like any other software development project. An unplanned or poorly executed automation effort will not only be a waste of resources, it can have a negative impact on the schedule if time is spent debugging automation rather than testing.

In their book, *Automated Software Testing*, Dustin, Rashka, and Paul (1999) describe common false expectations for automated testing as well as the benefits that can be expected if automation is implemented correctly and follows a rigorous process. The false expectations are summarized in Table 3.1, and the achievable benefits of automation are summarized in Table 3.2.

Table 3.1
False Expectations of Automated Testing [adapted from Dustin, Rashka, and Paul (1999)]

False Expectation	Comment
Everything can be automated.	There are several instances where automation doesn't make sense. If a test is only going to be run once, it makes no sense to automate it because it will take longer to automate the test than to run it. If the requirements or code are unstable such that the application is in a state of churn, it doesn't make sense to automate tests that will continuously be broken. Also, tests that require manual intervention, such as changes to hardware in the middle of the test, may not make sense to automate.
One tool can do it all.	Currently no commercially available tool can automatically generate a test plan, support test design, and manage test execution. No single tool is available that supports all operating systems and all programming languages. Automation tools need to be carefully selected for the job at hand.
The test schedule will be immediately reduced.	Automation can reduce the time required to test, but a substantial investment in training, automation development, and process improvement may be needed to realize the schedule reduction. When automation is first adopted, expect the schedule to expand to support the initial investment of resources.
Modern automation tools are easy to use.	Tool vendors are continuously improving the ease of use of automation tools, but you should not assume that a tool can be used effectively without a significant learning curve. Training time and ongoing vendor support should be carefully evaluated when planning an automation strategy.
Automation permits 100% test coverage.	Even with automation, you cannot completely test a computer program. See the sidebar earlier in this chapter for more detail.

If you decide to invest in automation, you should realize how it impacts the rest of your testing strategy. For example, the task of setting up a test environment may depend on whether the tests to be run are automated or manual. While the same hardware must be procured, cabled, connected to the network, and made operational for manual or automated tasks, you may decide to make the automated test environment a permanent configuration so that the automated tests can be run without manual intervention. If the automated tests are to be run for regression or maintenance purposes, it will certainly make sense to build a dedicated, static test setup that remains in place as long as the product is supported. However, this might represent a more substantial investment in hardware and space for the test environment than for manual tests that are configured on the fly.

Another consideration in developing an automation strategy relates to process. It is generally true that the software testing needs to be mature before automation is adopted. By "mature" it is meant that testing is integrated into the software development life cycle, that test objectives and test cases are based on requirements, and that a standalone test organization exists. An attempt to use automation when the testing process is in a chaotic state is not likely to be effective. Automation is best added as part of a continuous process improvement initiative rather than by taking a "big bang" approach of automating everything at once. (See Chapter 6 for more information on test process improvement.)

Your plans for automation should be included in the Approach section of the test plan documentation. If a substantial automation effort is anticipated, you'll probably want to have a standalone automation planning document that includes all aspects of the automation project: benefits tradeoff analysis, scope of the effort, responsibilities, tools analysis, and schedule.

Table 3.2
Benefits of Automated Testing [adapted from Dustin, Rashka, and Paul (1999)]

Benefit	Comment
Improved system reliability	
• Improved requirements definition	A variety of tools are available that support the development of testable requirements. Some tools require the use of a formal language for requirements definition, while others model requirements graphically.
• Improved performance and stress testing	Load-testing tools are available that allow the test engineer to develop scripts that automatically

Benefit	Comment
	capture performance statistics related to response times, multiple users, multiple transactions, and large transaction volumes. Stress tests can be run in which extreme loads can be applied to determine ways in which the system breaks.
• Improved testing repeatability	Automated tests run the same way each time, which reduces testing errors caused by variations in a manual test procedure. Test repeatability is important when reproducing bugs and verifying fixes.

Improved quality of test effort

Benefit	Comment
• Improved build verification testing	Automated tests can be used as a "smoke test" on a build before it goes from development into system testing. Entry criteria often call for the passing of a smoke test, thereby reducing wasted effort on a build that is not yet ready to test.
• Improved static and dynamic testing of code	Code can be analyzed for memory leaks, excessive complexity, runtime errors, unreachable code, and other problems. See Chapter 9 for more information on such static testing.
• Improved regression testing	Automated regression testing is used to verify that previously working code has not been broken in a new build.
• Improved compatibility testing	In some cases automated tests can be ported to a different hardware configuration or operating system, thus supporting a broadened range of test coverage without increasing the amount of manual testing.
• Improved execution of mundane tasks and after-hours testing	Automation of monotonous, mundane tasks reduces the likelihood of test errors and contributes to a reduced test schedule. Automated test runs can be made at night and on weekends, freeing up test engineers to focus on less mundane tasks during prime-time hours.

Reduction of test schedule

Benefit	Comment
• Less time required to run tests	Automated test cases, once developed and debugged, usually require much less time to run than manual tests.
• Less time required to analyze results	Automated tests usually generate test logs and test reports.

(continued)

Table 3.2
Benefits of Automated Testing [adapted from Dustin, Rashka, and Paul (1999)] *(cont'd)*

Benefit	Comment
• Less time to determine test status and report test results	Most automated test management tools can quickly generate status reports that show number of tests run, number of passed and failed tests, and other statistics.

Defining the Test System

Once the test strategy has been defined, you are ready to move to the next level of detail in the test planning process: defining the test system. The test system refers not only to the hardware that is to be used in testing, but also to the test architecture, the test tools, and the test configurations. We begin our discussion with the test architecture.

Test Architecture

Test architecture refers to the organizational structure of the test cases. It is a good practice to organize your tests so that each test isolates a specific part of the software functionality. If the test fails, it is easy for a developer to run your test and reproduce the failure, then analyze the failure and find the fault. Ideally, the scope of the test has been reduced to the minimum set of steps necessary to cause the failure.

If you are basing your tests on product requirements, the rule of thumb for the scope of a test is that at least one test be written for each requirement. In addition to keeping the tests to an efficient size, this notion of "at least one test per requirement" also supports test planning. By reviewing the requirements document you can get a good idea of how many new tests will be needed for a new product. Once you start writing tests in this orderly way, you can estimate how long it will take to develop and run a test based on past results.

Requirements-based testing lends itself well to test organization. Requirements are generally grouped together by functionality. You can organize your tests in the same way. Tests related to customer provisioning can be grouped together, as can tests for installing or upgrading the software. A group of related tests is called a *test suite*.

A requirement can involve more than one component. For example, a requirement for editing the database entry for a given customer might involve a number of different scenarios. The fields that need to be entered might be different for silver, gold, or platinum customers, so you would want to test differently for different customer classes.

One way to handle this situation is to allow the test to consist of different test cases, one for each class of customer. A *test case* is a set of test inputs, execution conditions, and expected results that are developed for a particular objective. The test case is the smallest unit of testing that can be independently executed from beginning to end. The relationship between test suite, test, and test case is shown in Figure 3.3 and Table 3.3.

Once you have defined the organizational structure of your tests, you need to specify a repository for storing the tests and a means of version control so that the tests can be reproduced. This repository should have the following characteristics:

- It should be readily accessible to all test engineers who develop and run tests. A shared network drive is often used as a repository.

- It should be regularly backed-up, and the backed-up files should be periodically restored to verify that the backup/restore functionality

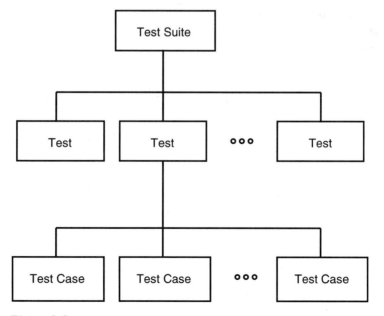

Figure 3.3
Test architecture.

Table 3.3
Test Hierarchy

Level	Definition
Test suite	Collection of tests used to validate a related group of requirements or functions.
Test	One or more test cases that focus on a single requirement or function.
Test case	Smallest unit of testing that can be independently executed from beginning to end.

works. As obvious as the need is for backing up all test plans, test cases, and test results, it is sometimes neglected.

- It should have version control so that older tests can be easily retrieved. Version control ensures that any test ever run on a product can be reproduced if the need arises.

Test Tools

Earlier in the chapter it was noted that the decision to invest in automated testing impacts all of your testing strategy. In this section we focus on test tools that can be used to implement test automation. Your overall automation strategy should not be limited to testing a single product; it should be a global strategy that will span multiple projects and be thoroughly integrated into the test process.

The plan to test a specific product should therefore consider what part of the overall automation strategy will be implemented in the current project. Perhaps you will add automated load testing, or will automate GUI testing, or will have automated test reports that post test results and metrics to a Web page. When you assess the time and cost associated with evaluating and procuring (or building) the tool needed to accomplish the desired automation, and then assess the effort for training and gaining familiarity with the new tool, you are likely to decide that only one or two new tools can be added per project. Trying to adopt several new tools at once is counterproductive as well as costly.

There is a wide variety of tools that can be used to support software testing. Some of these tools are summarized in Table 3.4. The table maps the tools to the software development life cycle phase in which they might be used.

Further information on test tools can be found in Dustin, Rashka, and Paul (1999), Lewis (2000), and Perry (2000). Each of these references contains useful information on test planning as well.

Test Environment

The test environment consists of the physical test facilities, the operating system on which the product runs, and the computing platform on which the product runs. Many companies that test software products have labs that are dedicated to testing. Like automation, the development of a good test lab is a long-term investment that spans multiple projects and requires a dedicated effort. Of course, good testing can be done in a single cube with a single computer, but it has become common to have a dedicated test lab to provide a controlled environment where the product can be evaluated under repeatable, well-defined conditions.

Rex Black (1999) provides a useful discussion on stocking and managing a test lab in his book, *Managing the Test Process*. He suggests that you consider the following questions when deciding if you need to establish a dedicated test lab. A business case could likely be put together if you answer "yes" to any of the following questions.

- Do you require large, nonportable equipment such as environmental test chambers, data generators/analyzers, or electromagnetic radiation measurement gear?

- Do you have special security requirements to protect proprietary information or expensive investments?

- Do you need to carefully monitor and control your test conditions? This could mean, for example, that you need to keep all nontest personnel away from your test systems to prevent unexpected changes in the test conditions.

- Do you need to maintain a set of fixed test configurations for an extended period of time, for example, to support the maintenance of an iterative set of releases?

When planning to test a specific product release, you'll need to determine what part of the overall lab strategy will need to be implemented. For example, you may need to add a particular type of data generation equipment, or may need additional computer platforms to implement load or stress tests.

Table 3.4
Representative Test Tools

Test Tool	Helps the Tester to:	Life Cycle Phase
Defect tracking tool	Enter and store bug reports Generate metrics and summary reports	All phases
Test management tools	Store test plans, test cases (manual and automated), test results Communicate test status	All phases
Requirements management tools	Organize and track requirements Trace tests to requirements	Data initially entered in requirements analysis and evaluation, but can be used throughout life cycle
Memory leak and run-time error detection tools	Test for memory leaks and run-time errors	Typically used during coding, unit, and integration test
Source code testing tools	Test complexity, cyclomatic complexity, and standards compliance	Typically used during coding, unit, and integration test
Code or test coverage analyzers	Use source code instrumentation to measure the portion of code covered during dynamic testing	Used with dynamic testing in integration or system test phase
Source code comparator	Compare two versions of source code to see if they are identical, or if not, to determine the differences	System and regression testing

Test Tool	Helps the Tester to:	Life Cycle Phase
Test data generators	Generate test data and populate databases	All testing phases: unit, integration, system, regression
GUI record/playback tools	Record keystrokes and mouse clicks of a user, play back the actions, compare results of test to expected results	System and regression testing
Load/performance/stress tools	• Run a number of clients simultaneously to load a server • Run clients in high-stress scenarios to see if the system fails	System and regression test
Network test tools	Assess performance of server and network to accurately transfer data	System and regression test
Command-line scripting	Automate commands to perform test setups, test data loading, or test results analysis	All testing phases: unit, integration, system, regression

Test Configurations

Suppose the product that you are testing is specified to run on a variety of network configurations, use several different configurations of client machines, and is to work with a variety of operating systems and browsers. When you analyze the number of possible test configurations, you come up with the following combinations:

- 5 network configurations
- 10 combinations of browsers and operating systems
- 20 combinations of client configurations (CPU, hard drives, video cards, and peripherals)

The number of possible test configurations is therefore $5 \times 10 \times 20 = 1,000$ configurations. If you expect it to take two people three weeks to run the planned system tests for a single configuration, then you're looking at taking 240,000 person-hours or 125 person-years to completely test all configurations! Unless you have very deep pockets and a big test staff, or you can take a very long time to test the product before releasing it, this kind of test effort is not practical.

Earlier in the chapter we derived a basic principle of testing that states "you cannot completely test a program." It is equally true that when you have several combinations of system configurations, you cannot completely test all possible system configurations. The trick is to prioritize the configurations and then decide which configurations require complete testing and which ones can be partially tested.

Prioritizing configurations usually depends on factors such as:

- Frequency of use: How many instances of a given configuration are likely to be in use?
- Risk of failure: Are there any mission-critical configurations for major customers?
- Likelihood of failure: Have any particular configurations demonstrated failures in the past?

Once you have identified candidate configurations for complete or partial testing, the next step is to determine which tests to run on the configurations that will not be completely tested. Assuming that you have prioritized the tests (see "Defining the Scope of Testing" earlier in this chapter), you can run only high-priority tests on some configurations and run tests that have a high likelihood of failure on configurations that have shown problems in the past.

When the configurations to be tested have been identified, you need to define them in enough detail that they can be set up by a test engineer or technician and reproduced at any time that the test needs to be run. Each test configuration might be defined by a block diagram and a parts list, or, if the connectivity between components of the system is obvious, the configuration might be defined by a list of components.

Estimating the Test Effort

One of the most critical components of planning is estimating the effort and time required for testing. The cost of testing can be a substantial portion of the overall project, and it is vitally important to the success of the test effort that enough people and time be available to do the job properly.

There are five steps in preparing an estimate for a project:

1. **Identify the tasks to be done.** Estimation begins by defining the work that must be done to test the product. In some estimation methodologies, constructing a work breakdown structure will fulfill this step. If a less formal method is used, the output of this step might simply be a list of tasks.

2. **Determine the effort required for each task and for the overall test life cycle.** Each task identified in the first step will have an associated effort, which is the amount of work required to perform the task. Effort is the product of people and time, and is measured in units such as person-days or person-months. There are a variety of ways to estimate effort; we will examine some of them in a later section.

3. **Determine the time required for each task and for the overall test life cycle.** The time or duration required to perform a task can be determined in days, weeks, or months. The time that it takes to perform a task depends on the number of people assigned to work on the task, but as we shall see below, the relationship is not necessarily linear. The total duration of the test effort will depend on the durations of the individual tasks, but it is not a simple sum, because some tasks may be performed in parallel.

4. **Construct a detailed schedule and a milestone chart for the test effort.** Put together the results from the previous three steps to create a

schedule, perhaps in the form of a Gantt chart, and summarize the important dates in a milestone chart.

5. **Assess schedule risks and formulate mitigation plans.** Anticipate problems in accomplishing key tasks in the allotted time, and plan for how to deal with the problems.

Before we begin discussing these steps in more detail, it is important to understand how accurate we can expect our estimates to be. At the start of a project (before requirements are elicited and analyzed), it is very difficult to understand how much a project will cost. It is only at the end of a project that the actual cost is known. At the start of a project it is not uncommon to overestimate or underestimate the actual cost by as much as a factor of four. By the time that the requirements have been analyzed and initial project planning is complete, it is more typical to be within a factor of two of the final, actual project cost (Boehm, 1981). The accuracy of an estimate is illustrated in Figure 3.4.

Due to the inherent inaccuracies of the estimation process, it is a good idea to periodically revisit the estimated effort and schedule as part of managing the test effort. If the time or cost starts exceeding the original estimates, it is better to alert project management about the problem quickly rather than waiting for the situation to become a crisis.

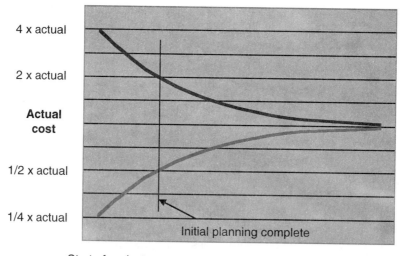

Figure 3.4
Accuracy of estimation. *Adapted from Boehm (1981).*

The next few sections of this chapter present an overview of the estimation process. Alternate strategies for performing the three main steps listed above are presented along with an assessment of their pros and cons. More details of estimation techniques, particularly those that relate to algorithmic estimation, will be presented in Chapter 12. Two good references on estimation are Boehm's classic book, *Software Engineering Economics* (1981), and his recent update on the COCOMO II estimation model, *Software Cost Estimation with COCOMO II* (2000).

Identify Tasks

The simplest way to come up with a list of tasks is to scan the requirements documents, writing down all the work that needs to be performed in order to test the features defined in the requirements. Once the tasks are identified, the list should then be prioritized. The requirements documents should give guidance as to the relative priority of the features, but there may be additional considerations for defining priorities. For example, some of the features may be minor modifications of code used in an earlier release of the product, whereas some of the features may be completely new to the release to be tested. You would probably want to devote more effort in testing the new code than the modified code. You will also need to dedicate enough time to design, build, and debug tests for the new code.

In addition to a simple scan of the requirements, you need to consider tasks that are not directly related to the requirements documents but that enable the testing. For example, you might consider including the following tasks in your list:

- Write test plan
- Review test plan
- Develop test cases
- Review test cases
- Debug test cases
- Validate bug fixes
- Identify test and product metrics and a process for their collection and use
- Static testing: inspections and reviews of software design and code
- Implement a suitable portion of your test automation strategy
- Review user documentation

- Procure equipment needed for this project as part of an overall test lab strategy
- Hire test engineers and technicians with needed skill sets
- Train test engineers on new technology and new tools
- Run tests and report results
- Conduct readiness reviews
- Perform post-project assessment

Once an initial task list is built, it's a good idea to review the list with the test team and mentally walk through the entire development life cycle, identifying things that the test team needs to do and the deliverables that need to be produced. The task list is likely to be a dynamic document throughout the planning stage, and perhaps throughout the testing life cycle, as you continue to refine your understanding of what needs to be done.

Another name for a task list is a *work breakdown structure* (WBS). A work breakdown structure is often a little more formal than the simple task list just described. A WBS can be a simple list of tasks, or it can be a hierarchical arrangement of activities in which a "tag" or identifier is attached to each task. The tag allows progress on the task to be tracked throughout the development life cycle, and allows effort or cost measurements to be associated with the various tasks so that a set of metrics can be collected for the actual effort expended during the project. Of course, more formality and more accounting means more overhead in terms of time and cost, so you'll need to make intelligent tradeoffs about how much detail you want to use in your project planning and management. A common middle ground is to use a project management tool such as Microsoft Project in planning and tracking the test effort. If you do use a tool, you'll want to make sure that its input and output is compatible with other tools used by other teams in the management of the overall project.

For rapid testing, the task list needs to be carefully built so that it contains all major tasks, especially those that require preparation time, such as equipment procurement, hiring or training of personnel, and test design. Forgetting to prepare for a major task before testing can readily lead to schedule slips. Another good investment of effort during planning is to coordinate the tasks that you have identified with other teams. Clearly identifying and communicating responsibilities for each task on the list is an effective way to keep the schedule on track, particularly if you expect someone who is not on your team to perform some of the tasks.

Determine Effort

Once you have defined the tasks that need to be done in testing the product, the next step in planning is to estimate the effort associated with the tasks. Effort can be measured in people-days, people-months, or people-years. Whatever the units, *effort* is a measure of the people and time required to perform a set of tasks. Some care needs to be taken when estimating effort, because there are common situations where linear arithmetic cannot be applied. A classic mistake made in planning is to assume that a task that can be performed by one person in four weeks can be performed in one week by four people, since both approaches have an effort of four person-weeks. The fallacy of this approach is discussed in Sidebar 3.2.

SIDEBAR 3.2

CLASSIC MISTAKES IN ESTIMATION

Regardless of the estimation technique that is used, there are a number of factors that can lead to inaccurate estimates. Here are some of the factors that can lead to classic mistakes in the estimation process:

- Incomplete requirements
- Changes to requirements
- Overestimating time that people can work on assigned task
- Not accounting for problems in integrating system components
- Not accounting for the time required to fix defects
- Not accounting for time required to handle unexpected problems
- Ignoring time required for training
- Including overtime work as part of the initial plan
- Not obtaining buy-in from the people who do the work
- Unrealistically adding people to a task in an attempt to shorten its duration

The first two items on the list relate to requirements. It cannot be stated enough that a complete set of requirements is essential to the planning and estimation process, and if requirements continue to change after they have been "frozen," the job of planning has to be done again.

The remaining items on the list deal with unrealistic expectations. For example, it is unrealistic to assume that each person will be fully dedicated to his or her planned tasks for 40 or more hours a week for the duration of the project. This leaves no time for meetings, training, or informal peer communication. Time needs to be allocated for debugging tests, time for medical or personal problems, and so on.

The last item, unrealistically adding people to shorten a task, needs some explanation. Before people can be added to shorten a task, it needs to be determined that the task is *partitionable* (Brooks, 1982). For example, no more than one person should drive a car at the same time, therefore, the task of driving is not partitionable. For tasks that are partitionable, there are two elements of overhead to be considered: training the additional people that are added to the task, and intercommunication between the people who are simultaneously working on the task. Training the new workers is not partitionable, so the added effort of training more workers increases linearly with the number of people added.

The possible communications paths between workers are shown in Figure 3.5. For one person on a task there is no added effort due to communications. If one additional worker is added, there is an added bidirectional component of communications between the two workers. If a third worker is added to the task, there is three times as much communications as for two workers. The effort associated with communications between workers does not increase linearly with the number of people added, but rather increases as $n(n-1)/2$ (Brooks, 1982).

In summary, two common mistakes of adding people to a task to shorten the schedule are applying people to a task that cannot be partitioned, and ignoring the overhead due to training and communications that are associated with adding workers.

The way to overcome the problems listed above and achieve better estimates is:

- Start with well-defined and "frozen" requirements.

- Base expectations and risk mitigation plans on results from similar, previous projects.

- Be realistic about how much time can be saved by adding people to a task.

One person

Communication between 2 people

Communication between 3 people

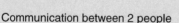

Figure 3.5
Communications between workers.

Here is an overview of some common effort estimation techniques, arranged more-or-less in order of sophistication and complexity. Be warned, however, that the more sophisticated techniques don't necessarily give more accurate estimates. Any estimation technique will depend on the skill and knowledge of its user, and will need to be calibrated against historical data to assess its accuracy.

1. **Fitting a constrained budget or schedule**. Sometimes there is no freedom in determining the number of people or the time that can be applied to a project. For these situations an estimate is still needed, but the outputs may be different. For example, you may know that the product must be tested by a given date, but there is some flexibility in how many people may be applied to the problem. In this case you would look at performing only tasks that have the highest priority, and running as many tasks in parallel as possible. In this situation, however, it is as important to define the limitations and risks associated with the test effort as to come up with the effort estimate.

2. **Analogy to previous project.** If the product under development is one in a series of iterative releases, or is similar to a finished product, it may be possible to use historical data from the earlier project to estimate the new one. It is important that the actual costs of the earlier project are available, and that the conditions of the earlier project be similar to the new one. For example, the same people or people with similar skills need to work on both projects.

3. **Expert judgment**. One or more experts estimate the people and time needed to perform the defined tasks. This method can be as simple as one person writing an estimate on the back of an envelope, or it can be as complex as using a team-consensus method such as the Wideband Delphi technique. A brief description of Wideband Delphi is given in Sidebar 3.3.

4. **Decomposition techniques**. If the product is large and complex, the estimate for developing and testing the product is likely to be time-consuming and complex. It is likely in these situations that a project manager will be assigned to develop the budget and schedule for the project as a whole, and the test team will need to provide input to the project manager in a specified format. The project manager may count on each team to come up with its own estimate using one of the techniques mentioned above, or may use a more unified approach where the product is *sized* in terms of lines of code or function points, and an estimation algorithm is applied to generate the estimate. If this approach is used, it is a good idea for the test team to in-

dependently derive an estimate—for example, using expert judgment—to insure that the result from the algorithmic approach makes sense.

5. **Empirical estimation models**. There are a variety of estimation models that can be used to predict the effort of a software development project. These models are usually based on the number of lines of code (LOC) or number of function points (FP), and each model will give different results for the same input. The key to using any of these models is to calibrate it for local conditions by running the model against completed projects and then adjusting the model to give predicted results that match actual data. More information on a well-known estimation technique, COCOMO, is given in Chapter 12.

SIDEBAR 3.3

HOW TO PREPARE AN ESTIMATE OF TEST EFFORT

The recommended steps for conducting an estimation work session are listed below. This procedure, which is a version of the Wideband Delphi Estimation Process, needs to be done early in the planning phase so that you have enough time to do each step. Expect your accuracy to get worse if you skip steps.

Preparation. Prepare data input forms for use in collecting and documenting estimates. Prepare brief explanatory material that tells participants how the process works and what is expected of them.

Kickoff meeting. Call a kickoff meeting to explain the estimation process and to assign new features to team members so they can research the features and explain them as needed at the working session. When the team members leave this meeting, they should have a list of items to estimate and understand how to perform the estimates. Think carefully before skipping this step—it gets everyone on the same page and prevents estimation errors due to lack of understanding of the process or the items to estimate.

Homework. Participants make individual estimates. Allow enough time for participants to gain an understanding of the new features of the release, but you don't want them to dwell on their initial estimates so long that they are not open to input from other participants. Be sure the team members understand that they are estimating the number of hours (or days) it would take to do a task, assuming that the resources are available to do the job. The units of measure (person-hours, person-days) should be understood.

Working session. Call a working session meeting to review and revise estimates. The meeting moderator collects the estimates and puts them onto an estimate summary form. The summarized estimates are returned to the team for discussion and review.

The team discusses the estimates, which often widely vary from person to person, and then submit revised estimates to the moderator. This process can be repeated until no one is willing to change their estimates, the estimates are within reasonable agreement, or the time allotted for the meeting expires. You should take no longer than 2 hours for a working session like this—if you go too long, the results become flaky. During the working session some issues may come up that need to be resolved outside the meeting. Assign people to resolve them.

Resolve issues. If there are unresolved issues from the working session, get them resolved and then either call another working session or, if the ramifications are minor, discuss the new information with a knowledgeable subteam. Update the estimates based on the new information.

Roll up the estimate. Take the final estimate summary and decide the maximum and minimum estimates of effort for each task. You may want to apply your engineering judgment or historical perspective to throw away some outlying data points as being unrealistic. Add the individual minimum and maximum estimates to get totals. You will then have two results: an optimistic or aggressive estimate of effort (minimum value) and a pessimistic or conservative estimate (maximum value). Be sure to document all assumptions that have been made in reaching the final estimate.

Convert the estimate to a schedule. Now that you have an estimate of the effort required, you need to come up with the other information that you're bound to be asked: When will you finish? One rule of thumb (McConnell, 1996, p. 183) is

$$\text{Schedule duration in months} = 3.0 * \text{person-months}^{1/3}$$

Of course, you'll want to come up with a more accurate schedule than is given by this simple relationship.

Determine Duration and Construct Schedule

Once the tasks are identified and the effort for each task is determined, determine the time required for each task and take a first cut at the schedule. The time required to perform a task, also called the duration, will depend upon how many people are able to work on it. If you apply more than one person to a task, be sure that the task is partitionable—in other words, make sure it is a task that can be productively worked on by more than one person at a time. Some tasks, such as grilling a steak, are done no faster when more than one person is applied to the job. More discussion on this point can be found in Sidebar 3.2.

After each task has people assigned, it is possible to see what tasks can be done concurrently and which will need to be done in sequence. One of the factors to consider in scheduling tasks will be the use of common equipment. You may have enough people lined up to work tasks concurrently, but you'll need to remember to assess the availability of equipment as well. If there is a lot of shared equipment, you may want to construct a separate schedule for the equipment, or build a logistics database that tracks people, equipment, and test time (see Black, 1999, for more information on building a logistics database).

The tasks, assigned resources (people and equipment), and durations can be displayed graphically in a bar chart such as the one shown in Figure 3.6. The bar chart can also be used to display project milestones, which are significant events in the life of the project, such as start of testing, end of testing, or product ship date. In Figure 3.6, the milestones are shown as X's or crossed vertical and horizontal lines. While the chart in the figure only shows the names of the tasks and the associated dates, a more detailed chart might show the resources assigned to the task, text listings of start and end dates, and other project management information.

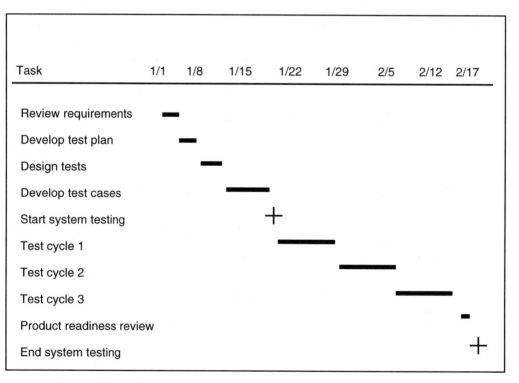

Figure 3.6
Sample bar chart.

Table 3.4
Sample Milestone Chart

Milestone	Date
Test plan complete	1/8
Test case development complete	1/18
Start of system test	1/18
Test cycle 1 complete	1/25
Test cycle 2 complete	2/1
Test cycle 3 complete	2/12
Product readiness review	2/14
End of system test	2/14

Often the project milestones are summarized in a separate table called a milestone chart. An example of a milestone chart, which can be used by test and corporate management to track testing progress, is shown in Table 3.4.

Assess Schedule Risk

Once you have developed an estimate of the people, equipment, and time needed to test a product, you'll need to assess the risk associated with your estimate. This can be done by considering what is most likely to go wrong during the test effort and then defining a plan for fixing the problems that arise. The amount of effort to perform the risk mitigation will give you an idea of how much your estimate might fall short in terms of time and cost. The risk built into your estimate is certainly something that you will want to communicate to upper management when the estimate is reviewed.

Examples of risks that can impact the testing schedule are:

- Hardware needed is not available at start of test
- Software to be tested is not available at start of test
- Test cases are not ready at start of test
- People scheduled to test are not available at start of test
- Requirements change during test development or during testing
- User interface changes during test development or during testing
- Training on new test tools has not been completed by start of test

Just thinking about a risk often directly leads to a risk mitigation plan. For example, if you decide that the test cases might not be ready in time to test, you have a basis for making a request to hire additional test engineers. If you depend upon critical new hardware for the project, by publishing the dependence and assessing risk to schedule, you put the project manager on notice that the delivery date for the hardware is start of testing, not the ship date.

It is a common practice in risk management to associate with each risk a probability that the risk will occur and a measure of the impact to the project if the risk occurs. For example, you might decide that it is very likely (probability of 90%) that key people will not be available to test at the planned start date, and you assess the impact to your ability of meeting the test schedule as critical (on a scale of critical, high, medium, low). A risk that has critical impact and a high likelihood of occurrence is obviously a risk for which you should have a contingency plan. In this case you'll probably want to negotiate for a change in the schedule or change in priorities of the people that are needed to perform the testing.

A suggested process for assessing risk is:

- List all risks that you think might jeopardize your ability to meet the test schedule. Consider historical data such as post-project assessments or anecdotal information about what went wrong in previous projects. Assess dependencies on other teams by discussing with them the likelihood that they will meet your test-entry criteria.

- Assess the probability of occurrence for each risk identified.

- Assess the impact of the occurrence of the risk to the success of your meeting the test schedule. Use a scale such as critical, high, medium, or low to describe the impact.

- Develop plans for reducing the probability of occurrence or the impact of risks, beginning with those that have high probability or high impact.

There is a lot of literature available on risk management. If you wish to learn more, Pressman (1997), Pfleeger (2000), and Boehm (1991) offer concise but useful information.

Preparing and Reviewing the Test Plan Documents

Test Plan Format

Once you have determined a test strategy, defined the test system, and estimated the effort, you are ready to create the test plan. The test plan is a document or set of documents that is the output of the test planning activities. It is a living document that changes as requirements change. A useful guideline for developing a test plan may be found in IEEE Standard 829, *IEEE Standard for Software Test Documentation* (IEEE, 1983). You may choose to use an alternate format, but you should consider including all the material in the IEEE standard in whatever format you choose. For other ideas and formats, refer to Dustin, Rashka, and Paul (1999), Lewis (2000), Perry (2000), and Black (1999). In this section, we use IEEE Standard 829 to construct a test plan template.

The outline of a test plan is defined in the standard to have 16 components (IEEE, 1983):

1. Test plan identifier
2. Introduction
3. Test items
4. Features to be tested
5. Features not to be tested
6. Approach
7. Item pass/fail criteria
8. Suspension criteria and resumption requirements
9. Test deliverables
10. Testing tasks
11. Environmental needs
12. Responsibilities
13. Staffing and training needs
14. Schedule
15. Risks and contingencies
16. Approvals

If you consider the list above, you'll see two things that the standard test plan is *not*—it is not a detailed specification of how the tests are to be performed, and it is not a place where test results are recorded. Some test organizations combine one or more of these items with the contents of a test plan in order to keep the test documentation all in one place. That can work very well, but in this book we will go for the more modular set of documentation that is set forth in the standard.

That the standard intends to keep test plans, procedures, and results separate is made clear in its definitions of the following documents (IEEE, 1983):

Test plan. A document describing the scope, approach, resources, and schedule of intended testing activities. It identifies test items, the features to be tested, the testing tasks, who will do each task, and any risks requiring contingency planning.

Test procedure specification. A document specifying a sequence of actions for the execution of a test.

Test summary report. A document summarizing testing activities and results. It also contains an evaluation of the corresponding test items.

The test procedure specification will be discussed in Chapter 4 as part of the work done in test development, and test summary reports will be addressed in Chapter 5, which deals with test execution. Ideally all these documents are linked together into an efficient, coordinated system that supports the test process from start to finish.

In this section we analyze the contents of the test plan and optimize its structure for rapid testing. For each component of the plan, we look for a reasonable way to satisfy the intent of the item quickly and efficiently. Of course, some of the decisions made here may not fit your needs, so you'll have to do the same analysis in the context of your development environment.

Each numbered item below corresponds to its counterpart in the outline presented in the previous section. Examples of a test plan, procedure specification, and test summary report are given in Part III.

1. Test Plan Identifier   You'll save time in the long run if you identify and track all your test documents. Generally speaking, here are three key points related to document tracking:

- Have a unique identifier for each test document to eliminate the possibility of someone spending time with the wrong document. The identifier can be an alphanumeric string that relates to the product name, release number, date, or any other information that helps you track the document. It is useful to use an identifier that fits into your overall system of document control.

- Set up a document repository (perhaps a shared network drive fronted by a Web page) that allows engineers and management to quickly locate any document related to testing. If you spin your wheels once during a crisis looking for the right version of a document, you'll be convinced that a document repository is useful.

- Set up a document tracking system that supports version control. Test documents, including test plans, may need to be changed at any time. You want to be able to quickly and accurately communicate the latest changes to engineers and managers. Version control can be as simple as documenting the revision history on the cover sheet of the document, and keeping the version in the document repository current.

2. Introduction   The purpose of the introduction is to briefly provide information to anyone who really wants to use the test plan. The trick is to identify the source documents that constitute the inputs to your test process in the introductory section of the test plan.

For example, you can list the product requirements document and the functional design specification for the product you are testing. When you list these documents, it is helpful to give their location (path to a shared network drive or URL to a Web page) so they can be quickly accessed. A great way to do this is to provide in your test plan a link to the source document so that a user can navigate directly from a soft copy of the plan to the reference. This has the advantage of automatically taking the user to the most current version of the input document.

Other than point to the input documents, you will probably need to spend very little time writing an introduction. The example supplied in IEEE Standard 829 includes objectives of the test plan, background of the product, scope of the test plan, and a list of references. The whole thing is done in about half a page. If there are special constraints that drive planning, such as time to market, you might mention them in this section.

3. Test Items   This is a high-level list of the product components that you are testing. Some of the things to mention in this section:

- Release/version identifier of the product under test
- Fixes to bugs found in previous releases; if the bug list is given in the functional spec, refer to the functional spec and save time by not duplicating it here
- Description of media used to distribute the product (e.g., CD, Web, or ftp site)
- End-user documents such as user guides, installation guides, release notes

Note that this is a list of inputs to your testing. You have to get these things in a timely way in order to meet the testing deadlines, so it is worth noting them in your plan as dependencies. You also want to be clear about what you're testing so that nothing falls through the cracks. For example, it is all too common to "forget" to test the user docs until the last minute.

When you try to fix this kind of omission at the end of a project, it's easy to cause a schedule slip or worse, ship a buggy product to the customer.

4. Features to Be Tested   IEEE Standard 829 offers the following definition of a *software feature:* A distinguishing characteristic of a software item (for example, performance, portability, or functionality).

The definition is very general because it has to cover a lot of ground. It may make more sense to define features in business terms. Consider a feature to be "something that can be sold to a customer." For example, if an application runs slower than customers like, then increasing the speed of its most-used functions can be sold as a feature. A slick new way to speed up data entry or query a database can be sold as a feature.

The key point for test engineers is that if something is promised to a customer, it needs to be identified in the test plan so that it can be tested before shipping the product. The source for finding out what the customer has been promised should be the product requirements document that you referenced back in the introduction.

The list of features in this section provides you with a checklist for estimating the effort required to test the product. Every item in the list should relate to an item in the requirements documents, and every item in the list should have one or more tests defined in the test procedures specification.

5. Features not to Be Tested   The purpose of this section is to explicitly state items that you plan in advance not to cover in testing. Some examples of items that you might list as "features not to be tested" include:

- Features that are being deferred to a later incremental release.
- Test configurations that you cannot test because you do not have the equipment. Sometimes operational setups are so expensive that they cannot be duplicated in a test lab. If you cannot reproduce the operational environment but you can simulate it, you should say so in the "approach" section. If you can't test against the operational environment at all, be sure to discuss this in the "risk" section.
- Combinations of settings or equipment configurations that cannot be tested within the time needed to get the product to market. If a business decision is made to limit the scope of testing for a particular feature, be sure to discuss the limit and the rationale in this section.

Near the end of the project, when the test group is being pressured to finish their job, it is very useful to have documented what you're planning to test and what you do not intend to test. People tend to forget in the heat of battle what agreements have been made—it is good to be able to point to this section of your test plan to fend off questions about why something isn't being covered. Of course, if a problem shows up in the field that was not tested before leaving your lab, it will have to be fixed and tested after release. Since the cost of fixing bugs after release is very high, it is important to make a careful assessment of risk before deciding to omit a feature or configuration from testing.

6. Approach   This section of the test plan is meant to provide a high-level description of how you will test the product. It is not a detailed description of all the test procedures that will be used. The approach described in the test plan should be based on considerations discussed in the earlier section, "Define the Testing Approach." Here are examples of topics that you might include in this section:

- Static testing of requirements and design documents
- Static and dynamic testing to be done in the code, unit, and integration test phases
- Feature testing
- Stress/load/performance testing
- Security testing
- Product installation/upgrade testing
- Data backup/restore tests
- GUI testing
- Regression testing
- Acceptance tests: alpha, beta, and other tests to be done in the field
- Bug fix verification
- Breakdown of automated and manual tests
- Testing to be done by third parties and other test organizations
- Use of defect tracking system to enter bug reports

If you are implementing part of a long-term strategy, such as automation of the test process and test cases, you can discuss what specific aspects of the long-term plan will be implemented in the current test project, and refer to the automation strategy document. For example, you may be planning to introduce a new tool, or you are trying to automate GUI tests for the first time. Or you may plan to use a third-party test organization to perform stress and load testing; this would be a good place to describe the plan at a high level and refer to any written agreements that you might have with the third-party organization.

If you are testing incremental releases of a product, the testing approach for each release is likely to be very similar. You should be able to save time by cutting and pasting large parts of this section from the test plan for the previous release, but should take care to think through any changes that apply to the current release.

7. Pass/Fail Criteria   There are two types of pass/fail criteria that are important to testing. The first relates to the individual tests. Each test case should have a defined set of expected results; generally speaking, if the expected results are obtained, the test passes; if not, the test fails. The pass/fail criteria for the individual tests should be included in the test cases themselves and can be omitted from the test plan. It may be appropriate, however, to mention that pass/fail criteria will be defined as part of each test case.

The second type of pass/fail criteria relates to the testing of the entire product. You need to state up front what constitutes success of the test phase—in other words, when can you quit testing and ship the product. In some cases the exit criteria for testing is defined in the program plan or even in the product requirements document. No matter who originates the criteria, it is good to state them clearly in the test plan. It is of course unrealistic to expect that any criteria that are stated in the test plan will automatically control the release of a product. Product release is a business decision that is made based on information about the quality of a product but also upon other business factors.

8. Suspension Criteria and Resumption Requirements   Earlier in the chapter we stated that entry criteria explain what needs to be done before you begin testing, and exit criteria describe what you consider to be necessary in order to conclude testing. Suspension/resumption criteria describe what happens if testing is blocked by bugs. For example, you might state that if a build contains showstopper bugs that block successful installation of the product, testing will be suspended until the blocking bugs are fixed. Of course you can't stop testing every time some of your tests are blocked, but you need to be able to notify management if a software build is so buggy that testing needs to be suspended.

9. Test Deliverables   This section is the place to define the outputs of the test effort; for example, you might list:

- Test plan
- Test design documents
- Test specification document
- Test results reports
- Defect (bug) reports
- Release notes (if you're responsible for them)

It is a good idea to show the person responsible for each document a deadline for having the document approved. To save time later, you might create some of these documents in template or "skeleton" form at the time that the test plan is written; then provide links or references to the "dummy" documents. For example, it may be useful to have a test results report ready and waiting on test data. In addition, a template for the test design might make the design effort start moving quickly. It is surprising how much time can be wasted in arguments over the format and desired contents of one of these documents.

Defining and getting agreement on what you plan to deliver from the testing phase early in the life cycle is a good practice because it supports the construction of a realistic schedule. To avoid adding useless overhead to the schedule, you'll want to avoid promising any deliverable that is not essential to the end goal, which is shipping a good product as soon as possible.

10. Testing Tasks   If you're using the test plan to document your estimate of the test effort, this is a place to list the individual tasks that are needed to prepare for and perform the testing. Better yet, if you document your estimate in a spreadsheet or with a project management program such as Microsoft Project, you can provide a reference here to the other document. This is another good time to use a link to the reference document or at least provide a path to the file on a network drive.

11. Test Configuration Information (Environmental Needs)
Describe the hardware and software needed to run your tests, and provide diagrams as needed to describe how the hardware components are connected together. The purpose of this section is to allow someone to reproduce the test setup if necessary to reproduce a failure or verify that a fix works. This section of the test plan should be based on considerations

presented in the "Test Environment" and "Test Configurations" sections earlier in the chapter. You may want to expand the scope to include a discussion of test architecture (how your tests are organized) and the test tools that will be used. Both of these topics are covered in "Defining the Test System" earlier in the chapter.

12. Responsibilities   If your test group has any dependencies on another group to get the testing done, here is a place to define who does what. For example, if you are counting on the software developers to include a particular suite of tests during their integration test effort, here is a good place to mention it. Perhaps customer support engineers are going to participate in the test effort by testing the user interface or the user documentation.

Another example of a responsibility that would warrant mentioning here is the case of a remote organization (for example, a contracted lab in another city or another country) that is going to assume responsibility for some of the testing. In all of these cases it can be useful to define a responsibility matrix that maps people to tasks.

If none of these situations apply, you can use a standard phrase stating that your team, the XYZ Test Organization, will run tests and report any defects found to development. This section is not intended to cover the responsibilities of individual engineers and technicians; that is covered in the next section of the test plan.

13. Staffing and Training Needs   This section allows you to list the people that you plan on employing to test the product. One reason for including this list is that your ability to meet your test milestones depends on these people being available throughout the test phase. If someone is diverted to another project or leaves the company, you have reasonable basis for hiring a replacement or slipping the schedule.

This is also the place to describe the training that you assume will be taken to get your test team the skills needed to perform the planned tests.

14. Schedule   This is usually not the place to put your detailed project schedule—it belongs in the overall project plan or as a standalone file that can be modified independent of the test plan itself. After all, the detailed schedule may be very dynamic, but the contents of what you're testing, the staffing needs, the testing work products, and other components of the test plan should be relatively static.

What you may want to include in the test plan is a brief list of testing milestones such as when testing begins, when the beta release goes to early users, and when testing is completed. Or you may simply choose to refer to the project plan or standalone schedule, using a link to a Web page or the path to a shared network drive.

15. Risks and Contingencies   Risks can be described in a table that shows the risk, the probability that the risk will occur, the impact of the risk, and the mitigation for dealing with the risk. A process for building this table was described in an earlier section, "Assessing Schedule Risk."

16. Approvals   This can be handled by listing the names of required approvers on the cover page of the test plan. You can have a meeting to review the test plan and obtain approval, or you can email each approver a copy of the test plan and solicit feedback. It is a good idea to store the email responses in a shared network directory that is regularly backed up, or attach all feedback and approvals as an appendix to the test plan itself.

Test Plan Reviews

The test plan is a major work product in the development life cycle, and it should be thoroughly reviewed. If possible, it should undergo a formal inspection (see "Static Testing Methods" in Chapter 2 and "Inspections/ Walkthroughs/Peer Reviews" in Chapter 9 for more information on inspections). Not only members of the test team, but representatives from development, marketing, and management should participate in the inspection or at least participate in a separate email review of the test plan. There are several goals of the reviews:

- All participants involved in developing the product need to understand and approve the objectives, coverage, limitations, and risks associated with the test effort.

- The test approach should be reviewed to ensure that it is technically correct and that it will succeed in verifying the requirements that are being promised to the customer.

- The entry and exit criteria for testing need to be understood by all participants in the project. Any dependencies upon work from other teams needs to be communicated clearly, and the responsible teams need to agree to provide their work products to the test team when promised.

Although communication between the test team and other teams should be maintained throughout product development, the review of the test plan is an excellent opportunity to ensure that all participants are "on the same page" early in the life cycle. Any misunderstandings or errors in test coverage that slip through the test plan review are likely to seriously affect your ability as a test group to make your schedule.

What's Next

In this chapter we discussed test planning and estimation. The amount of time and effort spent on planning can have a significant impact on your ability to successfully meet your test schedule and achieve your test objectives. The key steps in the test planning process are:

- Define the test strategy
- Define the test system (hardware and software)
- Estimate the test effort (resources and schedule)
- Assess risks to the schedule and prepare mitigation plans
- Prepare and review the test plan documents

The output of these steps is a set of test plan documents that should be used to guide the rest of the test effort.

In the next chapter, we look at what is involved in developing tests. The test strategy, test architecture, and test configurations that were defined during the planning stage will all play a role in developing a set of effective test cases.

References

IEEE. (1983). *IEEE Standard 829: IEEE Standard for Software Test Documentation*. Los Alamitos, CA: IEEE Computer Society Press.

Black, Rex. (1999). *Managing the Test Process*. Redford, WA: Microsoft Press.

Boehm, Barry W. (1981). *Software Engineering Economics*. Englewood Cliffs, NJ: Prentice Hall.

Boehm, Barry W. (1991). "Software risk management: Principles and practices." *IEEE Software*, 8(1) (January): 32–41.

Boehm, Barry W. (2000). *Software Cost Estimation with COCOMO II*. Englewood Cliffs, NJ: Prentice Hall.

Brooks, Fred. (1982). *The Mythical Man-Month: Essays on Software Engineering.* Reading, MA: Addison-Wesley.

Dustin, Elfriede, Jeff Rashka, and John Paul. (1999). *Automated Software Testing: Introduction, Management, and Performance.* Reading, MA: Addison-Wesley.

Lewis, William E. (2000). *Software Testing and Continuous Quality Improvement.* Boca Raton, FL: CRC Press.

McConnell, Steve. (1996). *Rapid Development: Taming Wild Software Schedules.* Redmond, WA: Microsoft Press.

Perry, William E. (2000). *Effective Methods for Software Testing* (2nd ed.). New York: Wiley.

Pfleeger, Shari Lawrence. (2001). *Software Engineering: Theory and Practice* (2nd ed.). Upper Saddle River, NJ: Prentice Hall.

Pressman, Roger. (1997). *Software Engineering: A Practitioner's Approach* (4th ed.). New York: McGraw-Hill.

Test Design
and Development

4

The key to successful testing lies in the effectiveness of your test cases. As we have shown in Chapter 3, good planning and preparation for testing is important, but in the final analysis, your test cases must be capable of finding bugs in the product under test, or all your planning and preparation goes for naught. The purpose of this chapter is to present a framework for designing and developing solid dynamic test cases that can be used in system and acceptance testing.

A diagram of the activities that make up test design and development is shown in Figure 4.1. The primary input to the process is the set of test plan documents that were described in Chapter 3. The test plan should give the approach that will be used and the scope of the test effort. It should have defined the test architecture, meaning that at least the test suites should be defined. It should have also defined a set of test configurations around which the tests can be designed.

The output of the design and development activities is a set of reviewed and debugged test cases that are ready to be used in system and acceptance testing. The test cases should map back to the customer requirements. They

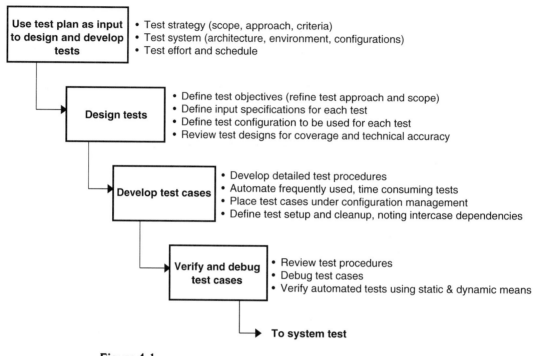

Figure 4.1
Test design and implementation.

should provide good coverage by testing at least all of the high-priority requirements, and ideally all of the customer requirements. The test cases should provide good code coverage by exercising most if not all the logic paths in the code. If possible, a substantial set of the test cases should be automated to provide good regression testing capability.

As shown in Figure 4.1, test case development has a life cycle of its own. It has a design phase in which the test objectives, input specifications, and test configurations are defined. There is a development phase in which the detailed test procedures are defined, and a verification and debug phase, in which the tests are reviewed and debugged. Each phase of the test case development life cycle will be discussed in this chapter. More detailed information about the techniques used in dynamic testing will be given in Part II, and examples of test cases will be presented in Part III.

Test Design

As we noted in Chapter 3, preparing to test is like peeling an onion—it is a layered process of successive refinement. Preparation begins by defining a high-level test strategy, and then more layers of detail are added that describe the test architecture and the test environment. Finally the detailed test procedures are developed and verified, the test system is assembled, and you are ready to begin system testing.

Designing test cases deals with one layer of the onion. Test designs are more detailed than the high-level test plan, but do not yet contain the detailed steps needed to run the test. The layered approach to test development is similar to the approach used in software development. In a mature development process, software developers don't jump directly from documenting requirements to writing code. They first perform a preliminary or system design to develop the concept of the product, and then perform a program or detailed design in which the design details are determined. In the testing world, the test plan corresponds to the preliminary design in the software development world, and the test design corresponds to the detailed software design.

One characteristic of good engineering design is *modularity*. In a modular design, a system is decomposed into discrete components, where each component has a clearly stated purpose and clearly defined inputs and outputs. Modular design principles are often used in software design, and they apply equally well to test design. The modular component of testing is the test case. This means that each test case should have a clearly stated purpose so it is clear what is being tested. Each test case should have a well-defined test environment with known initial conditions so that the test can be expected to give the same results each time it is run. Finally, each test case should have a clearly defined expected result (output) so that unambiguous pass/fail criteria can be applied.

Another characteristic of modular design is that the modules are organized in a hierarchy. The hierarchy is a result of decomposing the system into components, and it allows us to work with the system one level at a time. This is reflected in the test architecture, which may have a set of test suites that deal with high-level functionality in the system, and a set of tests or test cases that deal with the detailed functionality. For example, you might have one test suite that deals with the GUI and a second one that deals with system security. Within the test suite you might have tests that work with specific data input screens or data query screens. The test suite would map to one or more related requirements, whereas the more detailed test cases might map to items in the system functional specification. For more information on structuring tests, refer to the section "Test Architecture" in Chapter 3.

The last thing we'll note about modularity is that it supports catching bugs early in the development cycle. Theoretically each decomposed layer in a system can be reviewed for defects before proceeding to the next lower level. In practice, the test plan can be reviewed and corrected before proceeding to the next layer, which is the test design. The test designs can be reviewed and corrected before working on the detailed test cases. These intermediate check points help prevent bugs in the test work products from escaping downstream in the test life cycle, causing derivative problems that further impact the schedule.

SIDEBAR 4.1

ONE BIG TEST?—MORE ON TEST ARCHITECTURE

It is perhaps conceivable that you could design one giant test that would cover all aspects of a product, but there are several reasons why this is not a good idea. Suppose you run this one huge test and find some bugs. When the developer tries to reproduce one of the bugs so the root cause can be found and the bug fixed, what is the developer to do—run the one big test? Suppose this happens and the bug is fixed. How do you verify that the bug is really fixed— run this "super-size" test again? Obviously this is not a very efficient approach.

It is better, therefore, to structure your tests so that each test isolates a specific part of the software functionality. If the test fails, it is easy for the developer to run your test and reproduce the failure, then analyze the failure and find the fault. Ideally, the scope of the test has been reduced to the minimum set of steps necessary to cause the failure.

If you are basing your tests on product requirements, a rule of thumb for the scope of a test is that at least one test be written for each requirement. In addition to keeping the tests to an efficient size, this notion of "at least one test per requirement" also supports test planning. By reviewing the requirements document you can get a good idea of how many new tests will be needed for a new product. Once you start writing tests in this orderly way, you can estimate how long it will take to develop and run a test based on past results.

Requirements-based testing lends itself well to test organization. Requirements are generally grouped together by functionality. You can organize your tests in the same way. Tests related to customer provisioning can be grouped together, as can tests for installing or upgrading the software. As we saw in Chapter 3, a group of related tests can be put into a *test suite*.

Testing a requirement might involve more than one scenario. For example, if you are testing a requirement related to customer data entry, the type and amount of data required might change depending on whether the customer was a "silver class," "gold class," or "platinum class" customer. You would need to modify the test for this requirement for each class of customer.

One way to handle this situation is to allow the test to consist of different test cases, one for each class of customer. A *test case* is a set of test inputs, execution conditions, and expected results that are developed for a particular objective. The test case is the smallest unit of testing that can be independently executed from beginning to end.

Define Test Objectives

The first task in designing a test is to clearly state its purpose or objective. Suppose that you are designing tests for the Test Management Toolkit application described in Chapter 2 and in Part III. One of the requirements for the application is (see Figure 2.4 in Chapter 2 for other requirements):

```
2.2.1. The application shall provide a means for
creating, modifying, viewing, storing, and retriev-
ing test plan documents.
```

There is a great deal of functionality called for in requirement 2.2.1, but it all relates to management of test plan documents. One way to organize the tests that relate to this requirement is to create a suite called "Test_Plans" and collect within that suite all the tests for requirement 2.2.1. As an example, you might state the objectives for the tests in the suite as follows:

1. Verify that the program provides a means for a qualified user to create all valid types of test plan documents.

2. Verify that a qualified user can store and retrieve any test plan that has been created.

3. Verify that the program provides a means for a qualified user to modify all test plan documents that have been created and stored.

4. Verify that a qualified user can retrieve and view any test plan document that has been created and stored.

Each test objective states *what* the test will accomplish, but it does not state *how* the test will be performed. The *how* is the job of the detailed test procedure that will be developed as part of the test case. The test objectives present a refinement on the test plan, which might merely have noted that tests would be created to address requirement 2.2.1. Another distinction between test designs and test cases is that the test designs can usually be done using the requirements specification. The test cases, which involve detailed knowledge of the product, will need to have at least a functional specification and perhaps supplementary information from the product design documents.

Note that the example test objectives will require some clarifying information when the next "layer of the onion" is defined. Test objective 1, for example, does not define the characteristics of a "qualified user"—that is a detail that will depend on how control of program access is designed. Tests should be written to verify that qualified users can access the data, and that nonqualified users cannot. The test objective also does not say what constitutes a "valid type of test plan document," but the inclusion of this wording does remind the test engineer to consider both valid and invalid types of documents once validity criteria have been established.

In general, the following guidelines may be used when writing test objectives:

- Make a clear statement of the purpose of each test.

- Modularize the tests so that each test has a single purpose that can be mapped back to a tagged requirement in the requirements specification. Note, however, that more than one test may be needed to test a requirement.

- State what the test will accomplish, but don't explain how it will be done—leave that for the test case.

Define Input Specifications

Test input specifications include input data files, database records, configuration files, firmware images, or other inputs that are required to bring the test system to a desired known state so that a test can be executed. Input specifications do *not* include keyboard or mouse input from a user that is entered during the course of testing—those inputs should be specified in the detailed test procedures.

Each input file or image should be given a unique identifier and stored in a version-controlled environment that is regularly backed up. The repository for input data should be described in the test plan and referred to in the input specification for the test. For example, a set of test plan documents might be needed for the tests described in the previous section. These could be named TP_input1.doc, TP_input2.doc, and so forth, and stored in a managed directory such as D:\Test\Project_Name\Test_Plan\Inputs.

Define Test Configurations

Each test will need to run in a known test environment in order to give predictable, repeatable results. This means the hardware configuration, the operating system, the version of software under test, and the initial state of the system need all to be defined. As described in Chapter 3, the test planning effort should have analyzed options for test configurations and decided upon a set of possible configurations that would be used for system testing.

The task during the test design phase is to select one or more configurations that will be used to accomplish the test objective. Often the same test needs to be run on multiple configurations in order to simulate a variety of customer environments. For example, a major customer may predominantly use a standard configuration of operating system, processor, hard drive capacity, network operating system, and memory—this would certainly be a configuration to simulate as closely as possible in the test lab.

One way to track configurations is to specify them in the test plan with a unique identifier for each configuration. Then it is a simple matter to refer to one or more selected configurations in the test design document.

Test Design Document

The purpose of the test design document is to capture the information generated by the test design activities. The test design document could take the form of a spreadsheet, a table generated by a word processor, or a database. If you are using an automated requirements management test tool, you can get that tool to capture the test design information. An example of an entry in the test design document is shown in Table 4.1.

The table bears some resemblance to the requirements traceability matrix (RTM) discussed in Chapter 2 (see Figure 2.5). The first two columns in the table should correspond to entries in the RTM, and the remaining columns correspond to the data described in the preceding three sections of this chapter.

Once the test design document has been produced, it needs to be reviewed in the context of its related material: the requirements definition document, the test input definitions, and the test configuration. The purpose of the review is to perform the following verifications:

- Verify that all requirements are taken into account by the test design document. If a requirement is not being tested, an entry should be

Table 4.1
Example of an Entry in the Test Design Document

Requirement Definition ID	System Test Case ID	Test Input	Test Configuration	Test Objective
RD2.2.1	ST2.2.4	TP_Input1.doc	TC2.0	TO2.2.4 Verify that a qualified user can retrieve and view any test plan document that has been created and stored.

present in the RTM or in the test design document stating why the requirement is not covered.

- Verify that each test case has an appropriate set of input test data.
- Verify that each test case has a suitable test configuration, and that the test configurations being used are not redundant.

The test design document serves as a basis for developing detailed test procedures. Following its review, tests can be assigned to engineers on the team for detailed development.

Developing Test Cases

The test case is the basic component of dynamic testing. When stripped to its essence, the system test phase is little more than running test cases against a series of software builds for the purpose of finding and fixing bugs. This means that the most fundamental job of the test engineer is to write and run test cases. In this section we discuss how to design and develop good test cases.

In Chapter 1 we defined software testing as a process of analyzing or operating software for the purpose of finding bugs. We can now define a test as follows: A *test* is a set of operations designed to produce one or more expected results in a software system. If all expected results are obtained, the test passes. If the actual result differs from what is expected, the test fails.

The first thing to note about the definition is that every test has two components: (1) a set of things that you do, and (2) a set of things that should happen as a result. The things that you do are the test steps, which collectively form the test procedure. The things that happen as a result are called the expected results. Both the procedure and the expected results have to be clearly and unambiguously defined in order for the test to be effective.

The second thing to note is that, if the procedure and expected results are properly defined, the test will have a clear pass/fail outcome. If you enter two numbers to a program and expect to see their sum displayed, the test passes only if the correct number is displayed; otherwise, it fails.

As we have mentioned previously, a test may be further subdivided into test cases for convenience. If a test involves a lengthy procedure with multiple expected results, it may make sense to subdivide the test into test cases.

The test case, however, is the smallest unit of testing, and each test case must have at least one expected result.

Since the purpose of testing is to find bugs, a good test case is one that has a high probability of finding a bug. To design a test that has a good chance of finding a bug, the test engineer needs to adopt an attitude of "constructively breaking" the product. "Constructive breaking" means finding problems in the product for the sake of getting them fixed. The point is that the test designer is not trying to come up with ways of demonstrating that the product works; he or she is trying to find ways in which the product does *not* work. In designing a test case it is important to make no assumptions that any of the software functions will work. You should not assume that any build of the code will properly install, or that the database structure matches the design, or that the program will recover in the event of a power failure. It should not be assumed that because the program runs on a given platform, it would function the same on a computer with less memory or one running a different operating system.

Another quality of a good test case is that it is repeatable. If a test is run and fails, it is very important to be able to reproduce the exact conditions of the failure. For this reason it is important that the initial state of the system be defined by the test case in terms of software version, hardware configuration, number of users on the system, and so on. It is also important that the exact procedure used to obtain the failure be known. Ideally, the exact sequence of keystrokes, mouse clicks, and other events that led up to the observed deviation from the expected result would be precisely known. In practice all these details may not be known, perhaps because the test procedure is not spelled out in infinite detail or perhaps because some random or uncontrolled event occurred without the knowledge of the tester. That is why, when a failure occurs, it is important to immediately spend time reproducing the failure, noting in full detail the steps that lead to the failure if they are not explicitly spelled out in the test procedure.

A good test case has one or more clearly defined expected results and clearly defined pass/fail criteria. Usually the expected results and the pass/fail criteria are closely coupled. If an expected result or set of expected results occurs when the system is transitioned from one defined state to another, the test case passes. If the expected results are not observed after performing the defined actions, the test fails. For example, suppose you enter the value of a zip code into a data entry field and expect to see the corresponding state displayed when you click a "Show State" button. If you enter a set of zip codes and for each one see the proper state displayed, the test yields the expected results and therefore passes. If you enter a zip code for Seattle and get Florida displayed, you have succeeded in finding a bug; the expected result is not obtained.

At least one additional attribute of a good test case should be mentioned—it should not be redundant. An aggressive test schedule demands that you test enough to find many of the bugs before shipping, but that you waste no time running redundant tests. In the example just mentioned, you should not spend time displaying states for every known zip code unless this functionality is critical to your customer's business. If there is major liability associated with displaying zip codes, then you'll want to spend an appropriate amount of time testing the display feature. You should also consider automating such a tedious test. But if the feature is a convenience, you'll probably want to test a legal zip code and a few illegal zip codes to validate basic functionality. This topic is discussed further in the section "Equivalence Partitioning" later in this chapter and in Chapter 10.

In summary, a good test case has the following attributes:

- It has a high probability of finding a bug.
- It is repeatable.
- It has clearly defined expected results and pass/fail criteria.
- It should not be redundant.

Develop Detailed Test Procedures

Detailed test procedures can be developed from the test designs. The level of detail needed for a written test procedure depends on the skill and knowledge of the people that run the tests. Do you plan to bring in people to perform system testing that have little familiarity with the product? If so, the people will need some training and the test procedures will need to be clearly spelled out to ensure that the correct test steps are performed. But if the testers have detailed knowledge of the product, then the test procedures can be less detailed. The decision on how much detail to include in the test procedures is an important one, because time can easily be wasted in writing too much detail for experienced users. On the other hand, time can be wasted in teaching new testers how to run the tests if there is not enough detail, so a proper balance needs to be struck.

There is one special case that should be considered. If a test is to be automated, it is wise to spend time up front writing a detailed test procedure so that the automation engineer has an unambiguous statement of the automation task. A vague test procedure is likely to lead to an inaccurate or ineffective automated test. The amount of recommended detail for a test procedure will become more clear when we discuss expected results below.

There are a wide variety of techniques that can be used in software testing. In this chapter we focus on black-box techniques. Black-box testing is system-level testing that deals only with the "external" aspects of a program. Black-box testing assumes no knowledge of the internal workings of the software and is conducted by exercising only external interfaces such as the user interface or an application programming interface (API). More detailed discussions of black-box testing can be found in Beizer (1995), Dustin, Rashka, and Paul (1999), and Kaner, Falk, and Nguyen (1993). More information on black-box testing techniques is also presented in Chapter 10 of this book.

Two widely used techniques to design black-box tests are equivalence partitioning and boundary value analysis. Both of these techniques help reduce the total number of test cases or test conditions that are needed in order to fully cover the functionality of a program. Obviously these techniques are a valuable part of the rapid testing concept because the fewer tests that need to be developed and run to obtain the same functional coverage, the more efficient the testing becomes.

Equivalence Partitioning   Equivalence partitioning is a test design technique for reducing the total number of tests required to validate a program's functionality. The basic idea behind equivalence partitioning is to divide the input domain of a program into classes of data. By designing tests for each class of data rather than for each member of a class, the total number of tests needed is reduced.

As an example, consider the zip code program discussed earlier in the chapter. Suppose when the user enters a five-digit zip code and the shipping weight in ounces, the program returns the cost of shipping a package. The input domains for this simple program are the zip code and the shipping weight. The input domain for the zip code can be partitioned into classes of valid inputs and invalid inputs as follows.

- Valid inputs are all sets of five numeric characters that constitute an operational zip code.
- Invalid inputs include
  - Sets of numeric characters with less than five characters
  - Sets of numeric characters with more than five characters
  - Sets of five numeric characters that do not constitute a operational zip code
  - Sets of non-numeric characters

Similar partitions could be constructed for the shipping weight. For example, perhaps the program is required to deal with only those weights between 1 and 100 ounces. Then, numeric values that are between 1 and 100, including the end points, are valid entries. Values below 1 or above 100, negative values, and non-numeric entries all form invalid classes of input.

Test cases should be designed that test at least one member of each valid class of input and at least one member of each invalid class of input. For the test of the valid data, a clearly defined expected result should be obtained. For zip code 78723 and 20 ounces, a defined value of cost should be obtained, and that value should be defined in the functional specification. For tests of invalid data, a defined error message should be obtained if one is called for in the requirements and specifications. At least the program should not crash, cause data corruption, or lead to anomalous behavior when invalid data is entered.

More detailed discussion of equivalence partitioning can be found in Chapter 10, as well as in Myers (1979), Kaner, et al (1993), Pressman (1997), Kit (1995), and Beizer (1995).

Boundary Value Analysis   Boundary value analysis is a test design technique that complements equivalence partitioning. Rather than selecting any element of an equivalence class, boundary value analysis encourages the test designer to select elements at the "edges" of the class. It has been found empirically that bugs tend to cluster at the boundaries of the input domain rather than in the center. It is not clear why this is true; it is simply an observed fact.

For example, in the program that uses zip code and shipping weight to compute shipping cost, boundary value analysis leads us to use the minimum and maximum shipping weights (1 oz. and 100 oz.) and values just below the minimum (0 oz.) and just above the maximum (101 oz.) as test values. These values test the boundaries of the valid range of inputs, and test just outside the boundaries as well. For more information on boundary value analysis, see Chapter 10 as well as Myers (1979), Kaner, et al (1993), Pressman (1997), and Beizer (1995).

Define Expected Results

Dynamic testing relies on running a controlled set of operations on a software build and comparing the actual results to the expected results. If the expected results are obtained, the test counts as a pass; if anomalous behavior is observed, the test is considered to fail, but it may have succeeded in

Table 4.2
Examples of Expected Results

Step	Action	Expected Result	Pass (✓)
1	Click "Shipping Cost" in Main Menu.	Shipping Cost menu is displayed.	
2	Enter "101" in shipping weight field.	Error message "Invalid shipping weight" is displayed.	
3	Enter "0" in shipping weight field.	Error message "Invalid shipping weight" is displayed.	
4	Enter "100" in shipping weight field.	Shipping weight is displayed as "100 oz."	

finding a bug. The key to being able to determine if a test passes or fails is having a clear definition of the expected results for the test.

An excerpt of a test case for our example program that computes shipping cost based on zip code and shipping weight is shown in Table 4.2. The steps of the test procedure are numbered in the first column. A simple description of the action to be taken by the tester is given in the second column, and a clear description of the expected result is displayed in the third column. In this example it is intended that a hard copy (or interactive soft copy) of the table will be used to run the test, so a fourth column is shown in which the tester can check off each step as it is performed. Later we'll show how failed steps and other details of the test case can be handled. The point here is that for each step of a test procedure, the expected result needs to be clearly explained.

Setups and Cleanups—Testing from a Known State

One of the basic principles of testing is that the system under test should always be in a known state. If a bug is found but the tester doesn't know all the steps that led up to the failure, it becomes difficult to reproduce the bug. The need to test from a known state means that each test case needs to initialize the hardware and software to a known state. This doesn't mean that the tester needs to power down the system, reboot, and start the program from scratch for each test case—like all things in testing, there are limits to what we can do.

There are some practical measures that can be taken to avoid getting our test system into states that are not reproducible. One *is* to power cycle the system before the start of testing—perhaps this would be done at the beginning of the day's work. Another is to periodically refresh databases and erase test directories. With automation, cleaning up databases and data directories could be done frequently and without taking much time. Perhaps the system under test includes changes in firmware. If so, the firmware can be reloaded before running a set of related tests or at the start of a day to be sure that an uncorrupted version of the firmware under test is in the system. Ideally, automated tools would be used to inventory the state of the system under test, log discrepancies, and allow the tester to change the system to a desired state.

There are two approaches to dealing with test initialization. One is to use setup routines to bring the system to a known state at the start of test, and use cleanup routines that "undo" the changes made during testing. Another approach is to do setups only, and forget cleanups. If for each test there is always a setup operation, then it doesn't matter what happens at the end of the test—we're going to reestablish known conditions when starting the next test, and the effort associated with the cleanup may be wasted. Of course, a problem may arise if we add a new test that does not have a setup, because a previously run test could have put the system into an unexpected state.

A suggested rule of thumb is to perform cleanups when you run a test that intentionally puts the system into an undesirable state. For example, if you fill a data directory, corrupt a database, or put the system into an error condition, it is a good idea to restore the system to a normal state at the end of the test. Likewise, if you are running a test that is known to depend on the initial state of the system, it's a good idea to use a setup procedure to initialize the system under test.

Test Case Template

All of the ideas for test case design presented so far in this chapter can be combined into a single test case template. You may wish to create your own template, but a suggestion is shown in Figure 4.2. Test cases based on this template could be printed for manual testing, or a browser could display an HTML version so that the tests can be run interactively.

The main elements of the test case template are:

- Test case ID—include the version number of the test.
- Owner of test—name or initials of the person that maintains the test (may be different from the original author of the test).

Test Case Information	
Test case ID	SC03 ver3.0
Owner of test	Jean Douglas
Test name	Shipping Cost Range
Test location (path)	TestServer: D:\TestProject\TestSuite\SC03.doc
Date of last revision	mm/dd/yy
Requirement tested	SC101
Test configuration	ST02
Test interdependencies	Run test SC01 and its setup before this test.
Test objective	Verify that valid entries of shipping weight give valid shipping costs and that invalid values of shipping weight give error messages.

Test Procedure			
Test setup	None		N/A

Step	Action	Expected Result	Pass (✓)
1	Click "Shipping Cost" in Main Menu.	Shipping Cost menu is displayed.	✓
2	Enter "101" in shipping weight field.	Error message "Invalid shipping weight" is displayed.	✓
3	Enter "0" in shipping weight field.	Error message "Invalid shipping weight" is displayed.	X
4	Enter "100" in shipping weight field.	Shipping weight is displayed as "100 oz."	✓
5	Enter "1" in shipping weight field.	Shipping weight is displayed as "1 oz."	✓

Test Cleanup	None		N/A

Test Result		
Tester: JD	Date of test: mm/dd/yy	Test result (P/F/B): F

Notes:
- Test failed in step 3. No error message displayed.
- Bug report BR1011 entered against problem.

Figure 4.2
Example test case.

- Date of last revision—this helps you see if the test is current.

- Name of test—a descriptive name of the test that makes it easy to find the test and understand its objective. Nondescriptive names like "xxxLLL0123.tst" are not recommended.

- Location of test—this is the complete path name, including the server.

- Requirement tested—this should be a unique ID that maps to the requirements documents

- Test objective—a brief, clear statement of what the test should achieve. See "Define Test Objectives" earlier in the chapter for more discussion.

- Test configuration—input specs, output specs, test environment.

- Test setup—this would be similar to the test procedure; describe the action taken by the tester and the expected result. If the setups are automated, the setup might be a statement like: run setupSC03.pl.

- Test procedure—description of the action taken by the tester and the expected result.

- Test case interdependencies—identify any test cases that must be run prior to this one so that the test will begin with a known initial condition.

- Test cleanup—if you have placed the system into an unstable state or corrupted data, here is a chance to undo the damage.

Test Case Configuration Management

When a test is run, it needs to execute a known set of operations on a known system configuration. This ensures that the test is reproducible and that it is testing the planned functionality. As the software changes due to bug fixes or due to changes in the requirements, the tests need to change as well. The functionality of the software and the tests must maintain synchronization, or the tests will give erroneous results.

The way that software changes are often managed is through the use of configuration management (CM) tools such as the Control Version System (CVS) tool or the ClearCase tools. With these tools, files containing code or data are checked in for storage and checked out for modification. The tools provide version control so that previous versions of a file are archived and can be retrieved.

This type of CM system works very well for both manual and automated test cases. It provides a capability to baseline a set of tests so that a version number can be associated with a group of tests. For example, Version 3.0 of the data entry test suite can be used to test Version 3.0 of the software under test.

Verifying and Debugging Tests

Once a test case is written or automated, it needs to be reviewed to catch defects that can be quickly fixed, and then tested against a build of the product software. Static testing on test cases can be conducted using the same techniques that are used with requirements: inspections, walkthroughs, or peer reviews (see "Static Testing Methods" in Chapter 2). The methods can be combined if the complexity of the tests warrants detailed static testing. For example, you might use peer reviews on test procedures and formal inspections on automated scripts that implement the test procedures.

Here are some things to look for when reviewing test cases:

- Does the test or suite of tests fully address the functionality stated in the requirements?
- Do the test suites cover all requirements?
- Are the tests organized efficiently so that a minimum number of test configurations are needed?
- Are the tests checked into a configuration management system?
- Are any of the tests redundant? Can the redundancy be eliminated?
- Is there enough detail in the procedure that the test procedure can be automated?
- Does each test step have a clearly defined expected result (pass/fail criterion)?
- Do the automated tests faithfully reproduce the manual steps?

If you conducted static testing on the test plan, the review of the test cases should go a lot easier, because questions about requirements coverage should have been covered in the test plan review. The questions about test redundancy and efficient use of test configurations should also have been covered in the test plan review, at least in a preliminary way. Good reviews of the test plans and the test cases, just like static testing of the software product, will catch bugs in the tests early and prevent time from being wasted in test case debugging.

Following review, each new test needs to be run against a build of production code to ensure that the test procedure obtains its expected results.

Since this test is likely to be run against buggy code, some care will be needed when analyzing test failures to determine if the problem lies with the code or with the test. Debugging a test case often requires the same engineering and analytical skills that the software developer uses to debug the production code.

Test Case Automation

We noted in Chapter 3 that with proper planning and reasonable expectations, the use of automated tools and automated test cases is an excellent way to reduce the time required to test a product. In this chapter we briefly discuss some recommended guidelines that should go into automation of test cases. Automating tests is a software development activity that needs to be carried out with the same skill and discipline that is brought to the development of any software product. If you plan to invest in test case automation, you might want to look at a book dedicated to automation, such as Dustin et al. (1999) or Fewster and Graham (1999).

The following are some suggested guidelines for automating test cases. Of course local circumstances should be factored in as you consider these.

- Automate only test cases that will be repeated enough times that the automation is cost-effective. If you automate tests that will only be run a few times, the cost of the automation in time and effort may exceed the benefit.

- Develop a manual version of the test case first, and then automate the manual test. Test cases need to be debugged to make sure that the proper manual procedures are defined and that the test configuration works as expected. Trying to debug a test procedure and the code that automates that procedure at the same time can be inefficient and, in the worst case, can introduce errors to the test. If the manual test is debugged first, it becomes a baseline against which the automated test can be verified.

- The manual test procedure being automated needs to be clearly written and unambiguous so that the automation engineer can focus on generating code rather than trying to figure out how the test steps are to be conducted.

- Define and follow a standard coding practice. Automation is software that should be developed just as carefully as the software product you are testing. If automation scripts are going to be used as regression tests, they may need to be maintained for a long time. Eventually the person maintaining the test script may not be the person that originally developed it; in that case, clearly written code that is well documented is a must for efficient maintenance.

- Automated tests should be verified against the manual tests from which they were derived. Code reviews of the scripts are good for catching defects in the automation and for ensuring that coding standards are followed. The ultimate verification for an automated script, however, is that it provides the same testing functionality as its manual counterpart, and that verification should be conducted in the lab by running both manual and automated versions of the test side by side against all planned test configurations and conditions.

- Automated test scripts should be maintained under configuration control in the same directory structure as the manual tests. The configuration or version control system should allow only one authorized version of the script to be active at a time. This version control ensures that each test is reproducible and repeatable. When reproducing bugs, verifying bug fixes, and performing regression testing, having a single, known test that relates to a given defect is an essential condition of testing.

What's Next

In this chapter we discussed test design and development. The key steps in the test design and development process are:

- Define test objectives (refine test approach and scope)
- Define input specifications for each test
- Define test configuration to be used for each test
- Review test designs for coverage and technical accuracy
- Develop detailed test procedures
- Automate frequently used, time-consuming tests
- Place test cases under configuration management
- Define test setup and cleanup, noting intercase dependencies
- Review test procedures
- Debug test cases
- Verify automated tests using static and dynamic means

The output of these steps is a set of debugged test cases that can be used to conduct system testing. In the next chapter, we look at what is involved in running tests, documenting defects, and reporting test results.

References

Beizer, Boris. (1995). *Black-Box Testing: Techniques for Functional Testing of Software and Systems.* New York: Wiley.

Dustin, Elfriede, Jeff Rashka, and John Paul. (1999). *Automated Software Testing: Introduction, Management, and Performance.* Reading, MA: Addison-Wesley.

Fewster, Mark, and Dorothy Graham. (1999). *Software Test Automation.* Reading, MA: Addison-Wesley.

Kaner, Cem, Jack Falk, and Hung Quoc Nguyen. (1999). *Testing Computer Software* (2nd ed.). New York: Wiley.

Kit, Edward. (1995). *Software Testing in the Real World: Improving the Process.* Reading, MA: Addison-Wesley.

Myers, Glen. (1979). *The Art of Software Testing.* New York: Wiley.

Pressman, Roger. (1997). *Software Engineering: A Practitioner's Approach* (4th ed.). New York: McGraw-Hill.

System Testing

For the software testing professional, the system test phase is like game day for an athlete or show time for a stage actor. A lot of planning and preparation has been done, the stage is set, and it's time to produce. As shown in Figure 5.1, the first thing to do is to verify that everything is in place and ready to go. This can be accomplished by applying the set of system test entry criteria that was defined in the test plan. The entry criteria takes the form of a checklist: Is the test plan written, reviewed, and approved? Has the development team completed their planned unit and integration testing? Has a "smoke" test been performed to make sure that the program under test can be installed and at least displays an opening screen?

If the entry criteria are satisfied, system testing can begin. Start of testing is usually a significant milestone in a project schedule. Ideally a delay in start of system testing translates to a delay in product shipment, although the test team is often asked to figure out ways to accelerate the testing schedule so the product can ship on time. At the risk of using too many analogies, here's one more: If product development is like a relay race, the test team runs the last leg of the race. If the earlier runners in the race don't run well, it is unrealistic to ask the anchor person, in this case the test team, to become superhuman and make up for all the earlier problems. Unrealistic or not, business realities often lead to a need for acceleration during the system test phase, and it is very helpful in this situation to be prepared with a

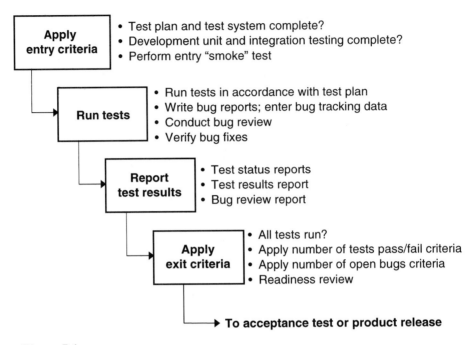

Figure 5.1
System testing overview.

set of prioritized tests and other contingency plans to mitigate the risk of a schedule slip.

Testing consists of running the tests called for in the test plan. As tests are run, bugs are discovered, bug reports are written, and bug-tracking data is entered into a bug-tracking database. Since the purpose of testing is to find bugs, bug tracking is a very important part of the test effort. The next section, "Finding and Tracking Bugs," deals with this part of the test effort in detail.

As tests are run, the results of testing need to be communicated to the rest of the organization. Anyone who is involved in developing, marketing, or managing the project should be informed of test progress and of the number and type of bugs that have been found. At the end of testing, a report should be prepared that summarizes the test results. The report should apply a set of exit criteria to assess the readiness of the product for release. For example, if all planned tests have been run and there are an acceptable number of bugs that remain open, the test team can state that the product does a reasonable job of meeting the requirements promised to the customer and is fit to ship.

Finding and Tracking Bugs

The objective of testing is to find bugs. It is not enough just to find bugs, however. They must be carefully reported so that developers can fix them, and progress on their repair must be reported so that the development schedule stays on track. Any inefficiency in bug reporting, tracking, repair, and verification will lead to lost time.

Therefore, there are two basic steps in finding bugs. The first step is to run tests in accordance with the test plan to see if any differences arise between expected and actual test results. The second step is to properly document any anomalies found in testing in a defect tracking system. Good documentation is important for two reasons—the first is that developers need solid information to debug and fix the problems, and the second is that testers need to be able to reproduce the problems so that fixes can be verified. The system that is used to document and track defects is an important, fundamental tool of software testing. In the next few sections we turn attention to the defect tracking system, looking at bug states, bug state changes, and other essentials of defect documentation and tracking. Then we return to the bigger picture of running tests and see how defect or bug tracking fits into the overall context of system testing.

Define Bug States

In Chapter 1 we noted that a bug is a fault in a work product such as the requirements document, the test plan, or the code itself. A bug goes undetected until the work product is reviewed or the program is run and fails to deliver an expected result.

Once the bug is found, it is analyzed to see if it represents a test failure, a code failure, or a defect in the design specifications. If the problem is with the test rather than the code, then the test needs to be fixed and the bug can be "trashed." The severity of the bug is also examined: Is it a catastrophic bug that must be fixed before shipment? Is it a major problem that seriously affects the functionality of the product, but which has a workaround that will allow testing and development to proceed? Or is the problem a minor one that can be deferred to a later release of the product?

A bug in the code will need to be assigned to a developer for repair. The status of the repair will need to be tracked carefully so that the bug is not forgotten. One effective way of tracking bugs is to define explicit states that a bug can assume as it goes from initial discovery to final testing. Each state needs to be unambiguous and have a set of defined entry and exit criteria.

Table 5.1 shows an example set of definitions of bug states. The names of the states vary from company to company, and additional states are possible. The table shows a generic set of names and states that you may want to use as a starting point if you are setting up a bug-tracking system from scratch.

As a bug is tracked through its life cycle of discovery, repair, and verification, it changes state according to a defined set of rules. Figure 5.2 shows an example set of state changes. The bug is discovered during a review or system test and is entered into the bug-tracking system in the "new" state. It is assigned a severity by the submitter and is passed to the bug review team for consideration. The bug review team (known in some circles as a change control board) determines if the bug should be fixed in the current release or deferred to a later release. If the development or test team has done further analysis since the bug was entered and has found that there is no problem in the code that can be fixed, the bug review team can decide to trash the bug. The action taken by the bug review team is documented, and the bug changes state to "fix," "defer," or "trash."

Table 5.1
Definitions of Bug States

State of bug	Owner	Description
New	Test	Bug is found in testing; bug report has been entered but developer has not been assigned to fix problem.
Fix	Development	Developer is assigned to fix problem and work is in progress.
Defer	Bug review team	Decision has been made to postpone fixing the bug until a later release.
Trash	Bug review team	The bug was entered in error, the product works as designed, or for another reason it has been decided that the bug will not be fixed.
Repaired	Development	A developer has identified and fixed the root cause of the defect and has done preliminary testing to verify that the problem is fixed.
Fix verified	Test	A test engineer has tested the fix using the same test procedure and test configuration that was used to find the bug originally.

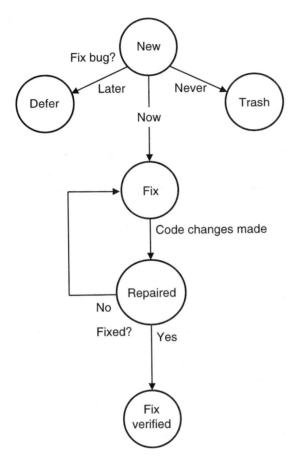

Figure 5.2
How a bug changes state.

If the bug is to be fixed, it is assigned to a developer, who makes appropriate code changes and tests that the changes work. Once the developer is satisfied that the bug is fixed, he or she changes the state of the bug to "repaired," and checks it into a build that is sent to system test. If the tester verifies that the bug is fixed, the bug enters its final state of "fix verified."

If you are new to testing or are working for a company that does not use an industrial strength bug-tracking tool, you might consider this state-based bug-tracking methodology to be overkill. And, if you are developing products that seldom have more than 40 or 50 bugs per release, you may be right. For many development projects, however, there are hundreds and even thousands of bugs that need to be tracked. If the tracking system is not effective and even a handful of known, high-severity bugs make it into the released product, your testing organization will have a very difficult time explaining why the bugs escaped.

Due to the importance of bug tracking to software testing, we devote the next few sections to a discussion of its essential points.

Bug Tracking Essentials

When a bug is first discovered, there is a good deal of data that needs to be captured to support its repair. An example of the data that should be recorded in the bug-tracking system for a new bug is shown in Table 5.2. The table shows a list of data items along with a brief description for each item and the reason that it should be captured. If you use a database tool to track bugs, the items shown in the first column will correspond to fields in the database.

Each bug in the tracking database should have a unique identifier, the bug ID. The bug ID is a key that supports database queries so that at any time status information about its repair can be determined. The tracking database should also maintain details about who found the bug, when it was found, its severity, and details about the problem caused by the bug. If the bug is found during system testing, then information about the test that found the bug should be recorded. For a well-documented test case, only the test ID is needed. If the test is not well documented, or if the bug was found by *ad hoc* testing, information about the test configuration and the detailed steps taken to find the bug need to be recorded. An example of a bug report that can be used to document this information will be shown in a later section, "Writing Bug Reports."

Once the bug has been entered into the tracking database, it will need to be examined by the bug review team (or change control board) to discuss any concerns about the bug. Is it really a bug? Has the correct severity been assigned? Does it have to be fixed in this release? The information that is entered into the tracking database after the work of the bug review team is shown in Table 5.3. The outcome of the bug review should lead the bug to being moved to one of three states:

- **Fix**—the bug goes to this state if the review team decides the bug needs to be fixed in the current release.
- **Defer**—the bug moves to this state if the review team decides to defer the fix to a later release.
- **Trash**—the bug goes to this state if it is determined that the bug was entered erroneously.

Table 5.2
Bug Tracking Data for the "New" State

Item	Description	Reason
Bug ID	Unique identifier for bug, usually an alphanumeric string.	Allows bug to be tracked through state changes and allows all work related to bug to be tagged to the bug.
Bug state	One of the allowable states; in this case the state will be "new."	Change to "new" state when the bug is discovered.
Found by	Name of person who found bug.	Provides point of contact for questions related to bug.
Date found	At least day/month/year; this field can include timestamp.	Allow bug's history to be tracked. Timestamp can help in debugging if it becomes necessary to reconstruct a sequence of test events.
Found in build	Unique identifier of the build of software under test.	This allows development to locate the source of the problem and allows a developer or tester to reproduce the problem.
Test ID	Unique identifier of the test that was running when the problem occurred. If the problem was found during *ad hoc* testing, this field can be marked not applicable (NA).	Allows the developer and tester to know what test to run to reproduce the problem. A test that finds a problem should become part of the regression test effort to verify that future builds do not regress.
Summary of problem	High-level description of the problem. This is typically a one-line description of the bug.	The summary is used in status and summary reports to allow management and other team members to understand the problem.
Description of problem	Detailed description of the symptoms of the problem and how it affects the overall functionality or performance of the system.	This is written for anyone who needs a detailed understanding of the problem, such as the developer who is working on a fix or a manager who is assigning resources.
Bug severity	A ranking of the significance of the bug. Example severities: • Catastrophic—causes system failure	Severity is often used to determine priorities for developers in fixing the bug and testers in verifying the fix.

(continued)

Table 5.2
Bug Tracking Data for the "New" State (cont'd)

Item	Description	Reason
	• Major—product not usable • Moderate—product usable; customer affecting • Minor—not customer affecting • Nuisance—repair as time permits	
How to reproduce problem	Detailed procedure for reproducing the problem, including the test configuration used. It may be sufficient to say "Ran test ID #" if the test is well documented.	A detailed procedure allows the developer to reproduce the bug and allows developer and tester to verify that the problem is fixed.

Depending on the outcome state of the bug, different data will need to be entered into the tracking database. For example, if the bug moves to the "fix" state, the name of the person responsible for the fix should be entered. If information regarding the bug is going to be communicated to customers, release note data needs to be entered. More information about the bug review will be presented in the section titled "Bug Reviews."

As shown in Table 5.4, a final set of data needs to be entered in the tracking system when the bug is fixed. The name of the person who fixes the bug should be recorded, as well as the date of the fix and an identifier for the build in which the fix was included. A detailed explanation of the root cause of the problem should be included so that the development team can reproduce and debug the problem.

Tables 5.1 through 5.4 summarize some of the essential features that you should look for in a bug-tracking system. It is possible to build your own bug-tracking tool, but there are a variety of commercially available tools that can save the great deal of time and effort that goes into the development of a good bug-tracking system. The feature set and usability of your bug-tracking system can have a significant impact on the efficiency of your test organization, and the selection of a bug-tracking system should be done with care.

The next section describes the format of a bug report that fits into the overall bug-tracking scheme just presented.

Table 5.3
Bug Tracking Data for the "Fix," "Defer," and "Trash" States

Item	Description	Reason
Bug ID (unchanged)	Unique identifier for bug	Allows bug to be tracked through state changes
Bug state	Fix, Defer, Trash	Change to "fix" state when the bug is assigned to a developer for repair; change to "defer" if the bug will be fixed in a later release; change to "trash" if the bug cannot be reproduced, or if the problem is not really a bug; also trash the bug if it is decided that the bug will not be fixed
Fixed by	Name of person assigned to fix the bug	Provides point of contact for questions related to bug fix
Deferred by	Name of person who deferred the bug fix (leave blank if not deferred)	Provides point of contact for questions related to deferring the bug fix
Trashed by	Name of person who trashed the bug (leave blank if not trashed)	Provides point of contact for questions related to decision to trash the bug
Start date of fix	Day, month, and year that the fix is assigned to a developer for repair	Allows the history of the bug to be tracked
Date deferred	Day, month, and year that the bug is deferred	Allows the history of the bug to be tracked
Date trashed	Day, month, and year that the bug is trashed	Allows the history of the bug to be tracked
Need release note? (Y/N)	Enter "Y" if a release note needs to be written and "N" if not	Flags the bug so that a list of bugs needing release notes can be generated
Release information	Description of the bug that will be communicated as part of the product's release notes (necessary only if the bug is *not* fixed in a release)	

Table 5.4
Bug Tracking Data for the "Repaired" and "Fix Verified" States

Item	Description	Reason
Bug ID (unchanged)	Unique identifier for bug	Allows bug to be tracked through state changes
Bug state	Repaired, Fix Verified	Change to "repaired" when the fix is checked into the code base; change to "fix verified" when the test engineer has verified that the fix works
Fixed by	Name of person who fixed bug	Provides point of contact for questions related to bug fix
Verified by	Name of person who verified the bug fix	Provides point of contact for questions related to verification
Date fixed	Day, month, and year that the fix is checked into the code base	Allows the history of the bug to be tracked
Date verified	Day, month, and year that the bug is verified	Allows the history of the bug to be tracked
Fixed in build	Unique identifier of the build that will contain the fix	Allows the tester to know what build to use to verify the fix; if the bug has been deferred to a later release, this field identifies the target release for a future fix
Description of fix	Explanation of the root cause of the problem and how it was fixed	Helps prevent similar problems from occurring in the future, and helps the developer and tester to look for additional bugs that might be related to the original problem

Write Bug Reports

Every time a new bug is discovered, a bug report should be written. If information about the bug is not captured quickly, it may be difficult to reconstruct the circumstances that led to the appearance of the problem. This is particularly true if *ad hoc* testing is being performed. If a documented test case is being run, it can be marked as a failure and the difference between actual and expected results can be logged as part of the test run. As soon as the *ad hoc* test turns up a problem, or as soon as a test run is completed, a bug report should be written.

An example of a bug report template is shown in Figure 5.3. The template might be implemented as a hard copy that is manually filled in by the tester, as a Web-based data entry form, or as part of a complete bug-tracking database system. The bug report template provides a means for capturing test data mentioned in Table 5.2.

The ability of test engineers to write effective bug reports will be a large measure of their success. It is often a good idea for testers to spend time studying bug reports that have been written on similar projects in their organizations. Ideally, a set of "golden examples" will be available that allow the new tester to understand what constitutes a good bug report and what makes a bug report ineffective.

Generally speaking, a bug report is poorly written or ineffective if:

- It is written in error—the bug described by the report does not exist.
- It is vague or ambiguous in its description of the problem—a problem may exist, but it is described so poorly that the behavior of the system is not clear.
- It does not contain enough information to allow a developer to reproduce the problem—the symptoms of the problem are described, but there is no explanation of the steps that cause the problem to appear.

A well-written bug report has just the opposite characteristics:

- It describes a real defect in the product.
- It clearly describes the symptoms of the problem in terms of the behavior of the system.
- It contains a step-by-step procedure for reproducing the problem.

Bug Reviews

If the process for finding and fixing bugs were perfect, there would be little need for bug reviews. Unfortunately, human error is just as likely to come into play in the system test phase as in any other part of the development cycle. Errors can crop up in test cases, in test configurations, or in the interpretation of test data. Once a bug has been found, care needs to be taken that it is assigned, fixed, and verified in a timely manner.

One way to verify test results and prevent bug-tracking errors is to hold a weekly bug review during system testing. The purpose of the bug review is to:

- Identify high severity bugs that need immediate attention

Bug Report
Bug ID:
Found by:
Date found:
Found in build:
Severity (catastrophic, major, minor):
Test ID:
Summary of problem:
Detailed description:
How to reproduce the problem: (If a documented test was not used, describe a detailed procedure. Sketch test configuration if appropriate.)

Figure 5.3
Bug report template.

- Identify bugs that require further investigation or that cannot be reproduced
- Determine state changes for bugs

A bug review is not conducted in the same way as reviews of code or other work products. It is usually not efficient to log the time that people spend preparing for reviews, and the roles of the participants are not as well defined as for a formal review of code or test cases. It is useful to have a set procedure for holding the reviews, however. A lead engineer in the test organization often conducts the review, and the bugs under review should be presented in a summary report that presents the high-level information regarding the bugs. An example format for the bug review summary report is shown in Figure 5.4.

The example report in Figure 5.4 lists all the bugs by bug ID and summarizes the state, severity, and date found. A brief description of the problem is given, but if full details of a particular bug are required, the original bug report will be needed. One of the key fields in the report is the "Action" column. A value can be entered for the expected action prior to the review, but one of the main outcomes of the meeting will be to determine the states that go into this column.

The report in Figure 5.4 provides places to enter the date of the review, to list the attendees, and a "Notes" field that can be used to document rationale for the decisions made in the meeting. If all the fields are correctly filled in at the review, the resulting report can be used as a record of the minutes of the meeting.

Project Bug Review					
Date of review: ddmmyy					
Attendees:					
Bug ID	State	Severity	Date Found	Bug Summary	Action
B1233	N	Cat.	DDMMYY	Data backup/retrieve functionality broken—cannot retrieve data after backup	Fix
B1234	N	Major	DDMMYY	Cannot open backup screen from menu; workaround is to use command-line interface	Fix
B1235	N	Minor	DDMMYY	Usability issue—keyboard shortcut to data retrieve function is missing	Defer
Notes:					
B1235—This problem will require an architecture change that needs to be deferred to the next release.					

Figure 5.4
Example report for bug reviews.

Running Tests

The emphasis so far in this chapter has been on bugs, because finding bugs is the reason for running tests. Now we focus more on the testing itself. In the next few sections, we be follow the overview diagram that was presented in Figure 5.1.

Entry into System Testing

When a new build is handed to the test group, a set of entry criteria are applied. Before testing begins, the test plan and test cases should have been written and reviewed. The development team should have finished unit testing and integration testing. They should have fixed any catastrophic bugs found in their testing before passing the build on to the test team.

The first test run on a new build is usually a "smoke" test that is used to verify that the program can be installed on the target platform, that any applicable upgrade procedures can be successfully run, and that at least some basic functionality of the program works. The idea behind the smoke test is simple: if the application doesn't run on the target platform, it can't be tested.

Unfortunately, it is not uncommon for a new build to fail the smoke test, particularly if little integration testing has been done prior to the handoff from developers to the test team. Developers can be so focused on getting their assigned functionality working in a development environment that system-level issues such as installation and operation in the customer environment are not given proper attention until the system test phase.

Test Cycles

The entry into system testing should mark the beginning of a cooperative effort between the development team and the test team. Testers will run planned tests, find bugs, and write bug reports. Developers will read the bug reports, reproduce the problems, and code fixes. The question is: How do the fixes get passed back to the test team?

The answer depends upon the software build cycle. Developers check their fixes into the software configuration management system in preparation for a periodic build. The build is commonly done on a daily or weekly basis and then passed along to the test team according to their needs.

There are several considerations for how frequently the test team accepts new builds. If the builds come too quickly the test environment can be destabilized—time is spent installing new builds, running smoke tests, and verifying that the few bugs found in the last build have been fixed. If the "build churn" is too great, there is not enough time to methodically run through enough tests to get efficient bug discovery.

On the other hand, if builds come too slowly, progress on bug discovery can be poor. Often the changes made to code when fixing a bug lead to new bugs being discovered. These new bugs could be due to breakage or regression introduced by the new fixes, or could be bugs that were previously in the build but which were masked by the earlier bugs. This means that new builds have to be injected into the testing cycle frequently enough for the next round of bugs to be discovered.

How often you accept new builds from development depends on several factors, including the complexity of the software, the number of testers, and the percentage of the tests that are automated. For example, if it is possible to run through all of your tests in three days, then you might want to accept a new build every four or five days. This would allow three days for the tests, and a day or so to verify bug fixes, run *ad hoc* tests in promising areas, prepare status reports, and conduct regular bug reviews.

Ideally, a *test cycle* consists of running a complete set of tests against a software build. The test plan will usually call for a set number of test cycles, each requiring a fixed amount of time. For example, the plan may call for three or four test cycles, each having one or two weeks' duration.

In practice the testing may not go according to plan. The first test cycle may last one or two weeks, but multiple builds may be needed to get the software stable enough to allow most of the tests to run. When each of these new builds is accepted into testing, a decision has to be made whether to rerun all the tests or to continue testing without starting over. It is usually more efficient to spot-check the new build by making sure that it installs and runs, that the previous bugs were fixed, and then proceed without rerunning all the tests. The time to start testing over again is at the start of a new test cycle. This means that an intermediate build may not have a complete set of tests run against it. The exception to this strategy is the final build of software, the "golden build," against which all tests are run.

One way to keep track of the tests that are run against a given build is to construct a build run list for each build of the software under test. An example of a build run list is shown in Figure 5.5. The list includes the build identification and the test date as a header; it then maps tests to test engineers. The build run list is essentially a "to-do" list for each test engineer. If there are shared test systems or workstations, the list can help

Build Run List				
Build ID:				
Date of test start:				
Test Number	**Test ID**	**Name of Tester**	**Test Configuration**	**Result (P/F/NR)**
1	A10	Jim D.	1A on System 1	Pass
2	A11	Jim D.	1A on System 1	Pass
3	B10	Bob Z.	2B on System 2	Fail
4	B11	Bob Z.	2B on System 2	Not Run

Figure 5.5
Example build run list.

eliminate conflicts by showing the test system that each engineer needs to run the tests. If there are conflicting demands on a test system, then a detailed schedule for the test system may be required. There is a column provided on the build run list that can be optionally used to summarize the test results.

A build run list can be very useful in situations where frequent builds are being delivered to the test team. By keeping track of what was run on previous builds, the list can be tailored to provide efficient coverage of the software features over a set of builds. The build run list also helps you adapt to a situation where a given build has bugs that block you from covering a particular area of the code. Once the blocking bugs are fixed, you'll know to focus on that area to ensure thorough coverage.

Log Test Results

When each tester gets an assigned set of tests to run against a particular build, he or she needs to follow the step-by-step procedure called for in the test case and log the result of the test. The example test case shown in Chapter 4 (Figure 4.2) provides a place for the tester to enter the results of each step of the procedure, as well as an overall pass or fail result, and a place to enter the bug ID of any bug discovered during testing. One way to log test results is to use a test case format similar to Figure 4.2.

An alternate way is to use the test log shown in Figure 5.6. The test log in Figure 5.6 is handy for storing the results of all the tests run by a single test engineer against a single build. It provides room for the pass/fail/not run result to be logged, as well as the ID of any bug found while running the test. There is space for comments—this would typically be used to log information that would be helpful in reproducing the problem or understanding the circumstances under which the problem is observed.

Regardless of the method used to log test results, it is very important that the result of each test be logged and stored in a safe archive. Archived test

Test Log

Date: mmddyyyy

Test cycle: 1

Build ID: B020202

Test configuration: 1A

Tested by: Jim D.

Test #	Test ID	Pass/Fail/NR	Bug ID	Comment
1	A10	P		
2	A11	P		
3	A12	P		
4	A13	F	XY1233	This problem appears to be specific to the test configuration.
5	A14	P		
6	A15	F	XY1234	
7	B1	NR		Test suite blocked by bug XY1234
8	B2	NR		Blocked
9	B3	NR		Blocked
10	B4	NR		Blocked

Figure 5.6
Test log.

results may be needed later for a variety of reasons: evidence of testing, support for reproducing a problem, or a historical record of the effort expended in developing a product.

Although the templates for build run list, test case, and test log are shown in this book as text on a page, they can be implemented as part of a Web-based data entry system or as part of a test management software tool. The use of automated tools for test case storage, test execution, and test reporting can be very effective in building an efficient system testing strategy.

Reporting Test Results

There are typically two types of test results that need to be reported. The first is a regular status report, often presented in a weekly meeting, in which representatives from all teams responsible for the success of the project are briefed on progress. The status report usually consists of a presentation of the testing status and a bug summary report. The test status report is designed to answer the question "how far along are we in testing?" The bug summary report is intended to give some idea of the success of the test effort in finding bugs. It also is meant to give a snapshot view of the quality of the product under test. These reports are discussed separately in the next two sections.

The second type of report of test results is a formal summary of the test results that is compiled at the completion of system testing. The purpose of this second type of report is to document the test results so that future questions can be addressed about what was tested, what results were obtained, and what recommendations were made by the test team regarding the readiness of the product for release. This report will be discussed in the section, "Test Summary Report."

Test Status Report

The report shown in Figure 5.7 gives an indication of the status of testing. The date, build ID, and test cycle tell the reader of the report what software is being tested and roughly how far along the testing is relative to the plan. The last entry in the report, the "% Run", is a measure of how many tests have been run against the designated build relative to the number of tests that were planned. The number of tests that have failed is shown in the column labeled "# Fail"—this gives a rough indication of how many bugs should be reported against the product. The "# Not Run" column gives an indication of how many tests are blocked by open bugs or other problems.

Test Status Report					
Date of report: DDMMYY					
Build ID: B123					
Test cycle: 2/3					
Start date: DDMMYY					
Test Suite	**# Tests**	**# Pass**	**# Fail**	**# Not Run**	**% Run**
Data entry	20	12	2	6	70%
Edit	15	10	4	1	93%
Backup and restore	25	12	6	7	72%
Communications	18	8	8	2	89%
Totals	78	42	20	16	79%

Figure 5.7
Example Test Status Report

Bug Status Report

Another view into the status of the test effort is to look at a bug status report such as the one shown in Figure 5.8. This report shows the total number of open bugs as a function of time in weeks. The time axis is often labeled with absolute dates rather than "week 1," "week 2," and so on. The number of bugs for a given severity (catastrophic, major, and minor) is shown in the report by stacking the values and by showing the values for each severity explicitly as labels. For example, there are 4 catastrophic bugs in weeks 3 and 4, and there are 32 minor open bugs in week 2.

The total number of open bugs is an indicator of the overall quality of the product. A lot of high severity bugs obviously does not speak well for product quality. The ultimate determinant of product quality is customer satisfaction, and customers tend to be unhappy with a buggy release. There are extenuating circumstances, of course—you may be in a situation where speed is essential, and the customer is willing to accept a buggy release just to get something going.

Generally speaking, as the test effort nears an end, you would expect the number of open bugs to decrease as development repairs them and they are verified to be fixed by the test team. It is also typical for the rate of bug discovery to decrease as testing winds down. The example shown in Figure 5.8

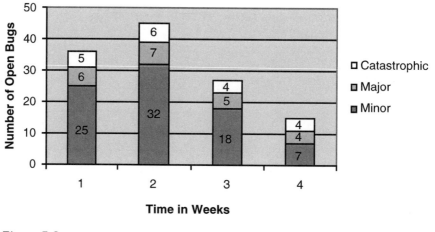

Figure 5.8
Example bug status report.

is unusual in that the number of open catastrophic and major bugs has remained fairly constant, while the number of minor bugs has been cut significantly. A more typical pattern is to see the higher severity bugs fixed quickly, while the minor bugs tend to languish, perhaps being deferred to a later release.

Another report that is often useful at a project status review is the bug review report shown in Table 5.5. The chart in Figure 5.4 is a useful indicator of test progress and product quality, but any decisions about what bug fixes to include in a release or how to prioritize bug fixes requires more detailed information about the open bugs. In some companies the functions of a project status review and bug review are combined, for example, in a regular meeting of the product's change control board (CCB). The CCB often consists of representatives of management, marketing, development, and test organizations.

Test Summary Report

The purpose of the test summary report is to address the following:

- What has been tested
- How the actual test activities deviated from the test plan
- How the schedule and effort compared to the test plan

- What bugs were found
- What bugs remain open at the end of testing and how they will be handled

The test summary report does not need to contain the detailed test results for each test run but it can refer to those results if they have been compiled and archived. The collection and archiving of all test results is one of the benefits of having a commercial test management tool. If the tool rolls up all the results into a single document, then that document can be referred to by the test summary report.

One way to report what has been tested is to include a final set of test logs (Figure 5.6) for each cycle of testing. This shows the results of each test without giving a step-by-step account such as that shown in Figure 4.2 in Chapter 4. Another useful summary is to compile a complete set of test status results, as presented in Figure 5.7.

It is important to understand how the actual testing deviated from the test plan because the test plan represents an approved definition of the scope of testing and an agreement as to how many people and how much time would be expended in the effort. It is particularly important to note test areas that were not completed, because untested areas of the program represent quality risks and possible escapes of bugs to the field. If testing went according to plan, you can simply say that in the summary report; if there were significant deviations from the plan, a statement of the deviations is needed. This information is useful in accounting of resources but also to provide input to future planning. If good historical data is collected regarding planned versus actual effort, the ability to improve accuracy of future estimates is enhanced.

Although the bug-tracking database should contain a complete set of information about the bugs found during testing of a product, it is a good idea to give a summary of the bugs found during system test in the summary report so that anyone interested in the outcome of the development will not have to query the bug database to get an idea of the success of the test effort and the quality of the product. Final versions of the bug review report (Figure 5.4) that shows all bugs found and their final states, and a final version of the open bug status report (Figure 5.8) are useful additions to the test summary report.

The test summary report should also contain a list of all open bugs with an indication as to whether they will be fixed in a later release or will be postponed indefinitely. Future releases of the product will still contain these open bugs until they are fixed, so it is a good idea to track them to avoid wasted effort in future releases by thinking something new has been found. The test plan for a future release can refer to this list of open bugs to give testers a heads-up on what to expect when testing a build of the new release.

An example test summary report that brings together the ideas discussed in this section is included in Part III.

Exit Criteria and Release Readiness

There are a variety of ways to determine when to stop testing, ranging from simple to sophisticated. Some of the means used to decide to stop testing are:

- **Run out of time**—if you are up against a fixed deadline, the day of reckoning may come when you simply stop running tests and ask the question, "How bad is it?" Almost any other method of stopping is likely to give you more confidence in the quality of the product that is shipped.

- **Completed all the planned test cycles**—if your test plan calls for three test cycles, then at the end of the third test cycle you are likely to ask the same question, "How bad is it?" If you've completed your plan, the test coverage is probably better than if you simply run out of time.

- **Bug profile meets exit criteria**—if you run an algorithm such as the Software Error Estimation Program (SWEEP) and see that the goal for the number of remaining bugs per thousand lines of code has been reached, then you may choose to stop testing. (See Chapter 11 for more information on SWEEP.) Once the goal for projected remaining bugs is reached, you are again likely to ask, "How bad is it?"

When you think it's time to stop testing, there are several factors that lead to a decision regarding the readiness of the product for shipment. A common set of factors that deal with the readiness of the product is:

- The number of catastrophic bugs found in testing that remain unfixed.
- The total number of bugs that have not been fixed.
- The percentage of planned tests that were run and that passed.
- The number of tests that cannot be run because they are blocked by bugs.

The usual forum for considering the readiness of the tested product is the release readiness review. In some organizations the test team conducts the readiness review; in other organizations a project manager or development manager holds the review. In any case, the job of the test team is to present the test results and make a recommendation as to whether or not the product is ready for shipment. Although the readiness review may not be conducted as a formal review in the same sense as a code inspection, it is important to record the names of the participants and the decision made regarding product shipment. In order to capture the results and recommendation of the test organization, the minutes of the readiness review should reference the test summary report.

What's Next

In this chapter we discussed tracking bugs, running system tests, and reporting results. Key points discussed include:

- Overview of system testing
- Finding and tracking bugs
- Defining bug states
- Bug tracking essentials
- Writing bug reports
- Bug reviews
- Running system tests
- Entry into system testing
- Test cycles
- Logging test results
- Reporting test results
- Test status reports
- Bug status reports
- Test summary report
- Exit criteria and readiness review

The input to system testing is a completed test plan, a set of test cases that are ready to run, and a fully configured and debugged test system. The output of these steps is a set of test results that allow management and the product development team to assess the readiness of the product for release.

The first five chapters of this book have defined a set of processes that cover software testing from elicitation of requirements to the completion of system testing. If you are new to testing or are trying to establish a new test organization, it is not easy to implement all of these processes at once; they need a phased introduction as part of a continuous process improvement program. In the next chapter, we look at how to put the test process together using a continuous improvement approach.

Putting It All Together: People and Process

Topics Covered in the Chapter

- ▶ The People Side of Testing

- ▶ Improving the Test Process

- ▶ What's Next

- ▶ References

In Chapter 1 we talked about rapid testing being a structure built on:

- People
- Integrated test process
- Static testing
- Dynamic testing

So far we have focused mainly on the second building block, the integrated test process. Part of the reason for the emphasis on process is that, no matter how good your people are, if they do not have a systematic, disciplined process for testing, they will not operate at maximum efficiency. The first part of this chapter will shift emphasis to address the people side of testing. It should be noted that entire books have been devoted to the people issues of software development; one that specifically applies to software testing is Perry and Rice (1997), *Surviving the Top Ten Challenges of Software Testing*. In their classic 1987 book, *Peopleware*, DeMarco and Lister provide a look at people issues as they relate to software development. In the first part of this chapter we will hit some high points of this important topic, which can truly make or break the success of your testing effort.

Although a good deal of discussion has already been devoted to the test process, there is still one matter that needs further consideration. At the end of Chapter 5 it was noted that the entire test process cannot be overhauled all at once. Process improvement needs to be a planned, phased activity. The second part of this chapter provides an overview of test process improvement.

Static testing and dynamic testing form the third and fourth building blocks of an efficient, effective test program. These two types of testing techniques were discussed in Chapters 2 and 3, and will receive more detailed treatment in Chapters 9 and 10.

The People Side of Testing

Barry Boehm (1981) states that personnel attributes and human relations activities provide by far the largest source of opportunity for improving software productivity. In other words, people issues have more impact than any other single factor on productivity. Boehm accounts for this in his COCOMO effort estimation tool by allowing analyst and programmer productivity to vary by as much as a factor of 4. It is the experience of the authors that similar variations in productivity apply to test planning, test development, and even test execution (finding bugs). If you are looking for the single biggest contributor to your team's ability to test a product quickly and effectively, the quality of people on your test team is an obvious first place to look.

In this section we look at the traits of a successful tester and then list some common traps that testers fall into that reduce the overall effectiveness of the test effort. We also consider some interviewing techniques that are specific to test engineers.

Traits of a Successful Test Engineer

There may be a few bright stars in the testing profession that are the perfect example of the test engineer. It is more common, however, for there to be excellent test teams that are built from people who have a wide variety of skills. In this section we build a list of the traits of an ideal tester, realizing that while no one person may embody all these traits, the test team as a whole should embody as many of these as possible. This list is based on experience and observation rather than hard scientific data; you might want to create your own picture of the ideal tester by using this list as a starting point. In our view, the ideal tester is:

- Able to break things and feel okay about it. Since the job of testing is to find defects, the tester must be comfortable in finding fault with another person's work.
- Able to design and follow step-by-step procedures.
- Able to communicate the sequence of events and the system configuration that leads to a problem. This includes being able to clearly document procedures and results, and being able to verbally communicate to developers, other testers, and management.
- Able to give and take criticism (for example, be able to explain bugs to developers in a way that they get resolved).
- Able to deliver bad news to developers and management. If the readiness for release of a product comes into question at the eleventh hour, the tester must be willing to stand up and deliver the bad news.
- Able to handle unrelenting pressure (testing is at the back-end of the process and will be done under stressful circumstances).
- Smart—able to learn new technology quickly.
- Patient—able to rerun tests as needed until a problem is resolved, and then rerun to verify that the problem stays fixed. (By the way, automation helps!)
- Flexible—able to shift gears quickly to test a new product or even abandon one product in favor of another, higher priority one.
- Able to both see the big picture and to focus in at a detailed level as needed; has a wide range dynamic range.
- Expert on a variety of subjects—your team may need experts on databases, communications, networking, GUI testing, test tools, automation scripting, or other areas.

This profile of the successful tester is useful when hiring and when evaluating people for potential work assignments. If you are building a team to take on a new project, it is useful to include people that contribute to a team profile that demonstrates as many of the traits listed above as possible. More about building productive teams can be found in DeMarco and Lister (1987) and in McConnell (1996).

Traps to Avoid

If all test teams demonstrated the qualities listed in the preceding section, life in the testing world would be easier. Few teams are perfect, however, and it is worth taking a look at some common mistakes testers make that rob their test effort of productivity. Sometimes it is possible to work with others (or yourself) to overcome some of these "efficiency robbers" simply by becoming aware of them and forming strategies for overcoming them.

Here, then, are some classic mistakes that testers make:

- **Assuming that a program is working OK.** The assumption of a tester should be that the program is *not* working OK; your job is to find out what the program does *wrong*, not what it does right. Any deviation from an expected result, no matter how small, should be seen as a potential symptom of a bug. No matter how nice or competent the programmer may be, you should not fall into the trap of giving the programmer the benefit of the doubt where potential bugs are concerned.

- **Not logging every problem seen.** This problem often occurs in the middle of a long test. You see a little problem and move on, thinking that you'll remember enough to write something up later. When later comes, you forget about the problem or can't reproduce the steps that led up to it. Keeping a running set of notes about little anomalies, even those that don't seem to directly relate to the test, is a good way to avoid this mistake. If you have good notes, it is possible at the end of the test to explore the problem in more detail in an *ad hoc* way to see if it's really a bug.

- **Ignoring or concealing a problem.** This relates to the first two traps, but is actually more extreme. Here you know there is a bug, but decide to ignore it. Maybe it will go away in the next build. Maybe it's not important. Perhaps you're pressed for time and don't think it's worth investigation. Falling into this trap can lead to some pretty bad consequences, including allowing defects to escape to the customer. It's worth remembering that any bug that you find could have a whole host of bugs hiding behind it—the hidden ones may escape if you don't conscientiously pursue the visible one.

- **Letting the developer talk you out of writing a bug report or trashing an existing bug report without solid reasons.** There's nothing wrong in talking to a developer and being convinced that your test has a bug or that your test configuration does not match a likely customer environment, but before you trash a bug, you should be sure you agree with the reasoning. If you have any doubts about the developer's reason for not writing up the bug or for trashing a bug report, it's worth checking the logic with a fellow tester or another developer.

- **Avoiding conflict with a developer.** This can relate to the previous trap, but can manifest in different ways. If you find a bug in someone's work, then there's a bug in your company's product, and the whole team is better off knowing about it and dealing with it—the sooner, the better. One of the benefits of a good defect tracking system and weekly bug reviews is that one-on-one conflicts are avoided. The personal sting of finding a flaw in someone's work can be reduced if tracking tools and proper review procedures are used professionally.

- **Not paying attention to test planning.** If your process does not support thorough test planning, it is easy to fall in the trap of spending too little time getting ready for the next build or preparing a hurried estimate of the time and resources required to perform a task. Hurried planning usually leads to big problems in test execution.

- **Writing bug reports on nonproblems.** This is a time-waster at the opposite end of the spectrum from most of the traps we've discussed. Got a bug quota in your shop? Is your performance rating tied to the number of bugs you find? If so, it is very tempting to write up nonproblems as bugs. It is a huge waste of time to try and squeeze a bug out of a program that is working as designed. Not only do you waste time writing up the problem, but development and management time will be spent tracking the bug and trying to reproduce the problem. Testers need to be aggressive about writing up every real problem they see but should not fall into the trap of writing up bugs that they know should be trashed. If more than 10% of a tester's bugs wind up being trashed, he or she may be falling into this trap, or may simply not have enough detailed knowledge of the system under test.

Interviewing Tips

One way to build a good test team is to hire experienced testers. Although a detailed discussion of interview strategies and techniques is outside the scope of this book, we list a few interview techniques specific to test engineers that have proven useful to the authors. These are all simple, common sense ideas, but if you've not tried them, you might be surprised at the information that can be gained with these techniques.

- **Ask about the candidate's experience with the testing process.** Have they written test plans? If so, what kinds of information went into the plan? Did they map test cases to requirements? Did they use a formal bug-tracking system? A few questions along with the follow-up discussion can give a reasonable gauge of the person's experience with the test process pretty quickly.

- **If the person claims expertise in a technology area, ask them to explain specifically how they have applied that area of technology in testing a product.** It is easy for someone to pick up a few buzzwords about an area of technology, but a solid explanation of how the person developed automated scripts, or configured a local area network, or used a capture and playbook tool can reveal a good deal about their working knowledge of the technology.

- **Ask questions that reveal how well the candidate matches the traits of a successful engineer that were listed above.** It's usually not very revealing to simply ask: "Are you smart?" or "Are you patient?" You can, however, ask someone to talk about some past experience that sheds light on one of these traits. For example, you might ask, "Have you ever had a change in project priorities where you were suddenly moved from testing Product A to Product B? If so, how did it go? Did you have trouble learning the new technology associated with Product B? In terms of lessons learned, what did you do well? What would you change?" If you are building a test team and specifically are looking for someone with one or more of the traits, you can construct some questions ahead of time that probe the area of interest.

- **If your hiring needs have focused requirements, you can pose a hypothetical situation to see how the person would come up with a solution.** For example, if you need someone to write test plans and test cases for a specific kind of product, you can generate a simple set of requirements and ask what kinds of tests the person would use to test them. By walking with the person through a solution, perhaps by sketching ideas on a whiteboard or just talking about the problem, you should be able to get a feel for how this person would go about writing tests.

- **Assess how vulnerable the candidate is to some of the "traps to avoid" that were listed above by posing situations and seeing how the candidate responds.** For example, you might pose a situation where the team is under pressure to finish testing. Do you abandon the test plan and do *ad hoc* testing? Do you log problems that you find while running tests, or just log passes and fails? Do you take time to plan what tests are going to be run for the final build of software, or just start running tests in hopes that you'll finish before the ending bell sounds? What has the candidate done in past situations like this, and what lessons were learned? Other possible situations to propose might involve repeated conflict with a developer or what to do if you find a colleague who seems to be writing bug reports on nonproblems.

This section has barely touched a few aspects that surround the people side of testing. In spite of the brevity, however, we have managed to touch three of the five basic principles of staffing that Boehm (1981) calls out in *Software Engineering Economics*:

- Top talent
- Job matching
- Career progression
- Team balance
- Phaseout (eliminating misfits)

The principle of hiring top talent is reflected in our characterization of a successful test engineer and the interview techniques that were presented above. Job matching and team balance were also addressed by the profile of the successful test engineer, where it was stated that no one person could provide all the skills needed on the team, but that a balanced team needed to be assembled that covered the needed skills.

Boehm's phaseout principle consists of removing people who don't positively contribute to productivity. One example of a negative contribution occurs if more effort is being spent fixing messes caused by the person than is justified by their productivity. Perhaps they fall into several of the traps to avoid discussed earlier. Perhaps they are not a good fit into the successful tester profile.

The principle of career progression is an important one in software testing. A person who takes on a new job in software testing should be made aware of the career path available to them. An increasing number of companies and individuals consider testing a viable career path, with specializations open in technical growth and with opportunities to manage. Software testing is a good place to learn a product line at the system level. Because it deals with all aspects of a company's products, it can also be a good launch pad for future work in development, field support, technical support, or technical marketing.

Improving the Test Process

An effective, mature testing process does not come about overnight. It takes planning and sustained effort over months or even years to develop a top-notch testing organization. Any attempt to improve an established testing process or to build a new process from the ground up should keep the following points in mind:

- **Testing is not an independent process.** In order be effective, the software test process must be well integrated with the rest of the software development life cycle. This means that it does little good to try to improve the test process by itself—test process improvement needs to be part of a larger, more comprehensive effort.

- **A good testing process must be built in stages.** There are distinct phases or levels in the maturity of any development process. The levels can be illustrated by a maturity model such as the Software Engineering Institute's Capability Maturity Model (CMM) for software development, the Illinois Institute of Technology's Testing Maturity Model (TMM), or the Test Process Improvement (TPI) model. Progression from one level of a maturity model to another must happen in an orderly way. An organization cannot jump from the bottom to top level of a maturity model by adapting a few procedures or tools; progression needs to move step-by-step through the levels without skipping.

- **Successful process improvement considers the people involved.** Setting up a process is not an academic or technical exercise; it affects the way people go about their day-to-day work and helps set the expectations that managers hold for their employees. Any process initiative that is to succeed needs input and buy-in from all levels within the company, from upper management to the person running tests in the lab. Once the process is defined, the people using it must be thoroughly trained to ensure consistency and efficiency.

The first point, that the test process is not independent, is evident throughout the development life cycle. As an example of cross-functional interdependence, consider the process for eliciting and defining requirements. We've said in previous chapters that testing should begin with requirements definition. Requirements definition is a broad cross-functional activity that should involve representatives from upper-level management, marketing, development, manufacturing, and customer support. Direct communication with the customer may not involve anyone outside of the marketing organization, but clearly the requirements that are defined impact the entire product development team. Therefore any process that is defined for requirements elicitation and definition should involve all participants, including the testing organization.

The second point, that a good process must be built in stages, is discussed in the next section in the context of the Capability Maturity Model. We do not discuss all levels and all key process areas within CMM, but focus on those areas in CMM that relate to test process ideas that are covered in this book. The maturity models mentioned above are discussed in the books by Humphrey (1990, 1997, 2000), the article on TMM by Burnstein et al. (1996), the book on CMM by Paulk et al. (1995), and the book on TPI by Koomen and Pol (1999).

The third point deals with the way that process improvement is carried out and is discussed near the end of this chapter.

The Software Engineering Institute's Capability Maturity Model (CMM)

The Software Engineering Institute (SEI) is a federally funded research and development organization established by the U.S. Department of Defense in 1984. It is maintained by Carnegie Mellon University. Information is available online about the SEI and CMM at the SEI Web site, *www.sei.cmu.edu.*

The Capability Maturity Model provides a framework that can be used to assess how capable an organization is to produce software. It classifies software development processes in terms of five maturity levels: Initial, Repeatable, Defined, Managed, and Optimizing. A brief summary of the characteristics of each level of maturity is shown in Table 6.1.

The characteristics summarized in Table 6.1 describe key features for Levels 1–5. The level of detail in the table is intentionally low; the idea is to give a quick idea of the state of an organization at each of the levels. For example, an organization at CMM Level 1, the Initial level, develops software using an undefined and unplanned process. It would be expected that such an organization would do a poor job of meeting deadlines, finding bugs in a product before its release, or being able to manage development costs. An organization at Level 2 has made a substantial investment in their process, and use solid project management principles of planning, estimating, and scheduling to achieve their goals. It would be expected that the Level 2 organization would better able to meet deadlines, find bugs, and manage costs.

Table 6.1
Characteristics of the Capability Maturity Model

Maturity Level	Name of Level	Characteristics
Level 1	Initial	The process is largely undefined and *ad hoc*. Typically there are no formalized procedures, project plans, or cost estimates. If such procedures exist, there is no management mechanism to ensure their use, and in a crisis formal procedures are abandoned. Change control is lax. Coding and testing are done without a sound plan. Designs, reviews, and test data analysis are considered expendable. Senior management has little understanding of the issues.
Level 2	Repeatable	Development is done according to a plan. A project management system is in place to support planning and tracking. A quality assurance group is established to ensure senior management that work is being done according to process and according to plan. Change control management is used for software. Estimates and schedules can be met as long as new tools, new methods, and major organizational changes are not introduced.
Level 3	Defined	In addition to the processes put in place at Level 2, additional improvements are made. A process group is put in place to support ongoing process improvement. A development life cycle is defined that is tailored to the specific needs of the organization and to the project at hand. A family of software engineering methods are in use, including inspections, formal design methods, and testing methods. At this level the organization achieves the basis for significant and continuing progress. Effective as it is, however, this level is qualitative. It does little to provide measures of what is accomplished or how effective the process is.
Level 4	Managed	In addition to previously established improvements, a set of measurements is established to quantify the cost and benefits of major process

Maturity Level	Name of Level	Characteristics
		activities. A process database is set up and maintained. Progress toward quality targets for specific products is tracked and reported to management. The focus at this level and previous levels is on product quality.
Level 5	Optimizing	At this level there is a shift of focus from product quality to process optimization. Data is now available that can be used to tune the process itself rather than be limited to the constraints of one or two projects. At the optimizing level, the organization has the means to identify and fix the weakest elements of the process.

Level 3 represents a significant improvement over the chaos of Level 1. By Level 3, the Defined level, most of the methods discussed in this book would likely be put into place in the testing organization: requirements management, test planning, solid estimation and scheduling, configuration management, and inspections and reviews. The Defined level of the CMM represents a very effective organization, but the process is still operated on a qualitative rather than quantitative basis. There is not yet an established, solid system of measurements for evaluating product quality or process effectiveness.

The final two levels of the CMM involve planned and ongoing measurements of product quality and process effectiveness. The main difference between Levels 4 and 5 is the shift in focus from product quality to process effectiveness. By Level 5, the organization has collected enough data that it has the means to tune its processes for optimum effectiveness. One of the key features of Levels 4 and 5 is the use of metrics. Testing metrics are discussed in detail in Chapter 11.

In addition to defining the five levels of maturity for a software development organization, the CMM further identifies 18 key process areas that are distributed across the five levels. The key process areas (KPAs) for a given level of maturity represent processes that need to be fully operational in order for the organization to reach that level.

For example, the titles of the KPAs for Level 2 are [see, for example, Paulk (1999)]:

- Requirements Management
- Software Project Planning
- Software Project Oversight and Tracking
- Software Subcontract Management
- Software Quality Assurance
- Software Configuration Management

While we leave the detailed definitions of these KPAs to books devoted to CMM, it may be useful to provide a high-level mapping of the Level 2 KPAs to the test processes that we've described in previous chapters of this book. We undertake this mapping in the next section.

Relationship of the CMM to Rapid Testing

The road from CMM Level 1 to Level 2 lies in implementing the key process areas (KPAs) listed in the previous section. The first process to consider is *Requirements Management*. The role of the test team in requirements management was the main topic of Chapter 2. There we noted that the test team needs early and accurate requirements specifications on which to base a test plan and test designs. We made a case for the test team getting involved in requirements definition by performing static testing on the requirements to verify that they are complete, consistent, feasible, and testable; and to validate that the requirements meet customer needs. We also advocated using a requirements traceability matrix to map each requirement to tests, design components, and code.

Chapter 8 describes the Joint Application Requirements (JAR) process, which is a methodology for requirements elicitation that fully integrates static testing into the elicitation process. Integration of static testing into requirements definition and tracing requirements through test planning and test case development are the key principles to bear in mind when considering the role of the test team in requirements management.

The second KPA for CMM Level 2 is *Project Planning*. For the testing organization this relates to effort estimates, schedules, and the test plan. Test planning and effort estimation was covered in some detail in Chapter 3, and additional information about test effort estimation techniques is covered in Chapter 12. An example of a test plan is presented in Chapter 14. In discussing test planning we have seen that the core activities that make up the test planning process are:

- Define the test strategy
- Define the test system (hardware and software)
- Estimate the test effort (resources and schedule)
- Assess risks to the schedule and prepare mitigation plans
- Prepare and review the test plan documents

While the order in which an organization tackles the KPA's depends on local circumstances, there is good logic to dealing with requirements management first and project planning second for the simple reason that the plan should be based on the requirements. As requirements change, the plan should be modified to accommodate the changes.

The third KPA in the CMM is *Project Oversight and Tracking.* For the test team, this means that information on test progress and the expected quality of the product as revealed in the bug reports must be readily available to management. This was covered in Chapter 5 in the discussions on test status reports and bug summary reports. If accurate, up-to-date information is presented at weekly (or in critical situations, daily) meetings, or if it is posted on an internal Web site, the test team should meet the purpose of this KPA. Since project tracking must have a plan to track to, it is apparent that this KPA depends upon good execution of the project planning KPA.

The *Subcontract Management* KPA is an area that we have not discussed, but it can be important to test groups using outside contractors to assist in any of the test activities: test planning, test development, and/or test execution. It is not uncommon to have one or more geographically remote teams working under contract to assist a testing effort. There are three considerations that should be mentioned regarding the use of contractors. One consideration is that they must be included in the effort estimation and test planning at the front-end of the project. Preferably they will be active participants in the estimation and planning exercise. The second consideration is that all the expectations of the plans must be included in a contract that is understood and agreed to by all parties. Finally, the project oversight and tracking task must include the work of the contractors.

The fifth KPA listed for CMM Level 2 is *Quality Assurance* (QA). The basic function of QA at Level 2 is to monitor product development to ensure adherence to process and to assess product quality. The QA group serves as a window for management into how a product is being built. The QA group needs to be independent of engineering in the sense that it should offer an independent, objective viewpoint. By "independent" it is meant that the QA group reports to senior management separately from the development team. Although the test group may be asked to serve in a QA role, such a role is not assumed in any of the processes described in this book. All the verification activities, such as formal inspections and informal reviews, are considered here to be part of static testing.

The final KPA for Level 2 is *Configuration Management*. A large part of configuration management involves placing selected work products in a protected repository under version control. Certainly the requirements documents, design documents, and code should be placed under configuration management. From the test perspective, the test plan, test cases, and test results (including bug reports) should go under configuration management. We discussed this in Chapters 3, 4, and 5, and mentioned that a test management tool is a good investment for supporting the configuration management needs of the test group.

An Approach to Process Improvement

Regardless of whether the SEI's Capability Maturity Model is used as a framework for improvement, or another approach is adopted, process improvement usually follows a systematic, disciplined approach that includes the following steps.

- **Assess the state of the current process.** The first step is to determine where you currently stand with respect to an established framework. The assessment might involve outside consultants who are trained to evaluate an organization in the context of a maturity model such as CMM. Alternatively, internal assessments may be conducted in the form of post-project reviews, which often have the combined purpose of celebrating the completion of a project and evaluating what was done well and what could be improved. Both internal and external assessments need full support from upper-level management and participation on the part of the people who will be implementing and using the changes.

- **Identify areas for improvement.** The results of assessing the current process should lead to a list of candidate areas to improve, but it is important that the candidate areas be prioritized and placed on an improvement road map. Attempts to fix all the candidate areas at once often leads to disappointment.

- **Plan the improvement effort.** Involve the people who will implement and use the improvements in the planning to obtain their ideas and support. The plan should include establishing a means of measuring progress toward the improvement goals. In the context of a maturity model, the measure of progress might take the form of another formal assessment 12 or 18 months down the road, with intermediate checkpoints to allow tracking of progress.

- **Implement the changes and monitor their effectiveness.** Once the plan is made, it is implemented, progress is tracked, and corrective action is taken to keep progress toward the goal on course.

Process improvement can take time. Large organizations can expect to take two to three years to move from Level 1 to Level 2. Smaller organizations may be able to move faster; see Paulk (1999) for thoughts on how smaller projects and organizations might apply CMM.

What's Next

This chapter concludes Part I, which has presented an approach to software testing that we call rapid testing. Rapid testing is a structure built on:

- People
- Integrated test process
- Static testing
- Dynamic testing

In this chapter we discussed the people side of testing and improving the testing process. With regard to people, we presented the traits of a successful test engineer, listed traps that testers should avoid, and presented a few interviewing tips that should help you select people to build a balanced testing team.

We noted that no matter how good your people are, if they do not have a systematic, disciplined process for testing, they will not operate at maximum efficiency. We presented three basic principles that should be kept in mind when trying to improve the testing process:

- Testing is not an independent process.
- A good testing process must be built in stages.
- Successful process improvement considers the people involved.

As an example of a phased approach to process improvement we considered the Software Engineering Institute's Capability Maturity Model, and mapped some of the key process areas to testing.

The next part of *Rapid Testing* is devoted to tips, techniques, and best practices that may be used to improve the efficiency of testing. As we have discussed in this chapter, however, it is not possible to change a development process quickly. In applying the ideas of Part I and Part II, you'll want to take a planned, phased approach to process improvement, changing first those things in your process that give the "biggest bang for the buck." Some examples of key testing work products are presented in Part III.

References

Boehm, Barry W. (1981). *Software Engineering Economics*. Englewood Cliffs, NJ: Prentice Hall.

Burnstein, Ilene, C.R. Carlson, and T. Suwanassart. (1996). "Developing a Testing Maturity Model." *Proceeding of the Ninth International Software Quality Week Conference*, San Francisco, May, 1996. *Note:* Ilene Burnstein is affiliated with the Illinois Institute of Technology, where work on the Testing Maturity Model is being conducted.

DeMarco, Tom, and Timothy Lister. (1987). *Peopleware: Productive Projects and Teams*. New York: Dorset House Publishing.

Humphrey, Watts S. (1990). *Managing the Software Process*. Reading, MA: Addison-Wesley.

Humphrey, Watts S. (1997). *Introduction to the Personal Software Process*. Reading, MA: Addison-Wesley.

Humphrey, Watts S. (2000). *Introduction to the Team Software Process*. Reading, MA: Addison-Wesley.

Koomen, Tim, and Martin Pol. (1999). *Test Process Improvement*. Reading, MA: Addison-Wesley.

McConnell, Steve. (1996). *Rapid Development*. Redmond, WA: Microsoft Press.

Paulk, Mark, Charles Weber, and Bill Curtis. (1995). *The Capability Maturity Model: Guidelines for Improving the Software Process*. Reading, MA: Addison-Wesley.

Paulk, Mark. "Using the Software CMM with Small Projects and Small Organizations." In Eugene McGuire (1999), *Software Process Improvement: Concepts and Practices*. Hershey, PA: Idea Group Publishing.

Perry, William E., and Randall W. Rice. (1997). *Surviving the Top Ten Challenges of Software Testing*. New York: Dorset House Publishing.

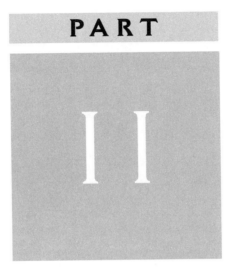

PART

II

Rapid Testing
Techniques and Tips

Introduction to Testing Techniques and Tips

Topics Covered in the Chapter

- The Scope of Testing Techniques
- Development Life Cycle
- Benefits of Rapid Testing
- Definition of Static Testing
- Definition of Dynamic Testing
- Life Cycle of a Bug
- Formal Test Phases
- Responsibilities of Test Team Members
- What's Next

The Scope of Testing Techniques

To understand the scope of testing techniques, Table 7.1 gives a list of techniques used in developing test cases. Some of these are static and others are dynamic testing techniques. Can you tell which ones are which? While this is an admittedly incomplete list, its intent is to convince you that if your test group is finding bugs using only a few of these techniques, it may be short-changing the project by missing bugs that might be easily found using one of the other techniques.

The next five chapters provide definitions of these terms, underlying objectives that apply to the techniques and examples of applications of some of them on a project. In some, we offer actual case studies or lessons learned

Table 7.1
Techniques for Testing

Facility	Volume	Stress	Storage	Configuration
Compatibility	Installability	Reliability	Serviceability	Documentation
Procedure	Acceptance	Environmental	Black-box	White-box
Inspection	Standards	Comparison	Boundary value	Side effect
Path	Segment	Thread	Module	Database
Logic	Validation	Verification	Proof	Assertion
Timing	Calls	Multitasking	Event-sequencing	Simulation
Performance	Accuracy	Stability	Consistency	Prior changes

from the experience of the author in order for you to better judge where to apply them on your projects.

Development Life Cycle

A hinged waterfall chart, shown in Figure 7.1, is helpful in understanding the difference between where static testing applies or where dynamic testing techniques should be used. This rendition of the hinged waterfall chart is consistent with the one shown in the latter part of Chapter 1, although some additional acronyms are included in Figure 7.1, which form a basis of the language used in this chapter and following ones. Documentation comes as inputs to the Integration Test, System Test, and Acceptance Test phases from the Detailed Design, Preliminary Design, and Requirements phases, respectively. This dependency is depicted with the double-ended arrows, and this is where some testing projects begin to fail. When the code doesn't meet the requirements, there are three things that could be found to be the cause of the bug, as follows:

- The requirements were changed and the documentation was not updated to reflect the change.

- One of the test cases, test scripts, or test results had an error in it that caused a false detection.

- The code has a bug in it.

Notice that in the first two out of the three possibilities, the bug should have been found through static testing means; they are failures that are caused by

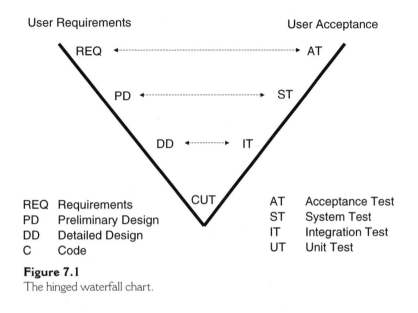

Figure 7.1
The hinged waterfall chart.

not following the life cycle process. Rapid testers who are on the job during early phases of software development, from Requirements through Coding, are the best guard against process failures of this sort.

As a general rule-of-thumb, dynamic testing techniques are applicable, starting with the software engineers who perform unit testing on their new code during the Code and Unit Test (CUT) phase, or earlier if a prototype is developed. Static testing techniques apply to both the development and test phases of the life cycle.

On some projects, there are no testers on the job until after the Code and Unit Test (CUT) phase has been completed and a complete source build has been performed. In fact, testers are sometimes brought in after partial completion of the Integration Testing (IT) phase. If this is true of your projects, you are, by definition, not employing the rapid testing philosophy. If testers are not engaged in developing test plans, test cases, test scripts, test results, and performing static testing of the documentation before and during the CUT phase, just think of the wasted development time caused by dealing with bugs introduced earlier in the life cycle of software development. Some people think that all the bugs are in the source code; this is absolutely untrue. For example, a bug introduced in the Requirements (REQ) phase may linger for months while development effort is expended on its architectural interfaces, its low-level design, and its low-level coding and documentation before it is recognized as a "not what we wanted" or "not the way we wanted it to be done" bug. We often lay blame on the requirements team, but who's on the requirements team finding bugs like this and eliminating them during the Requirements phase? Shame on us for not having testers on the job during the requirements phase looking for bugs like this and correcting them with the mere act of erasure or wadding up a piece of paper and throwing it toward the trash can. How much money is being wasted by not having testers on the job earlier in the life cycle? Chapter 8 presents a static testing technique, called Joint Application Requirements (JAR), which exemplifies the rapid testing philosophy, that is, how to integrate requirements-gathering with perfective testing.

In the early stages of the software life cycle, words are used to describe what the software is supposed to do, such as, requirements. This foundation in words is transitioned into architectural diagrams of some graphical form. The subsystems and subunits are allocated by the descriptive words of the requirements. Further along the development life cycle, process flows and data flows are described in other graphical forms, as well as tables that describe names and relationships that will form the basis of databases and queries. When the logic of a program is complete, state diagrams are often used to ensure the coders completely cover all cases. During each of these conversions from one problem description language into another, bugs are introduced. The role of a tester is to find bugs.

Strategies of developing test cases naturally break down into two categories, based upon what the tester has in hand:

1. **Black-box testing:** Knowing the specified function that a product has been designed to perform, tests can be conducted that demonstrate each function is fully functional. The term "black box" simply means the testers don't use any knowledge of the internal design or code to develop the test cases. The testing techniques that are applied during black-box testing are typically called dynamic testing techniques, and many of these are presented in Chapter 10.

2. **White-box testing:** Knowing the internal workings of a product, tests can be conducted to ensure that all the gears mesh, for example, the internal operation of the product performs according to specification and all internal components have been adequately exercised. The term "white box" simply means that the testers use any knowledge of the internal design or code to develop the test cases. The techniques that are applied during white-box testing are typically called static testing techniques, and many of these are presented in Chapter 9.

In the later stages of the software life cycle, the right half of the hinged waterfall, compiled software code is used to drive the computer system, peripherals, and communication subsystems to exhibit all of the functions that are documented as requirements, while satisfying all architectural and design specifications. Often, it's the first time that the application comes to life and can be performance-tested, compatibility-tested across multiple platforms, usability-tested, installability-tested, and other forms or techniques of dynamic testing discussed in Chapter 10 can be applied. The subsystems and subunits that were allocated with descriptive words of the architecture and design documentation are now implemented and hidden within the computer code.

Benefits of Rapid Testing

Many rapid testing techniques can be applied as early in the software development life cycle as requirements elicitation, and instantiations of these static-testing techniques are often repeated throughout the later phases of the life cycle (Chapter 8 is dedicated to a rapid testing technique for requirements elicitation). But, you say, "Won't it be more costly to have testers on the job early in the software development life cycle?" Figure 7.2 displays a software cost estimating model (Chapter 12 is dedicated to this software cost estimating model), which best fits empirical data between conventional versus rapid testing approaches. The percentages shown in the matrix to the left of this figure add to more than 100%. Those percentages that do add to 100% are for the development phases, namely, PD, DD, CUT, and IT, and this total staffing for the development will be referred to as the area under the development-staffing curve. It is traditional to not include the REQ phase, since the requirements must be completed before one can forecast the staffing needs of the development phases. The allocation of staffing for the REQ phase is 8% for rapid testing versus 7% for conventional, and this percentage is the percentage of the area under the development-staffing curve. It is also traditional to not include the first year after the release of the product, sometimes called the operations and maintenance (O&M) phase, in the staffing requirements of software development. The allocation of staffing for the O&M phase is 10% for rapid testing versus 15% for conventional, and this percentage is the percentage of the area under the development-staffing curve.

Notice that even though the phases of development are aligned, between the rapid testing staffing curve and the conventional staffing curve, the pie chart shows that the area under the total staffing curve for the rapid testing project is 56.25% (36%/64%) of the area under the total staffing curve for the conventional project. Because rapid testing projects require less total staffing than conventional projects, the time to deliver products is shortened considerably, as well.

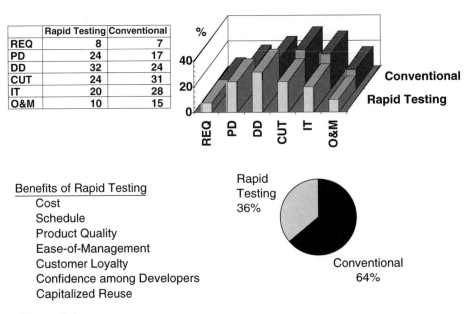

	Rapid Testing	Conventional
REQ	8	7
PD	24	17
DD	32	24
CUT	24	31
IT	20	28
O&M	10	15

Benefits of Rapid Testing
  Cost
  Schedule
  Product Quality
  Ease-of-Management
  Customer Loyalty
  Confidence among Developers
  Capitalized Reuse

Figure 7.2
A comparison between rapid testing versus conventional testing resources.

Imagine yourself as a practicing rapid testing software project lead, and that you are in the following conversation between yourself, and a fellow non-rapid testing software project lead. You say, "My new project is taking almost half the time during development and about half the staffing resources for about the same size product." The other project manager says, "Yeah, but I'll bet your quality has gone to the dogs." You say, "Actually, it's strange, but we are delivering only about a third of the latent bugs as we did in our last project that was of comparable size." The other project manager asks, "What on earth are you doing right?" You answer, "Rapid testing techniques are being applied from the first day to the last, in parallel and integrated with the development itself. It really is paying off for us. We are winning contracts against our competition and our end-users are winning, too!"

Definition of Static Testing

Static testing uses only the textual and/or graphical forms of the software to visually inspect or automatically process software documentation/code in order to find bugs. Text or graph processors like compilers, cross-references, discrete-event simulators, pretty printers, static checkers, path listings, and cyclomatic complexity counters all fall under this category and are called static processors. Many of these static processors are critical tools of the tester. Manual processes exist for static testing like inspections, checklists, and design reviews. These are the subjects of Chapter 8. It is optimum to find bugs up front or at the point that they are injected in a software development life cycle. A good example of an on-the-spot bug detection/correction process is a dynamic spell checker, running within a word processor. It actively looks for text strings that are not in its current dictionary and, when it finds one, it automatically replaces it with the closest word or highlights it so that the user can help by finding the correct word from a list of words with similar spellings. While static testing can be used throughout the entire life cycle of development and maintenance, it is particularly useful in the stages of development prior to the existence of executable code.

Definition of Dynamic Testing

Dynamic testing is the finding of bugs with the aid of the computer or an emulator of the computer to execute software created and integrated by software engineers to meet the product's requirements. Dynamic testing follows a natural tendency when one has an executing program, that is, to let the computer help find the bugs by running a series of examples or scenarios in the form of test cases. User-facing screens that may have been mocked up during the requirements and design phases of development suddenly become interactive with performance characteristics that may have been uncertain during earlier architectural studies. In performing dynamic tests, testers can truly put themselves into the user's seat and test the way each user will use the program. For the first time, testers can pay attention to timing and accuracy of the program's results. In the case of the development of a new subsystem, for the first time, other subsystems are enabled to access a shared database, communicate data between themselves, or whatever the new subsystem's added functionality provides.

Compatibility testing involves running the same tests against an executable program across multiple computer platforms and/or multiple configurations. Regression testing, by comparison, involves running the same tests against the $(n + 1)$th build and comparing the test results against those obtained from testing the nth build. By entering a variety of inputs and observing outputs, behavior, and performance of the computer system, testers can decide whether the program is ready for its end-users to start using. It's not always as simple as it sounds, since there are many variables to be considered in this decision, for example, correctness of hardware execution, correctness of the compilers and run-time support code and the operating system that enable the application's execution, the appropriateness of the data for the application, and many other factors, all of which can contribute to the root causes of candidate bugs that are to be found during dynamic testing.

Some applications have a wide variety of users with differing goals. For example, an order entry system may have users who are sales personnel whose job it is to get quotes on several proposed orders. An order processor uses a different portion of the order entry system to obtain status of an order or to edit a portion of the order. A credit card processor works off the exceptions of the automated credit-card processing portion of the order entry system. Multi-user applications require a great deal of preplanning work, organizing the logistics of setting up the terminals, communications lines, initial file structure, and coordinating the multiple testers in order to perform complete scenarios.

Life Cycle of a Bug

It is critical for the software developers to fix bugs as quickly as possible during the dynamic testing phases in order to remove test blocks. Test blocks are typically caused by logic errors, which prevent test data from being processed by the appropriate lines of code. It is natural to develop a tight loop between testers and developers, alternating between finding and fixing bugs in the early stages of the dynamic testing phases, but in the later stages of testing or in larger projects, a change control review board (CCRB) plays the role of a consolidation point, reviewer, and priority-setting entity, as shown in Figure 7.3. This figure shows the life cycle of a bug during dynamic testing. When a software build is ready for testing, the build master, working with the software configuration manager (SCM), performs the build operation. This creates an executable version of the product and the source is updated to point to the new version number.

The test staff is responsible for setting up the test environment for this executable program, including the computer systems, operating systems, databases, communications lines, and so on. The test staff also selects an appropriate set of test cases. The selection process for the test cases takes into account the nature and code locations of the list of bugs that have been fixed by

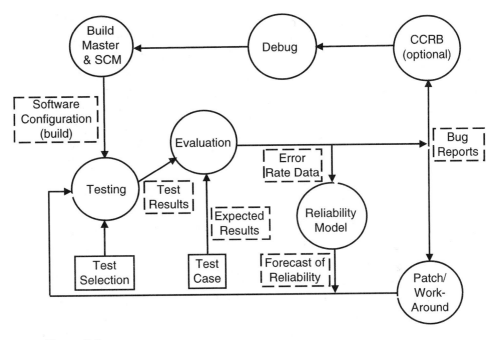

Figure 7.3
The developer/tester loop: A bug's life cycle.

the build. Following the test scripts, a tester exercises the program, and incrementally compares intermediate results against the test results documented in the test case. If there's a discrepancy found between actual results and expected results, either it means that the expected results of the test case needs to be updated to the actual results or another bug has been detected by the test case. After the selected set of test cases has been run, a regression test is run on against the build to determine whether changes that were introduced into the latest build have broken some function that used to work. Any new bug's characteristics are entered into the reliability model database, as well as in a bug report, and the cycle through the debug process continues the loop.

Figure 7.3 also shows a route back to continue testing the same build. It passes through the patch/work-around process. The test group may need to sort through the test cases yet to be run on the current build, dividing them into those that will hit the same bug again from those that should not be affected by the bug. This allows testing to progress until a future build fixes the bug. There are times when a patch of the executable program is required in order to resume testing. When a test block does occur, the priority for fixing the bug is automatically raised to the highest severity level as a means of prioritizing the need for an immediate fix.

The fact that a test team is busy performing dynamic testing does not preclude some of the team from performing additional static testing techniques. Static testing techniques are all just as applicable during the time that dynamic testing is being done. For example, the results of a battery of dynamic tests must be compared with the expected results. This comparative assessment may be automated or it may use a static testing process similar to an inspection. Several companies have discovered that during dynamic testing some of their test team members are not applying good static testing techniques to analyze their results. These companies say that many of their dynamic testers have a mentality that is summed up in the following quote: "Well, this test certainly didn't cause this computer to crash!" Such a mentality allows errors to pass through the dynamic testing processes undetected even though the test cases themselves present the opportunity to find the unreported bugs.

As an example of the "...it didn't cause a computer crash" mentality also seems to be prevalent with dynamic testers of products that use modem-based communications. Modem-based communications have a long history and a reputation for being fraught with faults, like busy signals, answering modem speed set different from calling speed setting, or even an "other" category that testers might use to mean the answering modem just hung up for no apparent reason. By not reporting this as a bug, testers are opening their company up to continuing communication bugs with the product that they are testing. Suppose such a product were released and installed into multiple locations within a hospital. These mysterious "answering modem just hung up for no apparent reason" failures would be just the sort of bug that becomes a major call driver from the hospital employees who, rightly so, believe that the modems should immediately negotiate a communication speed and interlock for communications to start, unless there is a busy signal. Not only would these failures become call drivers to technical support for the hospital, the telephone company, and the modem manufacturer who support the users, they frequently become call drivers for the company that released the product or its resellers.

Formal Test Phases

Dynamic testing can begin with the unit test phase of the development life cycle and finishes with the acceptance test. Dynamic testing strategies break down into the two categories, namely white-box testing and black-box testing. A white-box testing strategy is typically performed in the unit test and integration test phases of the development life cycle, while the systems test and acceptance test phases use a black-box testing strategy.

The purpose of unit testing is to ensure that what was designed was implemented in the code and that the overall scope and executing integrity of the code module is sound. Unit testing often uses drivers and stubs in order to provide run-time control of the test, while integration testing typically uses a GUI to control integrated functions made up of several modules or subsystems.

The purpose of integration testing is to ensure that all the interfaces between modules or subsystems match in terms of input versus output parameters, and in the correctness of other shared or passed data, for example, database records and fields, shared GUI screens, or shared communication pathways.

System testing can start when the integration of all modules, at least those of a major subsystem, have completed integration testing. System testing should be focused on the bigger issues of performance, scalability, installability, robustness to environmental conditions, and overall usability by the end-users.

Acceptance testing examines the software release candidate(s) to determine their acceptability to the end-users. All of these phases in the testing life cycle become less and less time-consuming under the rapid testing methodology, since a large majority of bugs have been found and fixed earlier in development.

Responsibilities of Test Team Members

Testers perform the work of test preparation, test execution, and test results reporting. There are many skill sets that are needed to support the testers within the test team. The same individual who is trained in multiple areas may fill these positions, especially in smaller projects. A brief summary of these skill sets is shown in Table 7.2.

What's Next

Chapters 8 and 9 cover static testing techniques. Chapter 10 deals with dynamic testing techniques. Chapters 11 and 12 cover testing metrics and cost estimating models for testing. The titles of these chapters are as follows:

Table 7.2

Responsibilities of Test Team Members

Job Title/Position	Duties/Responsibilities
Quality Assurance	Provides overview and detailed definitions of each test activity, including templates and examples. Provides instruction and coaching in the creation of test plans and test cases. Provides a review for compliance to standards. Provides ongoing monitoring and support during test execution with the precise role to be defined in each test plan.
Audit and Control	Provides input on additional conditions that would test controls and other audit-related features. Provides a review for compliance to audit standards.
Software Developer	Provides documentation on unit testing. Provides assistance to testers in writing baseline, integration, system, and user acceptance test cases. Provides problem/issue resolution leadership during test execution. Executes unit test.
Business Analyst	Writes user acceptance test plan. Writes user acceptance test cases. Writes baseline test cases in cooperation with tester. Executes user acceptance test. Reviews and approve acceptance criteria.
Test Developer	Writes baseline, integration, and system test cases. Executes integration and system tests. Provides technical support during user acceptance test execution for problems and issue resolution.
Tester	Executes the test cases. Records actual results. Fills out test problem reports. Verifies fixes for problems reported.
Debugger	Provides fixes for problems reported. Verifies validity of problems reported. Ensures fix addresses all aspects of the problem, including user documentation.

Job Title/Position	Duties/Responsibilities
Test Manager	Provides testing infrastructure, including test management and execution tools. Coordinates/manages all testing execution. Determines priorities for problem fixes as required. Reports to project and customer/user management on test progress. Tracks actual-to-plan progress.
Test Administrator	Logs the test problem reports. Creates daily status sheets of progress, relating the progress to the plan and to the test coverage.

8. Joint Application Requirements (JAR): A Method For Eliciting Requirements Using Rapid Testing

9. Static Testing Techniques and Tips

10. Dynamic Testing Techniques and Tips

11. Developing and Using Testing Metrics: Error Modeling and Forecasting

12. Testing Effort Estimation Techniques and Tips

Joint Application Requirements (JAR): A Method for Eliciting Requirements Using Rapid Testing

Topics Covered in the Chapter

- ▶ JAR Methodology
- ▶ Roles of the Test Engineer in a JAR
- ▶ Summary

One of the keys to success in software development is gaining an understanding of the customer's requirements. As we saw in Chapter 2, a clear definition of requirements is the starting point of an effective software development process.

There are a variety of methods for improving communication between the customer and development team. One class of methods used to elicit requirements is called fast application specification techniques (FAST), which were described briefly in Chapter 2. The Joint Application Requirements (JAR) is a FAST technique that is designed to fully integrate static testing with the elicitation process. The integration of static testing as part of the JAR is accomplished in the activity known as perfective maintenance.

Perfective maintenance is an organized way of interactively reviewing and revising elicited requirements. The activities associated with perfective maintenance are described later in this chapter.

The output of a JAR session is a set of carefully reviewed requirements that have been agreed to by the users of the end product or their representatives. The requirements captured in a JAR include both functional requirements and pertinent nonfunctional requirements; for example, the schedule and contents of a phased delivery.

JAR Methodology

The participants in a JAR form a core team that is established with representatives from the development team, a variety of users who are familiar with the variety of functionalities needed in the end product, a representative of the customer/buyer, and the JAR facilitator. A conference room with a lot of clear wall space is reserved for one or two weeks during all business hours to become the JAR room. The layout of a JAR conference room and the roles of the people invited to participate in the JAR are shown in Figure 8.1.

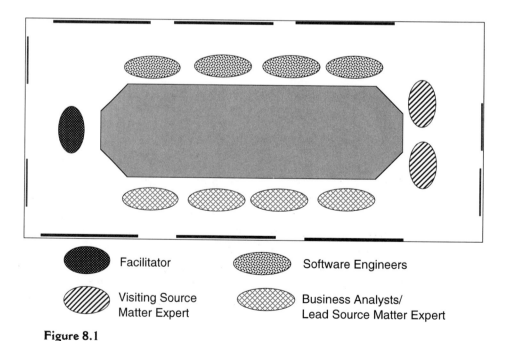

Figure 8.1
Core team seating in the JAR room.

Note that no managers, no vice presidents, no quality assurance personnel, no procurement personnel, and no supplier representatives are included in the core team. If any of these personnel appear at one of the core team meetings, they should be convinced to leave by the facilitator and be invited to walk the wall during one of the perfective maintenance sessions, which will be described later. Members of the core team cannot be absent from the JAR meetings and cannot be interrupted with messages and calls.

The role of the facilitator is to keep the core team focused on three tasks: eliciting requirements, wording the requirements clearly, and perfecting requirements. The facilitator should hold a training session on the day before the JAR in order to orient the core team to the goals and rules. In this training session, the JAR core team should agree to act in accordance with the following rules:

- Don't make personal jabs; for example, don't discount or discredit ideas from another participant.
- Remember that only one person has the floor at a time.
- Before you speak out, think about what value your idea has and whether it would change the end product.
- State your input well, and after it has been reviewed, document it in a final form.
- Pose questions only to the facilitator.
- Give the facilitator a time-out signal, like crossed arms, to be used by the core team whenever there are process exceptions/interruptions; for example, restroom break needed or a personal jab was noted.
- Allow no outside interruptions (email, pager, or phone) during a JAR session.
- Stay on task, focused, constructive, and helpful.

The facilitator presents the goals and limitations for the software development project and also defines the goals of the JAR, including:

- Elicit user needs, expectations, and measures of effectiveness.
- Analyze user needs and expectations to develop a verbal description of the operational flow of the system as well as individual functions that must be available within the product.
- Elicit delivery and update requirements for products that must be installed and updated for users.

- Develop a statement of the requirements in all areas to be covered in the requirements document.

- Obtain concurrence from the customer and users that they agree that the statement of the requirements will satisfy their needs and expectations.

- Construct phased deliveries with ever-increasing functional capabilities in order to meet the user's immediate and long-term needs, expectations, and measures of effectiveness of these phased deliveries.

There should be deeply experienced source matter experts (SMEs) on the core team that have historical knowledge of the business rules, use cases, and data flows that must be considered in developing the new system. The visiting SMEs are invited to requirements interview sessions that last 1.5 hours each. Up to two dozen visiting SMEs may be invited to these interview sessions, two at a time. Following each interview, time is allocated for the core team to document the requirements that were elicited from the SMEs and to perform perfective maintenance on the storyboards used to capture the requirements.

The schedule giving the "when-who-why" of a typical JAR is shown in Table 8.1. In this example, there are seven separate meetings: an orientation, three days of SME interviews, two days of walkthroughs, and one day to prepare the material for formal documentation. Since each SME session is conducted with two SMEs, this example has a total of 24 SMEs who participated in the JAR. Before the walkthroughs start, the core team may spend half a day reorganizing the storyboards on the wall. They may combine similar storyboards to reduce the feeling of redundancy. They may prioritize the requirements into two sets, for example, those requirements that might be implemented in a Phase 1 delivery project, versus a follow-on Phase 2 project. Since each walkthrough is held in a library-like environment, only 4 SMEs are invited to each of the 6 walkthroughs. In addition to the SMEs, a few persons whose management roles prohibited them from being on the core team can be invited to walk-the-walls during the walkthroughs. Between each walkthrough, the core team takes the time to perform perfective maintenance in order to incorporate the SMEs' comments into the base set of storyboards.

A seasoned JAR facilitator will have a JAR toolbox with at least 200 sheets of 8.5" × 11" blank paper, a dozen rolls of masking tape, a few dozen multicolored ballpoint pens, an easel with easel pad, multicolored felt-tipped markers, scissors, adhesive note pads (sticky notes), and cellophane tape.

Table 8.1
Typical JAR Schedule

When	Who	Topic	Facilitator-scheduled
Initial meeting	Core team and curious	Orientation	
Day 1	Core team	2 SME sessions	
Day 2	Core team	4 SME sessions	Perfective maintenance
Day 3	Core team	4 SME sessions	Perfective maintenance
Day 4	Core team SME groups	2 SME sessions 2 walkthroughs	
Day 5	Core team and SME groups	4 walkthroughs	Perfective maintenance
Day 6	Sub core team	Organize and meet with technical writer	Perfective maintenance

These materials will be used to prepare and maintain storyboards on which the requirements are captured.

The layout of the JAR conference room should correspond to the outline of the requirements document. Title sheets can be printed with the section names of the requirements document. They can be taped high on the wall, equally spaced and arranged clockwise around the room in the order of the document outline.

Each storyboard will have an associated title sheet. A storyboard template, shown in Figure 8.2, guides each core team member as to how to enter a requirement and file it on the wall under the appropriate title sheet, using masking tape. Training on how to construct such a storyboard from blank paper would be covered in the orientation sessions. The template should not be preprinted, since this would spoil the spontaneity with which the author should approach storyboarding of requirements. In taping the 8.5″ × 11″ page in landscape format onto the JAR wall, each core team member should be coaxed into taping only the top corners, perpendicular to the top of the storyboard. This technique allows a storyboard to be lifted upward from the bottom and moved to another section of the wall if it needs to be grouped with another requirement.

The subject line of the storyboard should be the same as the title sheet when it is placed on the wall. If a storyboard is moved from a group of

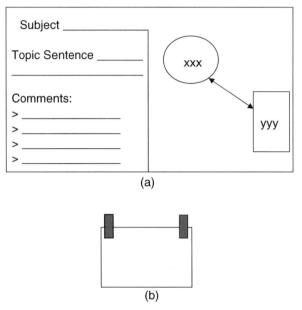

(a)

(b)

Figure 8.2
(a) Storyboard templates and (b) taping technology for the JAR wall.

storyboards under a title sheet to be with another set of storyboards under another title sheet, this subject line needs to be changed. The topic sentence is the essence of the requirement being stated. The comments section is an optional elaboration of the topic sentence. It could be an elaboration on the scope of the requirement, the interfaces that it applies to, or anything else that might be clarifying. The right side of a storyboard is a diagram that tells the requirement graphically. In one case, this might be a communications diagram showing what is connected to what. In another case, it might be stick figures of people in conversation, to depict a manual interview process. In another case, it might be one subsystem of a computer program that is interfacing through a database to another subsystem of the computer program. There is usually a title to the graphic diagram, placed under the diagram.

The core team members frequently walk the walls of the JAR room, doing perfective maintenance. This activity is not on the JAR schedule, since the facilitator will perceive the need for the activity and instructs the wall-walkers to spread out among the sections on the wall, read each storyboard carefully, and document suggested changes on sticky notes, which are stuck directly on the subject storyboard. This is a form of inspection that is thoroughly integrated with the requirements elicitation process. Rationales for writing up a sticky note are given in Figure 8.3. It should be made clear to

- **Perfective Maintenance – "StickyNotes"**
  - Helpful Criticism
  - Completeness
  - Clarity
  - Compound allowed
  - Redundancy
  - Clumping
  - Ranking/prioritization

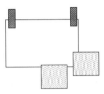

Figure 8.3
Perfective maintenance mechanisms.

all participants that this is the time to help find requirements bugs or to improve the clarity of the requirements statements or their organization on the wall. No changes are allowed to the storyboards themselves during this stage of perfective maintenance.

Following this activity, the wall is usually the color of the sticky notes, so the facilitator stops the activity in order to start up the next activity of the perfective maintenance process. The original owner of each storyboard that has a sticky note on it performs the update that is called for on the array of sticky notes, sometimes calling out "who said such and such about this requirement." The author of the sticky note and the author of the storyboard often get together to negotiate a satisfactory resolution. It is through this process that two important events happen: the requirements improve in clarity and independence from other requirements, while buy-in to the requirements by the entire core team and many of the SMEs who can participate in perfective maintenance is a natural occurrence. This act of working together should bode well for the project in that it will ensure that the product meets the true users' requirements. There will be many opportunities that arise during the product development where the development team and the end-user team or SMEs will interact, as shown in the following list:

- Interface control working group
- Technical control working group
- Interim program reviews
- Questionnaire, interviews, operational scenarios obtained from end-users (use cases in UML)
- Prototypes and models
- Observation of existing system, environments, and workflow patterns

- Make or buy decision and ensuing selections
- Alpha testing
- Beta testing

These opportunities will be more constructive and of higher quality when this cross-functional team has learned to work together and all know the baseline requirements. The outcome of the JAR is a set of storyboards containing functional and some nonfunctional requirements for the new project. To finish the requirements document, an experienced technical writer should be able to complete the template for this document with ease, because the JAR participants worked hard to clarify wording, graphic arts, prioritization, and title for each requirement.

CASE STUDY

A SUCCESSFUL JAR (GARY COBB)

Several years ago, I had the experience of intersecting a very important e-commerce development project that was on a fast track development schedule. It was clearly a candidate for using rapid testing techniques. The vision statement was that of quickly developing an applications programming interface (API) between internet-based orders and the company's standard order entry system. The funding that was allocated by management covered a 3-month development by a half dozen developers, including a manager/lead. The project lead set aside 6 weeks of the 13-week schedule for the documentation of requirements and appointed two of the developers to go off and get the requirements document ready, while the rest of the developers were to start prototyping the API. I stepped in and asserted that, if the project would follow a JAR process, then I could deliver a fully tested requirements document in 2 weeks, a full month earlier than scheduled, and it would have complete buy-in by the users, as well as fewer requirements bugs than the 6-week task that they were about to embark upon.

It was on Thursday that the project lead and his staff agreed to accept my offer of a JAR and on Friday, I started with the orientation meeting, during which the group developed a list of 28 SMEs. Also, during the orientation meeting, a conference room was booked and four of the most knowledgeable SMEs were booked as core team members for the following week (8AM–5PM each day). Appointments were also made for the 24 remaining SMEs to come in pairs to the 12 interview sessions, from Monday through Wednesday of the next week. Morning snacks and afternoon refreshments were to be catered in the conference room, but a noon–1PM time slot was reserved for private time for core team members to get lunch and answer messages.

Monday morning, the core team struggled with writing storyboards for some of the fundamental requirements. Some discussions were facilitated on the subjects of system architecture, user characteristics and usability, system performance, and external communication requirements. Then in the afternoon, the first two SME interviews were held. After the SME interviews on Tuesday, the first half of a perfective maintenance session was held, leaving the wall a pink color overnight, because the facilitator had pink sticky notes. Before the first SME interview on Wednesday, the authors of the storyboards worked the issues and the wall was back to white. Again on Wednesday afternoon, in preparation for the first walkthroughs on Thursday, a perfective maintenance session was completed and the core team moved some of the storyboards below the chair-rail of the conference room, thus indicating these requirements were of a lower priority and would be delivered later than those above the chair-rail. Also, a clean-up of the glossary was accomplished by one of the core team members. On Thursday afternoon, two managers were invited to walk the wall with pads of blank pink sticky notes. The core team was proud of the complimentary remarks from both of the managers.

By Friday, the JAR was winding down and the core team dispersed, except for the facilitator and the lead, who stayed to hold a session with the technical writer. The lead agreed to redo the project schedule to account for an earlier start to the design effort and have it ready by Monday. The technical writer agreed to have a draft of the requirements document and the new development schedule ready by Tuesday.

During this JAR, three incremental deliveries were planned, the first to be made at the end of the initial three months. It would pass Internet orders through to the order entry system, as planned. The second phase, developed in parallel with the first phase, was to develop an order validation ASP to run during the formation of the Internet order as a guard against bad orders from getting into the order entry system. The third phase, developed in parallel with the first and second phases, was planned to develop a Web-based order tracking system to automate the availability of order status information for Internet customers' orders. Releases of these phases were performed on time and were welcomed by the overworked staff of order processors, who previously manually entered and processed Internet customers' orders.

The most encouraging remark I heard later from the order processors was as follows: "On prior deliveries of software from this development team, they trained us on how to get our job done using their software and even they couldn't get the software to work during the training session; this time, when they delivered the software, we knew how to use it, since it exactly matched our needs. The only surprises were that there were very few bugs and the phased deliveries were always made on schedule." As I walked off, I said under my breath, "Yes! This is the result of doing development and testing together!" In other words, this is rapid testing that works.

Roles of the Test Engineer in a JAR

A test engineer has three roles in a JAR: (1) to participate in the perfective maintenance, (2) to become familiar with the testing requirements that would support resource requirements for the test staff and (3) to ask questions during the SME interviews regarding current maintenance test procedures of the legacy solution. One of the sections in the requirements document should address requirements for product testing and the tester should be a primary advocate of getting this section as complete and clear as possible in the requirements document. It will likely be the tester who will later decompose these testing requirements into testing resource requirements, the overall test plan, and numerous test cases with test scripts and test results. During the SME interviews, the tester should open with any of the following statements:

- Tell me about the failure modes of the legacy systems that are most noticeable to the users.
- Please describe the ways users work with the development team to document, fix, and test bugs in the legacy system.
- Describe how the users handle the transition to a new build from the development team.
- Name some product standards that the users want to impose on the developers of the new product.
- Please help by describing some of the platforms and spoken languages that the new product must function with, as well as any particular environmental considerations for the computer systems, including accessibility.

Regarding testing during the requirements phase of the development life cycle, remember that the requirements that are collected in the JAR and placed in the requirements document are both functional and nonfunctional requirements and they should be as complete and clear as possible. But, they are not the only requirements that are to be satisfied during the development and they are not the only requirements that should be tested. The following are some of the added requirements that must be accommodated by the development staff:

- **Project development standards**—these are requirements of the processes and procedures that the development staff will be required to follow during the development phases of the project; it is likely that these policies and procedures will be standard across all development projects, so the test staff should have tools and test cases that enable them to test each product against these requirements.
- **Derived requirements**—the SMEs in the JAR might say that the new product will need to be executable on one of three network clients in a normal professional work environment; when the software designers

see this requirement, they may set a parameter in the code for room temperature, and look up the upper limits and lower limits of temperature in the standard for a normal professional work environment; when the testers set up the test case to test the original requirements, they will have to refer to the derived requirement that the software designers came up with in order to set up a test environment for the product.

- **Interface requirements**—the software designers may make a series of make or buy decisions when implementing the new product; in order to interface with a purchased subsystem, additional nonfunctional requirements must be satisfied by the design in order for the product to work properly; when the testers set up the test cases to test the interfaces, they will apply tests to this subsystem's interface, as defined in the documentation from the vendor of the purchased subsystem, in order to verify the interface specifications.

Summary

In summarizing this section on integration of testing with requirements elicitation, please note that the JAR is really only one of many examples of requirements elicitation methods and that the lasting concept that should be taken from this section is that the entire development team will value testing if it is integrated directly into the development process from the beginning. The developers will appreciate not designing and implementing a complex design only to discover that the mainstream users will not be able to understand how to use this complex design and the buyer is not willing to pay the price for it either.

The system testers will appreciate not designing and implementing complex test cases for this complex design, too. The marketing staff will appreciate not selling against a lower-cost competitor who introduced their product into the market earlier because they didn't have the complex design in their product. And, finally, phased deliveries of products is a norm for the software industry, and the complex design that was eliminated from the original requirements may be a real boost that builds customer loyalty when and if the complex design is added and released as a value upgrade.

Static Testing Techniques and Tips

Topics Covered in the Chapter

- ▶ Cyclomatic Complexity and Its Relationship to Test Executions
- ▶ Example of Graphing the Design of a Module
- ▶ Formal Reviews
- ▶ Using Checklists
- ▶ Audits
- ▶ Inspections/Walkthroughs/Peer Reviews
- ▶ Inspection Team Roles and Responsibilities
- ▶ Reporting on the Inspection Process
- ▶ Metrics for the Inspection Process
- ▶ Using e-mail or an e-App to Streamline Inspections
- ▶ Formal Verification
- ▶ Specification-Based Languages
- ▶ Automated Theorem Proofs
- ▶ Testing Automation/Tools
- ▶ Requirements Traceability
- ▶ Physical Units Checker
- ▶ Symbolic Execution
- ▶ Cross-Reference Listings
- ▶ Pretty Printers
- ▶ Version Comparators
- ▶ Algorithm Testing
- ▶ Test Support Facilitator
- ▶ Shared Issues Databases
- ▶ Summary
- ▶ References

There are a number of techniques that involve analysis of the architecture and design of software developments. In this chapter, a number of these techniques are discussed. Rapid testing calls for these techniques to be applied as early in the development life cycle as feasible, and most can be applied before any coding begins. High complexity and high bug density are known to go hand in hand, so it's important to handle complexity reduction up front in this chapter. A major side effect of cyclomatic complexity measurement is that it prepares the test team with an estimate of the number of executions of a software object that will be required to test each path at least once. This can be a guide to both forecasting the testing effort and building an organized set of test cases.

Formal reviews, inspections, and audits are ways of ensuring that every developer is honoring a set of policies, procedures, style guides, and other standards used by the development organization, as well as a productive tool for finding bugs. Techniques that should be used to manage and execute reviews and inspections are also discussed in this chapter.

Cyclomatic Complexity and Its Relationship to Test Executions

Branches in software are error-prone, and as such, attract the attention of testers. Of course many software engineers considered the GOTO, that is, unconditional branch, as a language construct that caused code to be hard to understand. The GOTO statement has been banned in most of the structured programming languages. But, the decision point is a required construct even in structured programming languages; for example, the IF(...) or the DO WHILE(...) constructs both embody a decision point.

In procedural languages, a path is defined as the traversal of the program counter starting with a module entry point or a decision point and ending with a module exit point or a decision point. In some of the literature on this subject, other authors call a path a DD-path, which stands for a decision-to-decision path. Therefore, in a typical IF-THEN-ELSE-ENDIF construct, there are two paths, commonly called the THEN path and the ELSE path that both end with the ENDIF of the construct. Mathematics and graph theory have shown that the graph of a structured program is planar, and vice versa, all unstructured programs have nonplanar graphs. Early software practitioners learned to draw lines joining decision points to help them understand the program counter flow through the lines of code. They also learned to give up trying to understand programs that had too many paths and called for them to be modularized further into understandable chunks.

Logical complexity of software has captured the interests of testing staffs for a long time. Managers seem to be happier when the test staff says "Yes, we have tested every line of code at least once with our test plans." Thomas McCabe and Charles Butler (1989) defined the cyclomatic complexity number, denoted by V_g, as a metric to measure logical complexity. V_g can be computed in one of three ways:

1. Counting the number of regions of the planar flow graph of a structured program.

2. The cyclomatic complexity (V_g) for the flow graph g is defined as $V_g = E - N + 2$, where E is the number of flow graph edges and N is the number of flow graph nodes.

3. The cyclomatic complexity (V_g) for a flow graph g is also defined as $V_g = P + 1$, where P is the number of predicates contained in the flow graph.

Example of Graphing the Design of a Module

The planar graph shown in Figure 9.1 divides the plane into five regions, numbered 1 through 5, so it has cyclomatic complexity, $V_g = 5$. See if you can check off the four predicates contained in the code and in its flow graph. Finally, determine how many test cases you would need to create in order to test each line of code at least once.

The significance of the cyclomatic complexity to testing a program is that V_g is the minimum number of independent paths to be tested in order to attain complete coverage. A tester should be able to apply this fact to the graph labeled "a" on the left of Figure 9.2 and come up with the minimum number of test cases that should be run to ensure complete coverage of the application with this graph. Are the two test cases shown in the note box a complete test of the paths? Is there a path/DD path not included in test cases 1 or 2? If so, what should another test case be?

In two published papers, one titled "A Quantitative Evaluation of Effectiveness of Quality Assurance as Experienced on a Large Scale Software Development Effort," and the other titled "Central Flow Control Software Development—A Case Study of Effectiveness of Software Engineering Techniques," Peter Chase Belford described how his project at Computer Sciences Corporation used the cyclomatic complexity number to reduce the

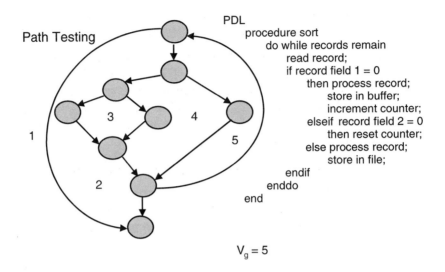

Path Testing

PDL
procedure sort
    do while records remain
        read record;
        if record field 1 = 0
            then process record;
                store in buffer;
                increment counter;
            elseif record field 2 = 0
                then reset counter;
            else process record;
                store in file;
        endif
    enddo
end

$V_g = 5$

Note: every structured program has a directed graph that is planar.

Figure 9.1
Planar graph of software showing the cyclomatic complexity number.

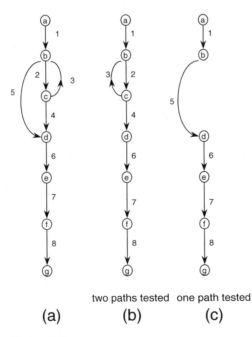

Example of path testing:
(a) program graph
(b) test 1 (1,2,3,2,4,6)
(c) test 2 (1,5,6)

two paths tested   one path tested

(a)   (b)   (c)

Figure 9.2
Determining a minimum set of test cases, guided by the cyclomatic complexity number.

cost of the project, while also raising the quality of the product by reducing the complexity of the code.

CASE STUDY

CENTRAL FLOW CONTROL PROJECT

These lessons learned are from Peter Chase Belford (1979). The Central Flow Control (CFC) project used pseudocode to document their algorithms. They built a parser for their pseudocode design language (PDL) and implemented a cyclomatic complexity number counter into this parser. They plotted the cost to develop each model and its cyclomatic complexity number and found that there was an S-shaped curve that best fit this data. Figure 9.3 shows Belford's S-shaped curve. It helped to show that there was a range of cyclomatic numbers of modules that represented acceptable—for example, nearly linear—cost measured in development hours; however, another region had unacceptable cost growth. The CFC project continually considered redesigning modules whose PDL measured more than 30 on the cyclomatic complexity scale.

The conclusions that Belford arrived at as a result of this software engineering research work is summarized as follows:

- Smaller units are better.
- The complexity of a software development system is better measured by the number of decision paths in the design than the number of executable source statements.
- The use of modern programming practices facilitates system understandability, system reliability, and development controllability.
- Spending more time on the design will produce more reliable software.

(continued)

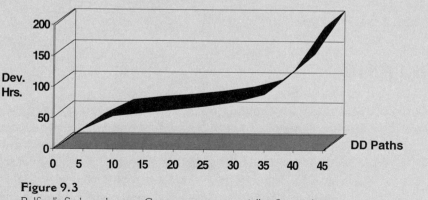

Figure 9.3
Belford's S-shaped curve: Cost grows exponentially after cyclomatic complexity of 30.

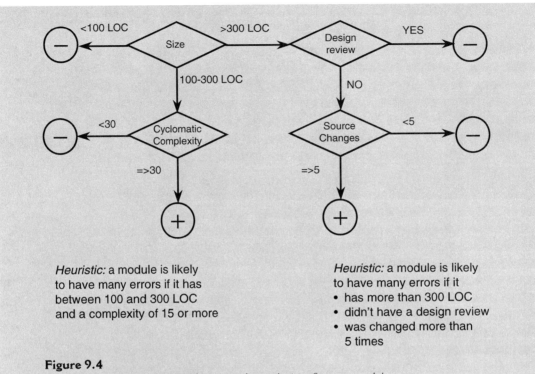

Heuristic: a module is likely to have many errors if it has between 100 and 300 LOC and a complexity of 15 or more

Heuristic: a module is likely to have many errors if it
• has more than 300 LOC
• didn't have a design review
• was changed more than 5 times

Figure 9.4
Establishing standards, limiting the size and complexity of source modules.

Some projects develop standards that attempt to limit the size of each module to a manageable amount of code. Figure 9.4 shows how a set of heuristics can be established and drawn as a decision tree that enforces the findings of Belford and other researchers. These standards might be assigned to the test staff to develop automated tools to measure all design or code modules.

Formal Reviews

There is value in holding periodic formal reviews of each facet of the software development project. You might ask what periodic formal reviews have to do with rapid testing. Rapid testing is a method that emphasizes doing each task as early as possible in the life cycle and simultaneously finding and fixing defects in the deliverables from each task. Typically, formal reviews are held when a development phase is nearing completion, and the deliverables plus the project database of metrics, schedules, defects lists, and so on from each phase of a development life cycle are the subjects of these reviews.

The purpose of formal reviews is to provide individuals on the development team with the manager's perspective/overview of all aspects of the development effort. Each developer should see and understand the dependencies between all deliverables, and in particular those for which he/she is responsible. Each developer should see and understand what metrics contain information that relates to the job that the developer does. The testers should pay particular attention to items being reviewed; for example, the status of the test hardware on order or the availability dates of new documentation, since this information can impact their test plan or test case development. In other words, every attendee of a formal review is looking at the phase deliverables from the viewpoint of whether or not they are ready to be used. While some people would say that these reviews are to maintain management control over the software development process, this author feels it's the other way around, too. The status data that is collected from team members, along with lists of defects/issues, should be compiled and organized by managers. This should enable them to walk through these data for the team and enable the team to tighten up their performance and to improve the quality of their deliverables.

For software developed under contract, terms and conditions of the contract are reviewed in each formal review on behalf of the customer. Summaries of these reviews may be presented to the customer, who needs the assurance that the development is proceeding within budget and on schedule along a well-managed path. The following is a list of items that could be prepared and monitored by the software lead or quality assurance specialist and presented at the formal reviews:

- The size of the software work products, or size of the changes to the software work products, is tracked and corrective actions are taken as necessary.

- The size of the software work products, or size of changes to the software work products, is managed according to a documented procedure.

- The project's software effort and costs are tracked, and corrective actions are taken as necessary.

- The project's software effort and costs are managed according to a documented procedure.

- The project's critical computer resources are tracked, and corrective actions are taken as necessary.

- The project's critical computer resources are managed according to a documented procedure.
- The project's software schedule is tracked, and corrective actions are taken as necessary.
- The critical dependencies and critical paths of the project's software schedule are managed according to a documented procedure.
- Software development technical activities are tracked, and corrective actions are taken as necessary.
- The software risks associated with cost, resource, schedule, and technical aspects of the project are tracked.
- The software risks associated with cost, resource, schedule, and technical aspects of the project are identified, assessed, and documented.
- Critical dependencies between software developments are identified, negotiated, and tracked according to a documented procedure.
- The project's software risks are identified, assessed, documented, and managed according to a documented procedure.

The attendance at formal reviews could include representatives from the company/agency doing the primary development, its subcontractor/partner team, the product acquisition team, and the user team. Management benefits from holding formal reviews by maintaining management control over the software development process, including reviewing reports and taking corrective actions pertaining to cost, people resources, computer resources, technical hurdles, critical dependencies, and risks. A recorder should take notes on action items that are agreed to during the meeting, and after the meeting, the action items collected must be distributed and tracked to closure. These action items will be worked after the meeting by lower-level managers who can mediate any conflicts that may arise between groups. Whether your company is a subcontractor or a prime contractor, it is important to hold well-organized formal reviews between prime and subcontractors (better known as *partners* in today's corporate language). The primary benefits of well-organized formal reviews are synchronization and sharing of lessons learned.

The primary value of formal reviews for the test team is to ensure that all partners are using the same pass/fail criteria, setting up compatible test environments across all testing partners, developing the means to immediately share bug reports as the bugs are uncovered, maintaining schedules for incremental deliveries of builds containing bug fixes, and reaching agreements on stopping conditions for testing.

Using Checklists

Because software developments can be very complex to manage, a compilation of lessons learned and best practices exists in the body of knowledge in the form of checklists. Checklists give that friendly reminder of things to watch out for as a team proceeds rapidly through the software life cycle. They are typically documented with predicated interrogative sentences, of the form "if…, then is…?" You shouldn't approach using checklists by searching for "checklists" on the Internet and picking one that seems interesting. Furthermore, checklists should not be deployed as an institutional standard. Unless the checklist is developed by the project from lessons learned within that project, it will not be useful. Checklists, done correctly, are very valuable tools for avoiding risks in a project.

In rapid testing, project-based checklists have different purposes, depending on the development life cycle chosen, the languages and tools used to develop the product, and many other factors. The following are examples of checklist entries:

- If the requirements include accessibility, then does the design call for text to be processed through the company's standard object that provides accessibility manipulations?
- If the requirements include accessibility, then has the project's standard accessibility test tool been called out in a test plan?
- If the company's standard inspection process is being required, then have all participants in each inspection meeting been through the 4-hour training course and passed its exit exam?
- If temperature is a required variable, then have provisions been made to allow the user to set an option as to whether to display temperature readings in either Centigrade or Fahrenheit?
- If "abc" is the chosen configuration management tool being used by the project, then are locks set on all versions of source modules that are currently checked out for update?

The author has seen a database of checklist entries, where the predicate is separate from the question and other fields are added as sorting keys in order that a project's checklists can be printed out depending on the phase and roles it has to support. Again, the most important thing to remember to do is to ensure that when a problem develops in a project, then it is the responsibility of all team members to ensure that there is a checklist entry created that says, if this were to happen again, what would our team make sure it has done?

How do checklist entries arise? A checklist entry for checklist maintenance is as follows: If a customer call driver is on the high end of the Pareto Charts, then is there a checklist entry that includes the call driver description in its predicate and a root-cause avoidance rule in the interrogative of that entry? Yes, it takes discipline to be able to do this, but the payoff is tremendous.

Audits

In order to ensure that company policies, procedures, and standards are being applied, a company audit can be done. Without the policies, procedures, and standards in place, an audit has no meaning and would be considered harassment. The notification, scheduling, interview sessions, and the reporting of an audit are all key actions in a successful audit. Interview sessions should be planned to isolate the following levels: leadership and support functions, for example, configuration control, quality assurance, customers/sponsors/business analyst, production control, database administrator, and other direct project developers/testers. Each interview session should have a lead auditor and a second auditor. The lead auditor leads the interview sessions and both the lead and second auditor capture notes of what is said. These roles can be interchanged from one interview session to the next. Table 9.1 organizes the tips for each of these key actions.

Table 9.1
Tips for Each Key Action in an Audit

No.	Key Actions	Tips
1	Notification of project leaders	Phone call to arrange a convenient audit time and a list of candidates for the audit interview sessions; later follow-up email arranging the project leaders' interview session, lasting 1.5 hours.
2	Notification of support functions	Compose an email message to between 6 and 10 participants, asking them to attend an audit interview session, lasting 1.5 hours, and bring artifacts that include communications between the developers and themselves, their reports to the developers, and communications with leaders.

No.	Key Actions	Tips
3	Notification of other direct project developers/testers	Compose an email message to between 6 and 10 participants, asking them to attend an audit interview session, lasting 1.5 hours, and bring artifacts that include schedules, deliverable documentation, and sample reports from project leads, support functions, and their own peer reviews.
4	Order of audit interviews	A minimum of three audit interview sessions shall be scheduled with the support functions first and the project leaders last. The other interview(s) should be scheduled.
5	Confidentiality assurance	In each audit interview session, after the introductions, the following statement should be made: "The information you present during this audit interview is aimed at process and product improvements, not at training you or in anyway harassing you. The auditors will be taking notes in order to aid their report-writing activities and they will be destroyed afterward. Our reports will be delivered to your project leaders, but will not have any clues as to who said what in the audit interviews, and certainly no attribution will be derived from these audit interviews. The findings documented in the reports will all be targeted at making continuous improvements in the processes and products."
6	Auditors meeting control	Auditors shall keep the tempo and tenor of each interview session professional, productive, and on schedule. No personal jabs shall be allowed and every attendee should be called on to give their view of each interview topic.
7	Findings report preparation	Both auditors shall meet for two or three hours after the three audit interviews have been completed in order to parse through the volume of "river-raft" notes, searching for continuous improvement findings and collaboration of these findings coming from at least two interview sessions. An initial draft of the findings shall be developed by one of the auditors and circulated for comments from the other auditor until consensus is reached on the wording and tone of each of the findings.

(continued)

Table 9.1
Tips for Each Key Action in an Audit (*cont'd*)

No.	Key Actions	Tips
8	Final findings review	In some cases, a final finding review can be scheduled for project leaders in order to clarify each finding, but it is the job of these project leaders to present the findings to the development team and the personnel involved with the support functions.
10	Final findings report and interview sessions notes	The auditors will destroy the audit interview session notes. They should file the final findings report in an audit archive and enter the completion of the audit in the audit logs.

The author performed an audit of over 25 software teams in 1999 to ensure that these teams, who had completed the appropriate Y2K program changes, had performed the appropriate testing and certifications, and that they had their application Y2K-compliant through the first quarter of the year 2000. The feedback that was received from the software projects that underwent audits was that the auditors were professional in their interview sessions, and the findings were accurate and helpful in pointing out any risk areas with their processes. The value to the company was that by auditing this 10% sample of its software teams, the Y2K project could reach a correct conclusion: that changes made to their production software between the time it was tested and certified as being Y2K compliant and January 1, 2000 had caused no Y2K noncompliant production software.

Inspections/Walkthroughs/Peer Reviews

Peer reviews are used by most software development projects in some form or other. One of the roles of the quality assurance personnel is to statistically sample, read, and mark up the user's or customer's software documents, and this qualifies as a peer review. Programmers sometimes furnish a just-completed module's source listing, along with its design documentation to another programmer to perform a code read and mark up, and this qualifies as a peer review. Programmers also share the debugging of a particularly hard-to-find bug with one another, and this share-a-bug club qualifies as a peer review. While these informal acts catch or fix many bugs, there are other bugs they may miss, mostly due to completeness and diligence that is lacking in informal peer reviews. Testers can employ peer reviews during the development of test scripts, test data, and the review of test results.

To improve over the informal peer review methods, walkthroughs and inspections have been formalized as a more complete and diligent means of finding, documenting, fixing bugs, and reviewing their fix. A walkthrough requires the author of a document or a program's source code to stand in front of his/her peers, presenting the approach he/she took in developing this portion of the software product. The peer group discusses the author's proposed solution approaches/algorithms, interpretations of requirements, or method of documentation while asking the author questions of clarification until the group is satisfied with the proposals of the author. Again, testers can employ walkthroughs during test planning, test case preparation, test data development, and test results reviews.

Michael Fagan (1976) first defined inspections while at IBM. An inspection qualifies as a form of peer review and has several features in common with an informal code read, as well as a walkthrough. An inspection starts with the author furnishing a just-completed source module's listing, along with its design documentation to an inspections coordinator.

Inspection Team Roles and Responsibilities

The inspections coordinator chooses an appropriate set of four or five inspectors, one of whom is named to the position of the inspections moderator. The inspections coordinator also chooses a time and place to hold the inspection. He/she also prepares the four or five inspection packets for the inspection team, by duplicating source module listings and the appropriate design documentation, along with some inspection forms and the appropriate phase-dependent checklist of lessons learned from prior inspections. These inspection packets are transmitted to the inspection team at least two days before the inspection meeting. Thorough training is required of each member of an inspection team. The inspection moderator and three or four inspectors know from their training that they must spend at least an hour and sometime up to two hours reviewing the materials in the inspections packet before the scheduled time of the inspection meeting. Mark-ups can be written on module's source listing by each of the inspectors, and other comments are made on the inspection forms provided in the inspection packets. Inspection forms are partially completed by each of the team members by the time they come to the inspection meeting, including a list of potential bugs, areas of improvements, failure to apply appropriate standards, and so on. As the time of the inspection meeting draws near, the inspection moderator prompts each of the other inspectors to be sure they have completed their review of the material before coming to the meeting, and where the meeting will be held. Table 9.2 shows the schedule for a typical inspection, but it can be accelerated to occur within a day, if it is deemed necessary.

At the meeting, the inspection moderator arranges the table as shown in Figure 9.5. The decision as to how many software developers or test engineers to have on an inspection team is up to the inspection coordinator and depends upon the nature of the contents of the inspection packet. For example, if the inspection packet is a test plan, then one or two test engineers and none or one software engineer might fulfill the needs, whereas if the inspec-

Table 9.2
Schedule of a Typical Inspection

Milestones	Responsibilities	Note
Day 1	Developer	Delivers target data for inspection to inspection coordinator.
Day 1–2	Coordinator	Develops and duplicates inspection packet, schedules a place/time for the meeting, invites 3–4 inspectors and 1 moderator.
Day 3–4	Inspection team	Spend 1–2 hours reading/studying the information in the inspection packet, developing a proposed bug list.
Day 4–5	Inspection team	Hold inspection meeting.
Day 5	Moderator	Organizes the output data from the inspection meeting, including entering reported bugs in the defect database, inspection metrics in the project's metrics database, and entering the results from the root-cause analysis that the inspection team has performed for the new types of bugs into the errors-by-phase checklists database.
Day 5	Coordinator	Receives the inspection packets and reports from the moderator, reviews inspection process failures, if any, and improves the inspection processes/databases.

tion packet contained C++ source code for a module, a dataflow diagram, and an entity-relation diagram of an object, then there might be two software engineers and none or one test engineer at the table. Finally, if the inspection packet contains a listing of all the components that went into a build, then the configuration on the right of Figure 9.5 might be more suitable, with the software build master or a software configuration management person taking the seat of the software developer or test engineer.

The role of the inspection moderator is one of a facilitator of the inspection meeting. In this capacity, the inspection moderator ensures that the documented and deployed, via training mentioned before, inspection process is completely followed. The role of the defects recorder is to accumulate all bugs that were found by the inspection team, remove any duplicates, lead the inspection team to clarification of wording of each of these bugs, ranking each of them by severity level, and assigning them a SEV number, before finally entering them onto the inspection forms that are turned into the inspections coordinator. The role of the metrics recorder is to ensure counts of bugs, along with their probable root cause or phase of the life cycle where they were most likely introduced, and any other inspection metrics currently being collected by the project, such as total time spent preparing for

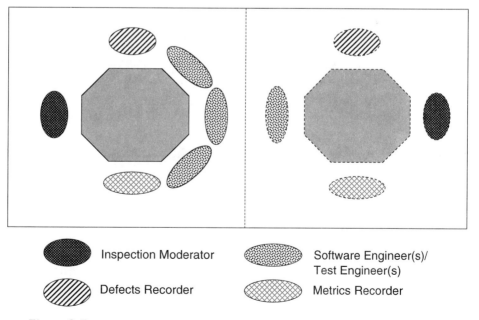

Inspection Moderator

Defects Recorder

Software Engineer(s)/
Test Engineer(s)

Metrics Recorder

Figure 9.5
Alternate arrangements of inspection table.

the inspection by the inspection team, number of inspectors on the inspection team, the total time the inspection took, the total number of bugs that were entered into the defect database, and so on. These data are entered into the inspection forms and the moderator collects the inspection forms from each of the members of the inspection team, later updating the defect database, metrics database, and checklist database and turning the paper copy of the consolidated inspections packet in to the inspection coordinator.

Reporting on the Inspection Process

The inspection coordinator ensures that the bugs that were communicated via the inspections packet are entered as quickly as possible into the project-wide defect database. Another rapid testing attribute is that some of these defects are marked as "blocking," which means that this bug directly hampers further testing of this function. The blocking bugs and the SEV 1 (catastrophic) bugs are communicated immediately to the development team for debugging.

The emphasis in rapid testing is on finding and fixing bugs at the earliest possible time. By keeping data on each bug, the inspection process can be greatly enhanced in accuracy and value. A checklist of lessons learned should be started for each phase of the life cycle. These phase-based checklists should become living documents, driven by new data on bugs that come from one of the inspections. An inspection team can perform a root cause analysis on each bug, seeking to locate at which phase the bug was injected into the product. The inspection team should add a lessons-learned item into the checklist for that phase so that the next inspection team that performs an inspection of material within that phase will find a bug that is similar to the one that was found earlier. This feedback that is performed on each bug causes the inspection checklist to be a living document, which is characteristic of a learning organization.

Metrics for the Inspection Process

The metrics that stem from the inspections directly feed into the project-based error model. The number of defects per thousand source lines of code is combined with other inspections completed within a time window, say daily, weekly, or per development phase, and added to the Software Error Estimation Program (SWEEP) input data. SWEEP is covered in depth in Chapter 11.

Using e-mail or an e-App to Streamline Inspections

For rapid testing, productivity improvements are to be generously used throughout the life cycle of the software development project. There have been several technologies that apply to the inspection process, as presented in this section, but also to other processes within the development process. The assumption is made that the software development team writes their code on computers that are linked together by local area networks (LANs). Either within the servers of the LAN or using storage area networks (SANs), any member of the project should be able to access the project's common storage facilities. Directory structures can be maintained that organizes the development and test data, which can be scheduled for backups on a regular schedule. As an alternate to the LAN/SAN technology, a project data repository can also be managed with an e-App running within the company's intranet on the project's Web site. This e-App can take care of storing the development documentation into a configuration management system that performs strict version controls and is backed up on a regular schedule.

By using integrated calendar and email messaging software on the company intranet, project personnel can reserve conference rooms and invite the participants of each inspection. For a project employing rapid testing methods, this productivity increase reduces the time required for the inspection coordinator to reserve the conference room and invite all of the inspectors at a time that will avoid any conflicts on schedule. This is accomplished by the inspection coordinator, who can look at all candidate inspectors' schedules along with the conference room scheduling to "book" a conflict-free meeting time and place. The corporate infrastructure, which forms the company intranet, also provides routing of the inspection packet, which might be in the form of a series of hyperlinks in an email to read-only versions of the forms and the inspection contents on the common storage facilities, or copies of the same shared files can be added as attachments to the calendar appointment notices that are sent to each inspector.

An inspection is a static testing tool, which can be used on all software documents, from the requirements phase to the acceptance test phase. Rapid testing implies a constant watch for bugs, which are to be caught and fixed as near the time that they are injected into the product as possible. Since an inspection is to be performed on a document that is developed in a given phase of the life cycle, all bugs found by the inspection should be mapped to root cause. The inspection team should then update phase-dependent lessons-learned checklists so that future inspection teams will not miss the same or similar bugs. The following lists attributes of inspections that meet rapid testing needs:

- Inspections that output bug lists, each having a severity number that gives the prioritization of the fixing process. The bug list is merged into the defect database and is used to manage changes to the legacy system that make up the successive build(s).

- Inspections that output revisions to the lessons-learned checklist for one or more phases, based upon root cause analysis performed by the inspectors. These lessons-learned checklists are ready for the next time the project passes by this phase in this or another software development project.

- Inspections that output metrics that drive the characteristic project error model and feed the Software Error Estimation Program (SWEEP), to generate the forecast of latent defects remaining in the current software product itself, as well as feed continuous improvements to the inspection process. SWEEP is covered in depth in Chapter 11.

- Inspections that output better inspectors who, when they go back to their developer role, are fueled with better understanding of the product or project requirements, product architecture, design, and programming algorithms, as well as the type of bugs to watch out for in their own work products.

From this definition of the inspection process, which was specially designed for rapid testing, you should be clear on just how integrated this form of static testing is with the actual development process and the emphasis that is made on rapidly increasing the quality of the resulting product. The rapid testing inspection process shortens schedules by fixing errors along the way, rather than at the end of the development.

Formal Verification

Verification is the act of ensuring at the nth stage of development that what was ordered at the $(n-1)$th stage of development has been fulfilled. While developing the architecture of the system and establishing the performance requirements, the tester should compare the architecturally allocated performance budgets against the overall requirements. While testing the detailed design documentation, the tester will verify this documentation against the architecture documentation, which was developed during the high-level design phase. During the coding phase, the tester will verify the code by comparing it to its detailed design documentation. If the detailed design document calls out, say, five modules to be written to perform some function, and one of these modules is a complex-valued Fast Fourier Transformation (FFT) algorithm, then one test case that the tester will write is one that tests the FFT code during execution, noting accuracy, performance, and built-in features it might have.

Specification-Based Languages

One of the tools in the tester's tool chest is called a software proof. This tool falls into the category called formal verification, in that code is proven to match its detailed design. The software proof is formulated by asserting a theorem or lemma (called specifications) directly into the code base, at the head of each main code block. Then the user interactively guides the automated theorem-proving tool to determine that the code meets the theorem or lemma as stated. Such a language is referred to as a specification-based language or assertion language and the tool is referred to as a formal verification tool. While the application of such a tool is a rarity in the software industry today, it is a viable testing tool to be considered in the testing arsenal.

Automated Theorem Proofs

The author has experience in software proofs, using a computerized mathematical theorem-proving utility called Gypsy (see Good et al., 1978) to prove about a thousand lines of code. The way Gypsy works is that the tester inserts statements of theorems and lemmas among the blocks of code, written in Gypsy language, a variant of Pascal, and then the theorem-prover within Gypsy proves that the assertions that are made in the theorems or lemmas are correctly implemented by the block of code. The algorithm that the author proved to be correct with this formal verification tool was called Collision Avoidance, which is in use in today's FAA in computer systems to warn one or more aircraft of an impending collision. Transponders are implanted in participating aircraft, as well as in tall buildings and tall mountains. Digital bursts of data are received from these transponders, which contain flight dynamics data, such as altitude, speed, and direction of flight. From the flight dynamic mathematical models, these digital packets of data are modeled to determine a probability of collision as well as the collision avoidance tactics that may be required. These are automatically fed back to the aircraft that are on a collision path in plenty of time for the collision to be avoided. It was clear that the collision avoidance code had to be correct— provably correct.

The collision avoidance program was first translated into the Gypsy language, and the theorems were specified around each block of code. The Gypsy theorem-proving capability was engaged, and all theorems were found to be implemented in the code. There was one bug found in this process, and the correction for this bug was inserted into the original code. The process was found to be painless and certainly productive.

Testing Automation/Tools

There are a number of automated static testing tools. Most of these tools are special purpose tools, rather than one large tool that can do it all. Another characteristic of these static testing tools is that they are language-dependent. Finding bugs in source language or in the documentation language includes highlighting errors that include spelling, language syntax, undefined variables or pointers, design constructs that are not closed, references that are not defined, including undefined URLs, and so on.

Requirements Traceability

Traceability for requirements means maintaining the statement of a requirement from its introduction to its fulfillment. From reading Chapter 8, you know that the outcome of the Joint Application Requirement (JAR) is a set of software requirements. Subsequent requirements decompose these requirements into a set of derived requirements, which are typically documented in the Software Design Specification (SDS). We have already covered the static testing opportunities that exist in this restated version of the requirements, looking for the missing, misstated, ambiguous, pair-wise conflicting requirements that form errors in the SDS. Finding bugs in requirements has the biggest payoff of any form of testing. In the rapid testing paradigm, using a Requirements Traceability Matrix (RTM), the development team, including the testers, show that they value the maintenance of their requirements and the completeness of the testing of those requirements, applying both static and dynamic tools, throughout the development life cycle.

On the other hand, if you come from a non-rapid testing paradigm and the start of testing comes after the software development is winding down, then you can perform requirements reverse-engineering in order to form an RTM that will be used to plan the testing activities throughout the remainder of your development life cycle.

Physical Units Checker

A tremendous aid in the development of scientific programs, the physical units checker is a static preprocessor of the source code that verifies that the output of each equation is in appropriate physical units of measure. Consider the equation for rate (R) or speed: $R1 = D1/T1$, where $D1$ is the distance traveled and $T1$ is the time of travel. This equation only applies when the physical units are compatible. Otherwise, it's the wrong equation. For example, if distance is in kilometers and time is in minutes, the rate that is computed by the equation $R1 = D1/T1$ is forced to be in km/min. If this rate is mixed into another equation that requires the rate be in physical units of miles-per-hour (mph), then there must be a conversion of $R1$, having physical units of km/min to, say, $R2$, having physical units of mph, before it can be used in that additional computation.

When implemented as a static checker, the physical units checker accepts additional typing specifications on all variables with physical units within specially formatted comment lines in the source. Then, with every use or definition of these variables, the formulas are verified that the left-hand side or receiving variable has the same physical units derived from order of computation and from the declared physical units of the variables on the right-hand side, or input variables, of the formula.

Symbolic Execution

Symbolic execution is a technique that puts symbols into formulas coded within a programming language, and a tool performs the algebra combining the symbols together, as specified in the algorithm. Consider the code for the SINE function shown in Figure 9.6. This algorithm is one that contains a minimum number of multiplications, as shown in the following equation: $\sin(x) = x * (1 - x^2 * (1/3! - x^2 * (1/5! - x^2 * (1/7! - x^2 * (\dots)))))$.

A symbolic testing tool performs the algebraic simplifications to show the steps of the algorithm in Table 9.3, which yields the familiar Taylor Series expansion.

```
REAL FUNCTION SINE (P,EPS)
ERROR = P
SUM = P
DO J = 3,1000,2
        ERROR = ERROR * (P**2) / (J* (J+1))
        SUM = SUM - ((J+1)/2) * ERROR
        IF (ABS(ERROR) .LT. EPS)
        THEN
        GO TO 30
    ENDIF
    ENDDO
30  SINE = SUM
    RETURN
    END
```

Figure 9.6
SINE function, coded using Taylor Series expansion.

This output can be compared to the one for the sine function that is found in most calculus books, namely: $\sin(x) = x - x^3/3! + x^5/5! + x^7/7!\ldots$ Again, this description substantiates why symbolic execution is a static test tool, in that it is not a requirement that the algorithm be executed with data inputs.

Cross-Reference Listings

A cross-reference listing is a language-dependent test and debug tool that indexes the use of variables within each module. Some cross-references include a list of source lines of code where a variable is used or defined. This allows a tester to be able to spot a misspelled variable name that would be a

Table 9.3
Symbolic Execution of Algorithm in Figure 9.6

J	ERROR	SUM
3	$P * (P^2/12) = P^3/12$	$P - (4/2)*(P^3/12) = P - P^3/6$
5	$(P^3/12) * P^2/30 = P^5/360$	$P - P^3/6 + (6/2)* P^5/360 = P - P^3/3! + P^5/120$
7	$P^5/360 * P^2/56 = P^7/20160$	$P - P^3/6 + P^5/120 - 4 * (P^7/20160) = P - P^3/3! + P^5/5! - P^7/7!$
	$\ldots$	$\ldots$
J	$P^J / (J! * (J+1) / 2)$ for $J = 3, n, 2$	$P - \text{SUM} (P^J / J!)$ for $J = 3, n, 2$

bug, since the misspelled variable would either be undefined or be involved in a computation it shouldn't be involved in. Some compilers offer this feature as an option.

Pretty Printers

A pretty printer is a structure-language-dependent test tool to ensure every structured construct is ended correctly. For example, if an IF-THEN-ELSE-ENDIF is missing its ENDIF, then the structure will be misaligned when the pretty print is observed. This would be a bug, since the ELSE clause would include computations that should not be involved. Many structured-language compilers provide this feature as an option.

Version Comparators

Configuration control tools ensure the latest version is the one that can be checked out for change. Such tools are designed to support the software developers. For example, if two developers check out the same version of the source and begin making changes, there is a dilemma when they want to come back together, unless they use a locking mechanism supplied by the configuration control tool to govern which source version must be checked in first. Then the two authors can reach consensus on how to combine the changes of one that are in conflict with the changes of the other. Another use of the version comparator tool is to ensure that a file is exactly the same as one of the versions maintained in the configuration control system, when it has been checked out.

Certain other operations of the configuration control tool support the testing staff in determining where changes have been made to the executable code or in data files between one version and the next. These operations are called *version comparators*. The version comparator operation makes a cell-by-cell comparison, highlighting the differences between two cells, where "cell" may mean source line or data field within a record. The testers and developers must communicate, typically through written records, about the areas of changes in the newer version, but this tool can be used as a failsafe in verifying these changed areas. Of course, areas that have not been changed may need to be regressed to determine whether there are side effects of changes that have taken place in the complement of the unchanged areas, but test cases that are targeted at the unchanged areas of the code certainly don't need to be rerun. So, the use of a version comparator tool can cause a productivity increase to the rapid testing staff.

Algorithm Testing

If a tester has been assigned the task of testing a module that implements a data transform using an algorithm, then the top-of-mind approach for the tester is to develop input data and expected results data that will exercise the algorithm's capabilities, options, and error conditions. For example, if a tester is assigned the job of testing a fast Fourier transform algorithm, there are a number of features of this transform that should be tested. Since the fast Fourier transform is a linear transformation, then the tester will develop a test case to determine whether $T(a*f_1 + b*f_2) = a*T(f_1) + b*T(f_2)$. Since the fast Fourier transform is reversible, the tester may then take a combination of pure frequencies through the forward transform into the power spectrum and then input this power spectrum into inverse transform in order to show that the inverse transform results are the original pure frequencies, that is, that $T^{-1}[T(f)] = f$. At this juncture, the tester could conclude that the code implemented a reversible linear transform, but there is still an open question as to whether this algorithm is truly a Fourier transform. The tester will certainly want to create data for a fixed frequency, which, in the power spectrum, has only one nonzero amplitude at the selected frequency and to ensure that its amplitude is correct in the power spectrum. This test case may be followed by another "pure" frequency after another until all frequencies and their amplitudes have been tested.

However, this top-of-mind approach falls under dynamic testing, which is the subject of Chapter 10. There could be a lot more testing done for this algorithm upstream in its development under the category of static testing. At requirements time, this algorithm was called out as a required feature of the delivered system, probably by someone saying "The user shall have a utility that will perform a fast Fourier transformation of complex-valued data of length a power of two up to and including 2^{10}." This is a clear statement to the engineering or physics laboratory, but to a software engineer, there is a lot of mathematics that may be lacking. During preliminary design, this requirement should be decomposed into understandable pieces. To start with, input and output data will be carried in two two-dimensional variables of length n, of type COMPLEX and of maximum length of 2^{10}, an error flag of type INTEGER, and the variable N of type INTEGER in the interval [2,10]. This preliminary design information sets the user interface so that a prototype or stub could be prepared and integrated into a graphical user interface (GUI) under preparation during preliminary design to obtain feedback from the engineering or physics laboratory personnel.

During the detailed design phase of development, a fast Fourier algorithm should be researched and selected, whether it is the original 1965 version by Cooley and Tukey, or another one. There are some decisions that must be made regarding the ordering of processing. For example, whether to apply a bit reversal of the output data before completing the transform, or to presort the sine and cosine data table using a bit-reversal algorithm, and store it in the fixed storage area in bit-reversed order. Also, decisions need to be reached regarding the accuracy requirement for this algorithm, and technical literature searches must be documented on this subject in order to support testing requirements on the resulting transformation algorithm's accuracy. Timing requirements must be addressed as well, to determine whether scalar central processing units (CPUs) will be sufficient to meet these requirements, or whether CPUs with vector instructions or other forms of array processors will be required.

The software design phases are the testing grounds for the requirements, and, except for dynamic testing of the prototypes, all the testing that is done during design is static testing. Many of the decisions that must be made during detailed design can be errant and lead to cost overruns or requirements that are unmet. A rapid testing approach to this issue is to concentrate on making trade-off studies on all such decisions during the detailed design phase of the development. Trade-off studies can then be used to defend against requirements volatility, one of the main cost drivers in traditional waterfall life cycle developments. Trade-off studies are a form of optimization prior to solidifying the final design that will prevent multiple costly software developments and dynamic testing to be done for discarded designs/implementations. In most SEI assessments, the assessors document many findings in the area of software design, and I have referred to this as a "chughole" of the development process—a dip in the road that sometimes can damage the projects that drive across it. Rapid testing is the art of stationing testers throughout the development life cycle, finding and reporting defects as soon as they appear.

CASE STUDY

GLOBAL ROUND-OFF ANALYSIS (GARY COBB)

Another area of static testing, particularly applicable to scientific programming, is global round-off analysis. In order to set a need for this form of testing in your mind, I will relate a true story. In the early 1970s, the company I worked for contracted with one of its clients to perform program conversion of their software from a scalar computer to a vector computer. In the area of the contract that dealt with the acceptance of the resultant products, the following is the essence of this term of contact: the converted programs will run 256 times faster on the vector computer over the scalar computer and they will get the same hexadecimal answers as the executions on the scalar computer.

Upon arriving on site for my two-year stint as manager of the program conversion staff, I performed a baseline of each of the major systems to be converted, both in terms of execution time and a captured printout of both major inputs as well as major output variables from runs that were deemed to be typical by the owners of the applications. This, I thought, would help fulfill the terms of acceptable performance for the conversion effort that ensued. It was not long after starting the conversion effort that one of my staff brought up a humorous issue: namely, that one of the hexadecimal outputs was named WWM, which stood for "worldwide mass," and it was the result of summing up the mass at each gridpoint proceeding around the world-spanning grid. Working together, we determined that this computation had a floating-point overflow about halfway around the world, since the summand that was accumulating got so large that adding the mass at the remainder of the grid points didn't cause any change in the summand. Now, the scalar computer had 36-bit floating-point operations, while the vector computer had a choice of 32-bit or 64-bit floating-point vector operations. We were clearly in a no-win position. If we performed the summation in single precision, it would overflow before getting even halfway around the grid (different hexadecimal answer). If we performed the summation in double precision, it would be slower (impossible to get 256X speed), and it would start getting a floating overflows condition about three-quarters around the grid (different hexadecimal answer). In order to negotiate our way around the acceptable performance term of the contract for this incidence, we had to prove that the baseline program got the wrong answer for the worldwide mass and that the converted program would therefore be exempt from getting the same wrong answer.

The application of global round-off analysis is a static testing technique that comes out of the field called numerical analysis, usually taught in advanced computer science courses in the university, by treating each input data variable as having an error term associated with it. If we let $X_i = C_i + c_i$ and $Y_i = D_i + d_i$, then the following shows the calculation of the error, E, due to summation:

$$\text{SUM } (X_i + Y_i) = \text{SUM } (C_i + D_i) + E(N) \text{ for } i=1, \ldots, N, \text{ where } E(N) = \text{SUM } (c_i + d_i) \text{ for } i=1, \ldots, N$$

Now, since the computer truncates the actual value of X_i and Y_i when reading in the input values, then c_i and d_i will always be the truncated value, which is non-negative. Therefore, the error function $E(N)$ is monotonic increasing and unbounded above. This numerical analysis can be performed on more complex algorithms in order to prove an algorithm's limits of stability.

To summarize this case study, testers who work on scientific applications must be able to perform numerical analysis on complex algorithms in order to define the boundary conditions of computer simulations, using such complex algorithms. While this may seem to be a high standard for testers, it helps to show the value of testers with numerical analysis or mathematical training and education in finding unstable algorithms and alternative stable algorithms that are clearly preferred for computer simulations, especially those used in scientific programming.

Test Support Facilitator

The concept of a test support facilitator is one of organizing and directing the day-to-day progress and status of testing, using the rapid testing paradigm. In small projects, this role may be assumed by the project lead. In medium-size projects, this role may be called "test lead." In huge projects, during dynamic testing, this role may be specialized in a full-time individual who works with the team of test engineers, network engineers, database administrators, test lab technicians, and business analysts who represent a user community. For usability testing, this role may be called the host or hostess of the usability lab. This host/hostess instructs visitors from outside of the company to exercise a new set of products and technologies for its user friendliness during live operation scenarios.

A test support facilitator's role is to study project test plans and coordinate the following:

- Set and manage the schedules of personnel who will be required to perform the complete ensemble of test cases.
- Ensure that the order of the test runs is compatible with the data flow in the software.
- Document the script for the test scenarios.
- Design test reporting forms that will be collected, analyzed, and compared against test result data.
- Collect and report real-time test status.

As you can see, the test support facilitator is somewhat like the role of the director of a movie or a multimedia product development. Without a test support facilitator, individual testers, each working with a subset of test cases, will create chaos and serialized activities due to the lack of coordination of test schedule, test platforms, file sharing, test results snapshots, and disk back-ups/restores that will be required to generate the environment of each test case. Parallel testing by multiple testers across independent or shared and networked resources requires an organized plan, a coordinated execution, and a summarization of the results. The facilitating and hosting of end-users, whether business analysts that support large legacy systems within information technology or surrogate end-users of a commercial product, requires a dedicated person, namely the test support facilitator, to ensure schedules, resources, and test data are all readied for a test period, and that after the testing is completed, the issues lists are combined, prioritized, and communicated with the development team.

Frequently, test plans require compatibility testing across a number of configurations, such as Wintel PCs, MACs, Linux, and PDAs, all with a myriad of peripherals, such as scanners, printers, modems, CD-RW drives, video cameras, joysticks, and remote controlled keyboards or game I/O devices. Also, several projects may be required to share their test facility so that the configurations may have to be set up or torn down in between test sessions. In order to optimize and control the test lab, a test support facilitator's job is created, often supported by several test lab technicians. The facilitator directs the hardware technicians to set up the hardware and software platform along with network resources that are called out in the test plans of multiple projects, and he/she schedules both the lab times as well as the support personnel's work. For information technology departments, this might be a very complex job, being performed by multiple test support facilitators, involving a mainframe test computer system, along with many business analysts' terminals/PCs, attached through a corporate global intranet, involving EDI connections to multiple business partners' servers, called business-to-business (B2B) telecommunications, in order to simulate the production system.

Shared Issues Databases

When the test team finds an issue with the software, it must be logged, prioritized, scheduled for the development team to fix, scheduled for a build/release to the test operation, retested for fixing the original issue, and tested for not having side effects. The easiest way of managing issues is through the use of a shared issues database. Each record in this database represents one issue and it has fields that are filled in by everyone who deals with the issue. The shared issues database can be sorted and separated into a database for each software subsystem, for each software development staff, included vended software, and for each type of issue, so that routing can take place efficiently. Also, merging updated records back into the shared issues database is an activity that database administrators perform with high frequency.

Roll-ups and status reviews are held periodically to ensure that issues are being tracked and reported on by all development organizations. Multiple builds will be coordinated by the development teams and sometimes are co-ordinated or performed by an individual called the buildmaster. Scheduling of retesting revolves around these builds and the shared issues database will be updated with the current events of this retesting.

A modern implementation of the shared issues database should be a secure, database-driven Web site that is established on an extranet belonging to the prime contractor to display the shared issues database. Transactional application service programs (ASPs) were written to allow updates and changes to appropriate portions of the database records by personnel within each development project. This implementation allows complete authenticated collaboration of prioritized issues lists to be performed by the partners in a development and was declared to be a successful implementation of the rapid testing paradigm.

Summary

In this chapter there are a number of directly applicable techniques that a test organization should evaluate immediately in order to embark on the road to rapid testing. From Chapter 7, we saw that the value proposition for rapid testing techniques is to be able to complete developments in half the time with half the people and a quarter of the number of latent defects to the end-user. The most important concept from this chapter on static testing is to start early in the development life cycle finding bugs, entering bug reports into a shared database, correcting them rapidly, and learning from having found them by putting them into checklists and reliability models, and, finally, measuring your productivity based on their counts. Continuous improvements will lower the injection rates for bugs, lower the staffing for dynamic testing phases, and lower the call volume from your customers.

References

Belford, P. C, R. A. Berg, and T. L. Hannan. (1979). "Central Flow Control Software Development: A Case Study of the Effectiveness of Software Engineering Techniques," Proceedings from the Fourth Summer Software Engineering Workshop, SEL-79-005.

Cooley, J. W., and J. W. Tukey. (1965). "An Algorithm for Machine Calculation of Complex Fourier Series." *Mathematics of Computation,* Vol. 19, pp. 297–301.

Michael Fagan. (1976). "Design and Code Inspections to Reduce Errors in Program Development," *IBM Systems Journal, 15* (3), 182–211.

Good, Donald I., R. M. Cohen, C. G. Hoch, L. W. Hunter, and D. F. Hare. (1978). "Certifiable Minicomputer Project, ICSCA," Report on the Language Gypsy, Version 2.0. Technical Report ICSCA-CMP-10, The University of Texas at Austin, September 1978.

McCabe, Thomas, and Charles W. Butler. (1989). "Design Complexity Measurement and Testing." *Communications of the ACM 32,* 12 (December 1989): 1415–1425.

Dynamic Testing Techniques and Tips

Topics Covered in the Chapter

- ▶ Functional Testing and Analysis
- ▶ Equivalence Partitioning
- ▶ Boundary Value Analysis
- ▶ Negative Testing
- ▶ Risk-Based Testing
- ▶ Path Coverage Testing
- ▶ Use-Case Testing
- ▶ Bebugging/Mutation
- ▶ Tracing/Tracebacks/Snap Dumps/Post-Mortem Dumps
- ▶ Breakpointing/Patching
- ▶ Data Flow Testing
- ▶ Testing for Memory Leaks
- ▶ Human–Computer Interface Testing
- ▶ Load Performance Testing
- ▶ Platform Configuration Testing
- ▶ Summary
- ▶ References

You might be wondering, "What sort of bugs would have survived the extensive front-end static testing techniques that are typical of a rapid testing project?" The simple answer is that they are latent bugs. Latent bugs are bugs that exist but are yet to be found. We, in software developing organizations, ship latent bugs to end-users at a rate in the range from 0.2 to 20 per thousand delivered source instructions (KDSI). If your project uses many of the static testing techniques typical of a rapid testing project, then up to the point where you can start using dynamic testing techniques, you should have reduced the number of latent bugs by 65% to 80%, leaving another 20% to 35% latent bugs to be found during the Unit Testing (UT), Integration Testing (IT), System Testing (ST), Acceptance Testing (AT), and maintenance phases of the software life cycle.

The types of bugs found during dynamic testing are those that were introduced by the Requirements (REQ), Preliminary Design (PD), Detailed Design (DD) and coding processes. Another, sometimes forgotten, source of latent bugs is legacy and other reuse software. The types of bugs include logic, typographical, data organization, performance, usability, database query, file access, interface faults, load management, missing functions, erroneous algorithms, communications glitches, test scripting faults, test results miscalculations and many more. In short, there is a cascading of latent bugs, stemming from all prior development phases that are still latent at the start of dynamic testing. But, with a rapid testing approach, catching the largest percentage of the latent bugs and correcting them, as near the point of their injection into the product as possible, has saved time and effort.

Functional requirements are mixed with nonfunctional requirements during the REQ and PD phases of the development life cycle. A few examples of nonfunctional requirements are delivery schedule, installation kitting, database filling, algorithm timing, human factors, supported configurations, communication infrastructure, security, robustness and many more. Most of these are from the programming standards or style guides of the company. The programming standards are typically based upon the company's lessons learned. These lessons learned, along with marketing research on competitive software developers and products, are converted to programming standards, sometimes called style guides. If your company wants to spend some nonrecurring money on testing, spend it to automate the testing of your company's programming standards or style guides. If this investment is made, rapid testers can gain speed by reusing legacy test plans, test cases, test scripts, and test tools designed to test nonfunctional requirements. Testers still need to develop test cases, test scripts, test results, and test tools when preparing to test a product's new functions, that is, the functional requirements.

There are a large number of dynamic testing techniques presented in this chapter, but it's not an exhaustive set. The mission of having a repertory of these techniques is to reduce the number of latent bugs in the software product in an organized and efficient manner. It is up to the test team to include as many of these techniques as feasible during their planning effort. Test planning, test case preparation, test scripts, and test results are products of the test development tasks, which are critical to this goal of having an organized pursuit of the latent bugs.

Functional Testing and Analysis

Functions, sometimes referred to as functionality, are what users pay to have developed into products. They often are the bulletized lists that are compared against those of competing products in the sales and marketing literature for the product. These lists of product functions are identified during the requirements phase and carefully maintained throughout the design and coding phases of the development, for example, in a Requirements Traceability Matrix (RTM). These functions are a byproduct of that portion of the design phase called incremental refinement and are fragments of source code from which modules or objects are formed.

Functional analysis is the act of describing characteristics of a function that affect the design and testing of that function. Say, one has a Taylor series expansion of a function $y(x) = \sin(x)$ (refer back to Chapter 9 under "Symbolic Execution"). Functional analysis would be performed, during the design phases, to establish the computational accuracy of the expansion, both in terms of the word size for the floating point variables involved, as well as any intermediate results. For example, for the Taylor series it can be shown for some functions that the greater the number of terms of the series, the more accurate the partial expansion will be for the variable $y(x)$. The important point to make about functional analysis is that if it is not performed during the design phases, it will have to be done in preparing for dynamic testing. Those organizations that delay the evaluation of the accuracy of an algorithm, until the dynamic testing effort is launched, are not rapid testing organizations. In a rapid testing organization, the testers who are responsible for preparing for dynamic testing simply refer to the documentation of the functional analysis to guide the establishment of test cases, test data, test scripts, and test results.

CASE STUDY

UNDETECTED FLOATING-POINT OVERFLOW (GARY COBB)

The author remembers working on a large finite difference solution of simultaneous partial differential equations and being deeply involved in the functional analysis of the impact of round-off and truncation of intermediate results. In the middle of this study, it was discovered that the source code calculated the integral across the grid of a variable, called *mass*, but as the intermediate results were adding up the individual masses, it became so much larger than the individual masses that about halfway across the grid, adding the remainder of the individual masses didn't change the floating point value of the summation. It was due to the exponent of the intermediate summand growing rapidly causing the computer's floating-point instruction's exponent alignment instruction to ignore individual masses whose exponents were small when compared to the intermediate summand. This functional analysis was performed after tests showed that the program would get different answers when run in single precision versus with double precision floating point instructions or across multiple mainframes with differing word sizes.

Equivalence Partitioning

For two data to share the same equivalence class simply means that the function performs the same operations on each of them. For two data to be in different equivalence classes means that there is at least one line of code that is required to process one datum that will not be used to process the other datum. We often describe data in one of two equivalence classes as being *good data* and the other equivalence class as being *bad data* for the function. The paths through the code that the good data takes within a function are sometimes called the *happy paths* while the paths that the function executes when given the bad data are called the *unhappy paths*. Most functions have *good* input and *bad* input data as defined in the design documentation. The testers should read the design documentation to determine the equivalence classes of data for each function. If this information is not found in the design documentation, then the tester must apply functional analysis to reverse-engineer the equivalence classes' information. In some cases, the design documentation may also use the term *valid* versus *invalid* data for a given function. Testing with bad data is accurately called negative testing, in that bad data is designed to ensure that each function has exception handlers to take care of bad data. Negative testing can go beyond just testing with bad data (refer to a later section in this chapter on negative testing).

One of the principle characteristics of a tester who wants to apply rapid testing techniques is that he/she must always test for breadth and coverage, while weighing the risks of releasing bugs that may hamper the efficient use of the target software. A tester should pay close attention to equivalence classes of input data for functions in order to ensure both happy paths and unhappy paths are tested within each function.

Boundary Value Analysis

A very productive area to look for bugs is on the boundaries of the equivalence classes of a function. The analysis that leads to defining equivalence classes typically identifies these boundaries. Including several boundary values into the test cases for a function will validate that the user's expectations (requirements) are satisfied. Let's consider briefly why software engineers make mistakes in coding at boundary values. It's pretty easy to understand how boundary value bugs are introduced into software products by considering the number of translations that are made from the point of the requirements to the point of dynamic testing. First of all, the requirements are written at a high level; they do not contain a great deal of detail. Software designers typically add what are called derived requirements to the RTM translating the original nondetailed requirements into computationally accurate and detailed requirements, during the Detailed Design (DD) phase.

Rapid testing organizations have grown to realize the importance of the DD phase to the test team. If derived requirements are missing or are inadequate, then the coding or test staffs will be forced to supplement the high-level architectural design and the original requirements with these documented detailed designs, including the behavior of their software on the boundaries of equivalence classes, as they perform the coding or test planning, respectively. As an example, consider IF constructs. Over the years, many computer science researchers have pointed to the predicates of IF constructs as being the most bug-prone programming construct. The programmer often answers whether to use a less-than or less-then-or-equal-to in the predicate portion of an IF construct, when these decisions should have been part of the DD phase or else they should have been caught as missing specifications during inspections performed during the DD phase.

Negative Testing

Negative testing simply means asking the tester to think outside the box to determine just how many ways he/she can cause the software product to get wrong answers or abort execution. By asking the designers what has to be in place before executing the program, a good tester can identify a series of test cases that determine how the target software product would react if one of these prerequisite conditions were not satisfied. By focusing on this contrarian view, the tester will execute the program:

- on platforms it wasn't intended to execute on,
- with missing communication lines, or bad incoming or outgoing data,
- without missing data files, missing data records in databases, or scrambled data in data files
- with misspelled links, or undefined, wrong, or missing configuration parameters
- powered-off peripherals, like printers, scanners, external CD or CD-RW drives, external hard drives, external speakers, and so on.

Negative testing also encompasses inputting *bad* data, as mentioned under the proceeding section titled "Equivalence Partitioning." This *bad* data can come in the form of illegal user inputs, randomized seeded out-of-range data in communications buffers, illegal index values seeded into indexed files, log files that are full and at end-of-file, and many more.

Robustness of software is the quality of being able to withstand negative testing without failing. Certainly there is a limit to robustness, but software developers must be challenged to code and test for the *bad* data as well as the good data. They should code self-tests to ensure the minimum system configuration is present and ready to run the application. This self-test should be run at the beginning of its execution, since the configuration could have changed since the installation of the product. It's not sufficient to run the configuration self-test only when the application is installed.

The test staff has access to a wide variety of equipment configurations on which to perform system testing. This is not true of the development staff, which uses generic development machines. It is important that the test team be passionate about their responsibility to ensure that the product runs and gets the same results on all configurations that are itemized in the requirements document. In addition to the required configurations, the test staff should run some required configurations that are disabled or augmented in some way. If these configurations have test exceptions, then at least a disclaimer should be written about the configurations that are banned.

The strategy for negative testing should never be a shotgun approach. Instead, the test plan should be well thought out, consistent, complete, and productive in the finding of bugs. The test development staff must be measured on their completeness for test cases that address the test strategy that is documented in the test plan. Through this form of discipline, the system testing will be productive in finding and getting many bugs out of the product.

Risk-Based Testing

Another rapid testing technique is to define a risk-ranking metric and establish appropriate policies and procedures for its use. The risk-ranking metric should be employed throughout the project with absolute uniformity, as documented in the policies and procedures. The goals for the risk-ranking metric might be stated in some tailored form of that shown in Table 10.1.

For each subsystem of the target software product, a Change Control Review Board (CCRB) traditionally maintains, prioritizes, tracks status, and approves releases that fix a focused subset of documented bugs. Often there is a bug database that is maintained under the control of the CCRB but is shared as read-only records with both the development and test teams, who fix and retest bugs assigned to future builds of the target product. This infrastructure supports a risk-based rapid testing approach that can transition with the release of the target product to the maintenance organization. This infrastructure also scales to two software development partners who are geographically dispersed across the world.

The International Electrical and Electronic Engineers' (IEEE) Standard 1044 (IEEE, 1993) lays out additional definitions, flows, and processes for bug tracking process. This standard places the responsibility on a tester to perform bug classification at the time of its discovery (recognition). The bug report from the tester documentation is analyzed for its impact and a value of the risk-based metric is proposed (recognition impact). The development or maintenance team takes steps (investigation) to ensure that the bug is re-

Table 10.1
Risk-Ranking Metric

Risk Level	Standard for Selection of this Level
1	Bug results in termination of all applications/communications; a restart is required and session data may be lost or incomplete
2	Bug results in wrong answers that may impact future results, should the user continue using application
3	Bug results in correct results, but user requirements not fully met
4	User-facing information or performance does not meet user usability requirements
5	A feature that could be improved, but users are not negatively impacted

peatable and attempts to determine its root cause. An update to the proposed value of the risk-based metric and a plan, including resource assignments, identification of the first build that will contain a fix for the bug and estimates of costs (investigation impact). Upon execution of this plan, the corrective action is taken and the test team reruns the test case that found the bug in the first place, as well as some level of regression testing to ensure the bug fix didn't create other bugs. Based on the results of retesting, the disposition of the bug is documented in the release notes of the build that first contained the fix. A chart outlining this process is shown in Table 10.2.

Table 10.2
IEEE Standard 1044 Terminologies for a Bug Tracking Process

Recognition	Activity	What you were doing when the bug occurred?
	phase	What lifecycle phase is the product in?
	Suspected cause	What you think might be the cause?
	Repeatability	Could you make the bug happen more than once?
	Symptom	How did the bug manifest itself?
	Product status	What is the usability of the product?
Recognition impact	Customer value	How important the fix is to the customer.
	Severity	How bad was the bug?
	Mission/safety	How bad was the bug with respect to project objectives or human well-being?
Investigation	Actual cause	What caused the bug to occur?
	Source	Where was the origin of the bug?
	Type	What type of bug was it?
Investigation impact	Schedule impact	Relative effect on the product schedule.
	Cost impact	Relative effect on the budget.
	Project risk	Risk associated with implementing a fix.
	Quality impact	Impact to the product quality or reliability to make the fix.
	Societal impact	Impact to society of implementing the fix.
	Priority	Ranking the importance of resolving the bug.
Action	Resolution	What kind of action was taken before closing out the report?
	Corrective action	What to do to prevent failure from happening again?
Disposition	Disposition	In the final analysis, what became of the bug?

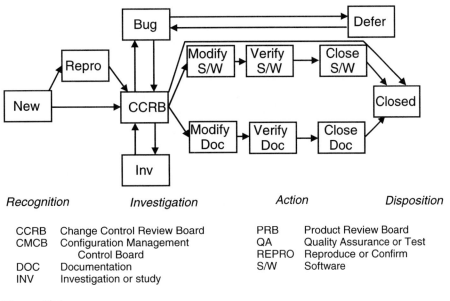

Recognition   *Investigation*   *Action*   *Disposition*

CCRB	Change Control Review Board	PRB	Product Review Board
CMCB	Configuration Management	QA	Quality Assurance or Test
	Control Board	REPRO	Reproduce or Confirm
DOC	Documentation	S/W	Software
INV	Investigation or study		

Figure 10.1
Information flow for a bug under the IEEE 1044 standard.

The information flow diagram, shown in Figure 10.1, helps to order the subprocesses within each phase and how they fit into an overall process. Typical configuration management and production control groups, found in many companies today, can support this bug tracking process comfortably. In order for a bug to be closed, both the software and its documentation, including requirements, design, detailed design, and users manual, must be synchronized.

Path Coverage Testing

There are several definitions of path testing within software engineering. The most traditional definition of a path is that it is the execution order of source statements starting at entry or conditional branch and ending at the next conditional branch or exit. This has been called a DD-path, which stands for decision-to-decision path. The rapid testing approach recognizes the impracticality of attempting complete DD-path testing coverage, but, instead, recommends that the development team utilize a software tool that automates documenting all the DD-paths in a source. Also, as part of unit or integration testing, they should prioritize their testing to include a higher-risk subset of DD-paths.

The computer listing in Figure 10.2 was created in the 1979–1981 time-frame when the author was developing the Software Testing System (STS), an internal product development by Texas Instruments, Incorporated, that was funded by the Advanced Software Technology (AST) organization. STS was a software tool that enabled the structured Fortran programmer to see an enumeration of the paths within their code. To the tester it was a helpful tool to determine the appropriate settings of program variables that were required to move the program counter through a particular DD-path. STS had the capability of installing probes into each DD-path. During execution these probes logged the DD-path numbers as the paths were executed. After a series of executions, the log files were analyzed to report that DD-path(s) had not been executed up to the point of the report. If an abnormal termination occurred during execution, the log file with its path trace was combined with the line-numbered source file, enabling a report to be generated listing the source in the reverse order of execution. This file was very useful to debuggers since they could bring it up in an editor and search for variable names that were involved with causing the termination.

In order to read the path listing, you need the following definitions:

- <line number> is a tool-induced numbering of every line of code
- JUMP <line number> means some form of GO TO, ENDDO, or IF construct
- THRU <line number> includes all lines until reaching the <line number>
- <line number> A means the THEN part of the IF construct
- <line number> B means the ELSE part of the IF construct
- EOP indicates the termination of the path

Also, in reading through this computer listing, note that a pair of cyclomatic complexity numbers are calculated and listed. The left number is the one defined by Thomas J. McCabe (1976). The right number is the complexity number defined by Glenford J. Myers (1977) in response to McCabe's original journal publication. Remember that the cyclomatic number is the minimum number of individual executions of a module that will be required to exercise each line of code at least once. This information can be an aid in cost-estimating a testing effort. You might challenge yourself to find all the paths in one of these modules and weigh the value of this software tool with respect to the amount of effort it saves.

Most computer scientists agree that over half the number of bugs that are found in new code are there as a result of bugs in the logic of the code. Path testing highlights the logic of the code and allows the tester to focus on testing the correctness of the logic. However, it should be only one weapon in the testing arsenal, since the lines of code within the THEN part of an IF construct can still have bugs that can lead the program to have wrong answers or terminate abnormally.

Another consideration is that many paths in delivered software are *dead paths*. It's a fact that few testers realize. Developers who design in debug code typically control its execution by a variable that is defaulted to a value that means no-debug. Upon the release of their code, the default remains in this no-debug state throughout the customer's use. The next section gives a priority-based scheme of mitigating the amount of work required to perform complete DD-path testing.

```
        ADVANCED SOFTWARE TECHNOLOGY -- FORTRAN SOFTWARE TESTING SYSTEM
--  (STS)
        12/08/80                TIME: 12:40:34              PAGE:     1

        THE OPTIONS IN EFFECT FOR THIS RUN OF STS STATIC ANALYZER ARE:

            LIST      = INPUT
            SCANONLY  = NO
            APPEND    = NO
            TYPE      = BOTH
            TIMEFIO   = NO
            DOPTION   = NO
            COPY      = YES


    1* C    THIS PROGRAM WILL SPLIT A FILE WITH <REP CARDS IN IT TO A
DIRECTORY
    2* C    AND LIST THE MEMBER NAMES OF ALL THE FILES CREATED.
    3* C
    4* C    UNIT5 -- INPUT (PARM1)
    5* C    UNIT6 -- OUTPUT DIRECTORY (PARM2)
    6* C    UNIT7 -- LIST (PARM3)
    7* C
    8*       IMPLICIT INTEGER*2 (A-Z)
    9*       LOGICAL HEQ,HNE,FIRST,NEWMEM,GETYNO,ASCII
   10*       DIMENSION CARD(80),PATH80(80),PATH40(40),CHARS(4),OLDMEM(4)
   11*       DATA CBB,FIRST,ASCII/2H  ,.TRUE.,.FALSE./
   12*       DATA LESSTH,R,E,P/2H< ,2HR ,2HE ,2HP /
   13* 1000 FORMAT(80A1)
   14*       CALL SCIINT(IERR)
   15* C
   16* C         OPENFL( LUNO,PARM,ACCESS,BKSZ )
   17* C
   18*       CALL OPENFL(5,1,1,80)
   19*       CALL OPENFL(7,3,3,80)
```

```
20*        ASCII=GETYNO(4,IERR)
21*        CALL BANNER(ASCII)
22*        CALL GETDIR(PATH80,NDEX,2)
23*        NDEXM2=NDEX-2
24*        WRITE(7,5000) (PATH80(I),I=1,NDEXM2)
25*        WRITE(7,6000)
26* 5000 FORMAT('   THE OUTPUT DIRECTORY',/,1X,79A1)
27* 6000 FORMAT(//,'   FILE WITHIN OUTPUT DIRECTORY       NUMBER
RECORDS')
28*        NRECS=0
29*        RECCNT=0
30*
31*
32*
33*
34* 1     CONTINUE
35*        DO INDEX I=1,80
36*        CARD(I)=CBB
37*        END DO
38*        READ(5,1000,END=100) CARD
39*        IF(ASCII) CALL EBCDIC(2,CARD,0)
40* C      WRITE(10,1000) CARD
41*        NEWMEM=(CARD(1).EQ.LESSTH.AND.CARD(2).EQ.R.AND.CARD(3).EQ.E.
                                          MODULE NAME --
MAIN
        ADVANCED SOFTWARE TECHNOLOGY -- FORTRAN SOFTWARE TESTING SYSTEM
--(STS)
        DATE: 12/08/80              TIME: 12:40:44              PAGE:      2

42*        &AND.CARD(4).EQ.P)
43* C      WRITE(10,111) CHARS,NDX,LEN
44* 111  FORMAT(' AT 111 '4A2,2X,2I10)
45*        IF(FIRST.AND.(.NOT.NEWMEM))
46*        THEN
47*        WRITE(7,1500)
48* 1500 FORMAT(' ERROR: FIRST RECORD IS NOT A <REP CARD')
49*        CALL ENDFIL(7)
50*        STOP
51*        END IF
52*        IF(NEWMEM)
53*        THEN
54*        NDX=5
55*        CALL HFIELD(CARD,NDX,CHARS,80,LEN,CODE)
56*        IF (.NOT.FIRST)
57*        THEN
58*        CALL ENDFIL(6)
59*        NRECS=NRECS+RECCNT
60*        WRITE(7,7000)OLDMEM,RECCNT
61* 7000 FORMAT(10X,4A2,26X,I5)
62*        RECCNT=0
63*        END IF
64*        DO INDEX I=1,4
```

```
65*       OLDMEM(I)=CHARS(I)
66*       END DO
67*       CALL SETMEM(CHARS,PATH80,NDEX,PATH40,3,6)
68*       FIRST=.FALSE.
69*       DO INDEX I=1,80
70*       CARD(I)=CBB
71*       END DO
72*       READ(5,1000,END=100) CARD
73*       IF(ASCII) CALL EBCDIC(2,CARD,0)
74* C     WRITE(10,1000) CARD
75*       END IF
76*       WRITE(6,1000)(CARD(I),I=1,80)
77*       RECCNT=RECCNT+1
78*       GO TO 1
79* 100   CALL CLOSEW(5,IERR)
80*       CALL ENDFIL(6)
81*       NRECS=NRECS+RECCNT
82*       WRITE(7,7000)OLDMEM,RECCNT
83*       WRITE(7,3000) NRECS
84* 3000 FORMAT(//,'  THE TOTAL NUMBER OF RECORDS SPLIT WAS:',I5)
85*       CALL ENDFIL(7)
86*       STOP
87*       END
```

(STS) -- STATIC ANALYSIS FOR MODULE "MAIN   ", BEGINNING AT LINE 14

```
        PATH   1:  14       THRU37      EOP
        PATH   2:  37       JUMP35      THRU37      EOP
```

MODULE NAME --

MAIN

ADVANCED SOFTWARE TECHNOLOGY -- FORTRAN SOFTWARE TESTING SYSTEM
-- (STS)
        DATE: 12/08/80   TIME: 12:40:56
PAGE: 3

```
        PATH   3:  37       THRU38      EOP
        PATH   4:  38       JUMP79      THRU86      EXIT
        PATH   5:  38       THRU39      EOP
        PATH   6:  39     A THRU39    B THRU45      EOP
        PATH   7:  39     A THRU45      EOP
        PATH   8:  45       JUMP52      EOP
        PATH   9:  45       THRU50      EXIT
        PATH  10:  52       JUMP76      THRU78      JUMP34      THRU37
                            EOP
        PATH  11:  52       THRU56      EOP
        PATH  12:  56       JUMP64      THRU66      EOP
        PATH  13:  56       THRU66      EOP
        PATH  14:  66       JUMP64      THRU66      EOP
        PATH  15:  66       THRU71      EOP
        PATH  16:  71       JUMP69      THRU71      EOP
```

```
        PATH   17:   71       THRU72      EOP
        PATH   18:   72       JUMP79      THRU86      EXIT
        PATH   19:   72       THRU73      EOP
        PATH   20:   73     A THRU73    B THRU78      JUMP34      THRU37
                              EOP
        PATH   21:   73     A THRU78      JUMP34      THRU37      EOP


        STS CYCLOMATIC COMPLEXITY INTERVAL = (   11 ,     9 )


                MODULE NAME -- MAIN



        ADVANCED SOFTWARE TECHNOLOGY -- FORTRAN SOFTWARE TESTING
   SYSTEM -- (STS)
        DATE: 12/08/80              TIME: 12:40:59          PAGE:     4

     88*        SUBROUTINE BANNER(ASCII)
     89*        IMPLICIT INTEGER*2 (A-Z)
     90*        LOGICAL ASCII
     91*        DIMENSION DATI(8),NDX(1),VAL(2,2)
     92*        DATA NOPTS,VAL/1,2H Y,2H N,2HES,2HO /
     93*        DO INDEX I=1,NOPTS
     94*        NDX(I)=2
     95*        END DO
     96*        IF(ASCII)NDX(1)=1
     97*        CALL DT(DATI)
     98*        WRITE(7,1000)DATI
     99*        WRITE(7,2000) ((VAL(NDX(I),J),J=1,2),I=1,NOPTS)
    100*        RETURN
    101* 1000   FORMAT('   SPLIT UTILITY',/,
    102*     &       '   DATE:',4A2,', TIME:'4A2,
    103*     &    //,'   OPTIONS SELECTED')
    104* 2000   FORMAT('       CONVERT EBCDIC->ASCII=',2A2,/)
    105*        END
   (STS) -- STATIC ANALYSIS FOR MODULE "BANNER  ", BEGINNING AT LINE 93

        PATH   22:   93       THRU95      EOP
        PATH   23:   95       JUMP93      THRU95      EOP
        PATH   24:   95       THRU96      EOP
        PATH   25:   96     A THRU96    B THRU100     EXIT
        PATH   26:   96     A THRU100     EXIT


        STS CYCLOMATIC COMPLEXITY INTERVAL = (   3 ,     3 )

        THIS IS A NORMAL COMPLETION OF STS -- STATIC ANALYZER RELEASE 3.1
```

Figure 10.2
Automated path listings and cyclomatic complexities from the Software Testing System (STS).

Use-Case Testing

For object-oriented programming, a design technique called use-case design (see example in Figure 10.3) is often in use today. Use cases depict what entities interact with one another, based upon a scenario. Popular scenarios of use occur in most designs. The strong mapping of scenarios to use cases allows us to conclude that there is a set of popular use cases within a design. John D. Musa (1993) noted this relationship and paired usage frequency data with use case charts. The concept of usage frequency data can be expressed as a relative value by dividing each by the total of the usage frequencies and expressing it as a percent. With this information about the design of a product, rapid testers can budget more than 50% of their test case development and test case implementation time on less than 50% of the code that has the highest usage frequencies, that is, the popular use cases.

Another similar approach is to probe the DD-paths, as described in the preceding section. After the probes are in, run a large number of test cases and stack execution logs of the paths, executed from run to run, by probe number. The volume of tests should be specified and implemented based upon the requirements, information flows, and experience with legacy systems in

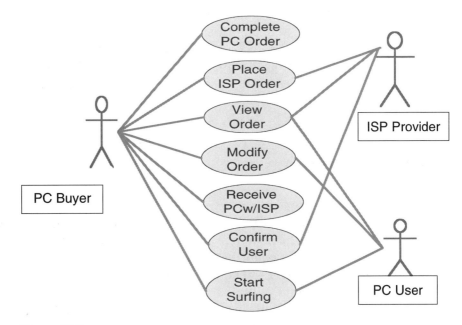

Figure 10.3
Use-case design example—Registering an ISP with a PC's purchase.

production, should such exist. The DD-paths whose probe has the highest hit rates form an empirical forecast of the main usage frequencies. The process described here qualifies as a rapid testing technique, since it is targeted at saving time and increasing productivity of finding bugs. What would be worse than to have several testers developing test cases for several paths in a new piece of code, only to discover the code is *dead code* and therefore cannot be tested, or that the new code was *live code* that wasn't executed except under some very obtuse condition. What a waste of time and resources for zero productivity, since no bugs will be found.

The use-case design, along with the estimated usage frequency of each, provides a rank order of the priorities for the test cases, which are to be based on the individual use cases or threads of associated use cases. Test case development and the order in which the tests are executed should be based on these priorities in order to optimize test resources and testing productivity.

Before applying the use-case approach to testing, the testers and developers must work together to ensure that the use cases match the requirements and the code. Letting requirements documentation get unsynchronized with the code has been a frequent audit finding for many software development projects. In some organizations, software documentation is not valued as highly as user documentation. If the use cases that were developed from the original requirements are given to the test staff without validating them against current requirements, volatility in the original requirements may have occurred. In that case, if the testers use the use-case information, they might get false detections of bugs, and, upon further investigation find out that the code satisfies the requirements, but not the use-case information. Bugs in test case design and test results will be likely and test case development effort will be wasted.

Bebugging/Mutation

Bebugging, which is a form of program mutation, is a way of determining the effectiveness of the testing strategies that are being taken on a project. Buy-in of both the testers and the developers should be won before launching a bebugging effort. How would you like to be able to answer the development manager's often-asked question: "How close are we to finding most of the bugs in this build?" Usually, the test manager's comeback is: "How many of those little bugs would we be looking for?" The primary test progress metric should be: number of bugs found divided by the number of latent bugs to be found, expressed as a percentage. The issue with this metric is that at the outset of the testing effort, both numerator and denominator of the metric are unknown quantities.

Bebugging is the act of changing the software to create bugs, creating a build that is tested by the test team, and then comparing the bugs found against the created bugs to determine test effectiveness. The ratio between the created bugs found divided by the number of created bugs should be the same as the ratio between the bugs found divided by the number of latent bugs in the product, which will be an estimation of the test progress metric introduced in the previous paragraph.

Rapid testing organizations find that the bebugging approach can speed up the testing process by defining the stopping condition. In fact, a high degree of creativity can be applied to the creation process for the inserted bugs. If each of the created bugs is typed according to the historic bug model of similar developments, using the same development language, and if the found bugs are typed the same way, analysis of the test progress metric can be applied by type. Not only can the test status report definitively answer that question: "How close are we to finding most of the bugs in this build?" but now it can say "We've found most of the logic bugs in the program and now we are developing additional test cases that focus on the robustness of the error handlers. Similarly, each of the created bugs can be typed by severity level, and if each of the found bugs is typed by severity level, the test status report can definitively answer the question: "How close are we to finding most of the bugs in this build?" but now it can say "We've found most of the SEV 1 and SEV 3 bugs and now we are developing additional test cases that focus on the SEV 2 and SEV 4 bugs."

Analogous approaches to program mutation can be created for non-source bugs, including bad data in a database, bad communication lines, corrupted communication data, bad user input data, bad process-to-process interface, and so on. Program mutation is a strong tool to use by a development organization that is reusing source code from another project. Part of the process for reusing source code is to place it under maintenance. Bebugging can be used to test the progress of this maintenance effort by providing test goals for development of new test cases.

Tracing/Tracebacks/Snap Dumps/Post-Mortem Dumps

Testers can benefit from some of the tools that exist and are used during today's developments. Four of these are traces, tracebacks, snap dumps, and post-mortem dumps. Older programmers from mainframe days may think this section will be addressing how to print or read system diagnostics, including hexadecimal sys-dumps, that a systems programmer uses, along with the linkage edit mapping to determine the nature, location, and source-level cause of a system bug. No, while we are using the same terms, we will be defining techniques based on today's applications and tools. For example, in a transaction-based software program, designers often design in a transaction trace function that can be selectively turned on by any user who picks this option in their profile. This option creates a trace file with transaction inputs and outputs, plus formatted snap dumps of query data. Of course, the tester should test the system without this option turned on, since the user's default is to not run with this trace on, but if there seems to be something wrong with a transactional application, the tester should see if there is a transaction trace option, select it, and save the log so that the bug can be repeatable when it is diagnosed. This trace should be attached with the bug report in order to help show the environment that exhibits the bug.

When a rapid tester finds a bug, it's not enough to scribble, "I couldn't download a file," on a notepad or put it in an email directed to the author of the code. Most testing trainers tell you to separate the jobs of testing from developing, so that the tester is a so-called *independent* tester and is responsible only for finding bugs. To such independent testers, it is the developer who is responsible for removing bugs. The spirit of rapid testing is to integrate these roles to the point that it speeds up the finding and fixing process. Rapid testers capture screen shots into a Microsoft Word file, and intersperse operational notes or test script pointers in between these screen shots, as shown in Figure 10.4.

The example in Figure 10.4 brings up the subject of a nonrepeatable bug. Several days after this bug report was sent, the tester repeated this test. The URL was found and the download was successful. The same client software worked at a later time. Does that mean that it was not a bug? No, it was a bug at the date and time the screen prints were taken. The fact that the bug was not in the client software simply means that it was fixed on the server and then all worked as designed. Client/server designs have distributed the bugs across the two code bases and maintenance of such designs is different from the maintenance of standalone software. These differences will be the subject of a later section.

Breakpointing/Patching

A *breakpoint* is defined as a way of stopping the progress of the program counter at some point in the source code. Debuggers, when applied to assembly language programs, enable breakpoints to be set in order to get

Bug Report

Time/Date: 9:40PM 6/13/2001

Report Date: 9:50PM 6/13/2001 via email to support@groove.com

Nature of the failure:

From the Groove Maintenance Update screen, I selected "Update Groove" and received an error message that the URL could not be found. This was repeated three times and the following documentation was captured on the fourth try.

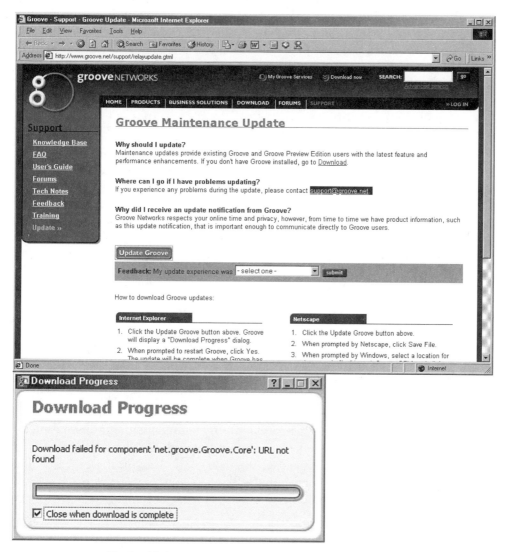

Figure 10.4
Annotated screen captures.

feedback on memory and register status in order to set up data in memory or to collect memory information that might help find a fix to a bug. *Patching* is another assembly language programming technique in which a branch instruction is overwritten, or patched, in order to branch to a patch area within the addressable space of the program, where it executes some auxiliary code, before branching back to the instruction following the first branch. Bugs used to be fixed in this manner in large assembly language programs, for example, Lotus 1-2-3.

How do breakpointing and patching apply to today's software testing? The attraction of these techniques is their speed of diagnosing and fixing a bug, especially one that is holding up testing. Sometimes, a tester finds a bug that prevents further testing in the area of this bug. This is referred to as a blocking bug, as defined in Chapter 5. If such a bug is not fixed as soon as possible then testing productivity could become stalled. For over 95% of the bugs, which are captured and reported to the development team for fixing, waiting for the CCRB to meet and rule on the priority and schedule of resources to be applied to each bug is quite acceptable. But for the less than 5% of the blocking bugs, there needs to be a team effort to determine a quick way around the blocked threads. A developer can provide a temporary fix to the offending object, followed by a partial linkage edit, in order to place this interim/modified build back into the hands of the testers. This temporary fix will be reimplemented and tested again in another upcoming full build, but in the interim, the test team can remain highly productive in finding more bugs downstream from the point of the blocking bug's location.

Data Flow Testing

One way of forming a test case for data flow bugs through a non-user-interactive portion of a program being tested is to make a baseline copy of the start-up data files. Then, verify that run after run, the output results are the same, as long as the program starts from this baseline copy of the start-up data files. Finally, insert probes into the source that log a unique probe number after each I/O statement in the program. Compare the probe logs from run to run to determine whether the flow through the probes is the same for each test that starts with the baseline copy of the start-up data files. This test case will then be armed to ensure that the same data flow still occurs in a new build.

Data flow testing that is more common is the approach used for transaction-oriented applications, for example, a business order entry, order processing, manufacturing, billing, shipping, and returns cycle. The data from each test transaction can be traced through all of these processes and validated by interim test results between each of the processes.

For the testing of modifications of legacy systems, data flow testing is easily planned and accomplished, since snapshots can be taken before and after each of the processes first using the legacy system. Then later when the modifications are introduced into a new build and the same data is entered into the new build, new results can be compared (sometimes automatically) to the prior legacy test results.

Another example of a blocking bug that also exemplifies data flow is the statement:

```
IF (I > J) THEN B(I) = A(J) ELSE B(I) = 0 ENDIF.
```

If the greater-than operator (>) is the bug and it should have been less than or equal to (< =), then the wrong subset of B was set to zero. All computations that are downstream from this IF statement may operate with these zeroed values of B, when they needed to operate with the non-zeroed-out values copied from A. This may mean that all test results that depend on B will be wrong, so the tester cannot determine whether the program has a bug or not following this IF statement. The tester could follow the flow of data for all values of I and J or a subset. Knowing the flow of data through multiple processes enables the tester to capture interim test results, thereby speeding the process of detecting and then recreating bugs.

Testing for Memory Leaks

A memory leak is a type of bug that causes an application to fill up the virtual memory, which is managed by the operating system. Several modern languages allocate the application's stack and heap in virtual memory to allow more efficient and convenient management of temporary memory. There are other names used for memory leaks, namely, memory aliasing, smash the stack, memory smash, overrun screw, and others. The root cause for a memory leak bug is failure to reclaim virtual memory that is dynamically requested by the application. There is no external repair that can be made for a memory leak, except to avoid the operational area of the application that causes the memory leak. Most technical support personnel simply suggest terminating the application or rebooting the operating system. Figure 10.5 gives an example of an announcement from Microsoft's technical support group regarding a memory leak in the retail version of Windows 95.

Memory Leak in Windows 95 Kernel Using Windows Sockets

- **SYMPTOMS**

  –When you run a program that uses Windows Sockets in Windows 95, a gradual increase in the memory used by the operating system may occur over time, especially if the program opens and closes a large number of sockets.

- **CAUSE**

  –There is an error in the Windows 95 Kernel (Kernel32.dll) that prevents the proper freeing of certain small data structures associated with Windows Socket processes and allocated sockets. Over time, these small memory leaks can result in a significant loss of available memory.
  Note that you can free the resources associated with a program by closing the program. If you quit and restart Windows 95, the memory is freed.

Figure 10.5
Retail version of Windows 95 with OS memory leak.

Microsoft placed workarounds and fixes for these memory leak bugs on their respective download Web sites.

Typically, the memory leak is found in a small function that is written correctly for its *happy path*, but incorrectly for its *unhappy path*. If virtual memory allocation is accomplished at the start of the function, but a user entry causes a program interrupt, the error handler for the interrupt may not have been programmed to release the virtual memory. Whether the memory allocation is large or small, the repetitive nature of the function may ultimately cause virtual memory to be exhausted and the program can no longer function. Particularly vulnerable are applications that run 24/7. Even the smallest leak ultimately will cause a program or system crash.

Memory leaks are especially hard to find in an object-oriented (OO) source, but by tracing the execution and observing the *Object Histogram*, the developer can see which object creates and releases memory and which calls are made between these memory manager calls. In the Java runtime, one can add the command line option *–tracepopulation* before the program in question is loaded for execution. Remember to apply static testing techniques once the leaking object is isolated to speed up the root cause. It is more important to understand the design and any potential interruptions that could happen in the *happy path* that might cause the object to miss freeing the memory. For C++, there is a *debug_malloc* object, which can be very useful to track down a memory leak. While memory leaks are not intermittent, they show up on small memory diskless systems way before they show up on configurations that have larger memory and large disk systems that are not rebooted frequently, for example, server-based applications.

A rapid testing tip is that once a developer has found and fixed a memory leak, then he or she should inspect the new code to help look for other memory leak candidate bugs in the same area. It seems to be traditional to treat the first-found cause as being the only bug, while overlooking the other ways that the same code does not free dynamically allocated memory can occur. This rapid testing tip is also counter to most testing trainers and configuration manager's admonitions to only fix the problem identified by the bug report. If you're employing rapid testing tips, you have to break the mold some times and just get the application redesigned and reimplemented.

Human–Computer Interface Testing

The human-computer interface (HCI) of today's computers may involve a wide assortment of peripheral devices like a keyboard, keypad, mouse, stylus, touch-screen monitor, voice, scanner, and many more. Also, for large production control systems running on a mainframe computer, there are likely to be many persons required to operate the program, each having his/her own personal computer that runs a terminal emulation to the mainframe. Test planning is crucial to the coordination of HCI testing, because it may be the only testing that views the product from the exact view of a user. Many of the user's functional requirements are testable from the HCI of the product, and that is the focus of system testing.

There is a word of caution that should be considered when using an HCI that tests the user-eye-view. If your test team starts testing with the system test phase and uses the HCI exclusively, your testing scope will be very limited. HCI testing is only one of many ways the rapid test team searches for bugs. In fact, typically, the HCI testing process is not very productive in finding even the most basic bugs, because it is more of a data-flow-based pathway through the product, and this pathway has already had a lot of unit testing performed with well-designed scenarios.

In organizing the HCI testing, it is always valuable to have a database administrator plus several end-users working with members of the test team. They can develop input test cases, test scripts, and test results that ensure that input data is screened and then stored correctly into the appropriate record(s) in the database for future processing and reporting. They can also develop output test cases, test scripts, and test results that ensure the output data is formatted and communicated to the appropriate media or communications buffers.

End-users are very helpful in working with the test group to design a valuable acceptance test. In larger organizations, there is a job function called business analyst. A business analyst is typically a surrogate end-user, who is paid from project funds and who fashions HCI tests to assess a software build's acceptance. The acceptance testing performed by the end-users will typically be scenario-driven and will exercise only happy paths. When end-users develop test cases, test scripts, and test results, there may not be the same rigor that is used within the project, but, regardless, the bugs that they find are documented by the test team, fixed and retested by the test team, and then tested by the end-users in a follow-up to the acceptance test. Testing performed by business analysts, on the other hand, should include both the unhappy and happy path testing, in order to ensure that the software build's robustness is high and that test cases, test scripts, and test results cover primary use cases.

Load Performance Testing

A cost-effective way of scaling applications is to employ distributed computing. There are two main components of a networked architecture, namely, server and client. A network can have thousands of servers and tens of thousands of desktop personal computers, mobile laptop computers, wireless and handheld clients; each with connectivity to the servers via the network. Client/server designs are prevalent and much of the testing that goes on today is involved with the client/server/network environment. Security and access rights are testing considerations that are of a systems nature, rather than an application nature. Replication processes may be required for databases so that an application running in one city/country receives the same results for a query on a database, as the same application running concurrently in another city/country.

Testing client/server applications requires a thorough understanding of the software's architecture, including data warehouse servers, communication pathway characteristics, and load-balancing servers. Frequently, establishing test data is of primary importance to the success of the testing effort. Several examples are given in this section, but analogies exist in other applications as well.

In testing communications-rich applications, there are two approaches that should be used, namely, test patterns and randomized data streams. If the focus is on the reliability of the communication pathway, then pattern testing is applicable. Detecting an aberration in a repetitive graphical pattern is much easier than looking at a listing of data values to determine if any are in error. Electronics engineers use oscilloscopes in a similar manner, looking at test frequencies to ensure that a connection or process is operating properly. Testers should take advantage of this technique in a start-up self-test process for a communications pathway. Once the communication pathway passes a start-up self-test process, then a known set of transactional data can be passed through the pathway with the intent to measure the correctness of the execution, as well as the performance of the transactional processor. Output data, stored in output records or log files, can be automatically compared to expected results. This sort of test is typically designed as a regression for the transactional system, something that is constantly updated as new or revised transactions are added to the production system.

Client/server applications support a test design option in which a high-tempo emulator server, along with a test storage emulator, is programmed/loaded in order to exercise a bank of operational servers that are front-ended by a load-balancing server, as depicted in Figure 10.6. The high-tempo emulator server forces transactional data through an alternate communication pathway to the load-balancing server, which, in turn, fans out these transactions across the bank of operational servers at a tempo higher than normal operational rates. Bottlenecks in performance can be uncovered by this test. If there is a feedback pathway from the test storage emulator back to the high-tempo emulator server, automated comparisons can be made between the production server's transactional outputs versus the expected outputs of the tests. This closed-loop system can be used as a preproduction test of new builds before they are implemented into production. It applies directly to most Web applications as well.

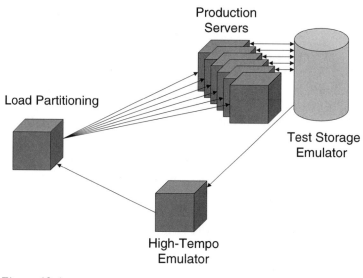

Figure 10.6
High-tempo emulator server plus test storage emulator exercise production
client/server application.

CASE STUDY

TEST DATA CREATION (GARY COBB)

While I was in a Software Engineering Process Group (SEPG), a test engineer approached me to ask whether I knew anything about Coriolis forces. I acknowledged that I knew it was a force caused by the earth's rotation, which had an effect on any moving body on or above the earth's surface, causing it to drift sideways from its course. We talked about how it is the Coriolis forces that cause ships and airplanes to drift to the right of their heading in the northern hemisphere or to the left of their heading in the southern hemisphere. It also is a motion driver for ocean and air currents in the sea and air, respectively.

The test engineer asked if I would help create some test data to be used to feed a series of test cases that he was responsible for to be applied to a newly developed shipboard meteorological forecasting system. I said yes, and decided to use a spreadsheet approach to develop the test data. One rationale for choosing a spreadsheet is that all numeric computations are carried out in 64-bit floating point arithmetic. Figure 10.7 shows all of the test data that the test engineer needed to develop his tests.

There is a distinct advantage to using a spreadsheet like this one for developing data for test cases; once these calculations are validated, they can be reused to calculate the test results for other, in this case, areas of interest (AOI).

G E O S T R O P I C   W I N D   C O M P U T A T I O N
D U E   T O   C O R I O L I S

    CONSTANTS:

    EARTH RADIUS (3437.911nm*1852.44m/nm)   6368523.85284 m
    EARTH'S GRAVITY   9.8 m/sec**2
    EARTH'S ANGULAR VEL. ("Omega")   7.2920E-05 per second

    DEFINE AREA OF INTEREST (AOI):

    CENTER OF AOI   C.LA   C.LO
    CENTER (DEGREES)   30.199998   -97.800000
    CORIOLIS FORCE AT CENTER OF AOI   7.3360E-05 per second
    AOI WIDTH (3200nm*1852.44m/nm)   5927808 m
    M=MESH=1/64   5788.875 m resolution
    GRID SIZE   1024 X 1024

DL = DELTA LONGITUDE (DEGREES) = (AOI WIDTH)/((PI/180)*(EARTH RADIUS))
    DL   53.330785596795 degrees

    AOI POINTS: x.LA   x.LO
    CENTER(C) (AUSTIN)   30.199998   -97.800000
    EAST(R.C.X)   30.199998   -124.465392
    NORTH(U.C.X)   56.865391   -97.800000
    WEST(L.C.X)   30.199998   -71.134607
    SOUTH (L.C.X)   3.534605   -97.800000

                                             MX   MY
    CENTER(C) (AUSTIN)   0   0.553340844437
    EAST(R.C.X)   -0.46539890067 0.553340844437
    NORTH(U.C.X)   0   1.212368963348
    WEST(L.C.X)   0.4653989006696 0.553340844437
    SOUTH (L.C.X)   0   0.061729665232

ANGLE SUBTENDED BY ARC 100 NM LONG ON THE EARTH SURFACE:
100nm*(1852.44m/nm)/(earth radius (m))*(180/PI)
    Angle(deg) =   1.6665870498998 degrees

    SCALE FACTOR(SF)= MD/SD = ABS(U.C.MY-L.C.MY)/SY.MAX
    SF =   0.00112477 (earth radii)

    AOI CORNERS: x.LA   x.LO
    U.LE.X   29.36670447505 -96.9667059751
    U.RI.X   31.03329152495 -98.6332930249
    L.LE.X   9.36670447505   -96.9667059751
    L.RI.X   28.5334109501   -98.6332930249

	MX	MY
U.LE.X	-0.575319649058	1.212368963348
U.RI.X	0.5753196490579	1.212368963348
L.LE.X	-0.575319649058	0.061729665232
L.RI.X	0.5753196490579	0.061729665232

BOX CENTERS (DEGREES):	x.LA	x.LO
ENTER BOX	33.3166666667	113.7500000000
EAST BOX	33.3166666667	111.6166666667
NORTH BOX	35.0833333333	113.7500000000
WEST BOX	33.3166666667	115.8166666667
SOUTH BOX	31.5833333333	113.7500000000

	MX	MY
CENTER BOX	0	0.617329479414
EAST BOX	-0.037233690709	0.617329479414
NORTH BOX	0	0.654613029744
WEST BOX	0	0.0360701378745
SOUTH BOX	0	0.581477015532

dX=ABS(DELTA LON.)*(EARTH RADIUS IN m)*COS(LAT.IN RAD.)*(PI/180)
East-West dX   390111.37991131 m

dY=ABS(DELTA LAT.)*((EARTH RADIUS IN m)*PI/180)
North-South dY   389030.98403348 m

Test Case 1. Assume following heights of the 300 Mb constant pressure
field:

CENTER BOX	9000
EAST BOX	9100
NORTH BOX	9100
WEST BOX	8900
SOUTH BOX	8900

GEOSTROPHIC WIND VECTOR COMPONENTS (Ug directed East, Vg directed North)
Ug = -(GRAVITY/(2*OMEGA*SIN(LAT.(RAD)))*(PARTIAL OF H WRT Y) =
Ug (in m/sec)   -62.72030217113   -51.39

Vg = (GRAVITY/(2*OMEGA*SIN(LAT.(RAD)))*(PARTIAL OF H WRT X)
Vg (in m/sec)   62.89448561333   51.69

Figure 10.7
Coriolis test data.

Platform Configuration Testing

Variations in configurations create complexity in testing. Peripheral devices can be one cause. With each of these peripheral devices comes the vendor's driver, chosen from an ensemble of candidate drivers for use with the appropriate operating system. Personal computers are that, personal. Testing an application for all personal computers has become too costly, due to the complexity and expense of operating systems and their peripherals. The rapid tester should treat this like path testing, where completeness is not feasible, and apply the test cases to those operating system/peripherals combinations that are most prevalent in the user base for the application.

In order to manage an ensemble of test platforms, a technique of developing a test configuration matrix speeds the planning and implementation of the testing process, while also organizing the reporting of results. Table 10.3 suggests a format for the test configuration matrix. The items listed under the H1 or H2 columns should have lengthy specifications on file describing version numbers for all firmware and switch settings for any hardware reconfigurable parts.

If the matrix of platforms is large and complex, this test configuration matrix can become a database with dated transactions and logs to provide configuration control. Inspections can be held at a given frequency that

Table 10.3
Test Configuration Matrix

Id.	Components	H1	H2	Others (add columns)
1	Hardware	PC-100, Pentium III	PC-100, Pentium III	
2	Operating System	Linux 7.0 Windows	Win98SE, SP-2	
3	Keyboard	Happy Hacking Lite	Standard Querty	
4	Keypad	——	——	
5	Mouse	IntelliPoint	Three button	
6	Stylus	——	——	
7	Touch-screen	HP	——	
8	Voice	——	Via	
9	Scanner	Plustek	——	
10	Modem	Psion V.90	Xircom 56 Baud	
11	Database	MS Access	Oracle 7.0	
12	Target of Testing	Build 2.4.3	Build 2.4.4	
13	Add more items by inserting additional rows			

Table 10.4

Basic Platform Requirements

ID	System Requirements
1	Personal computer with a Pentium 166 (or higher) processor is recommended
2	Microsoft Windows 95, 98, or NT
3	30 MB of free hard-disk space
4	At least 32 MB of free RAM
5	A keyboard and a pointing device
6	A CD-ROM drive (4x speed or faster recommended)
7	A 16-bit or TrueColor card
8	A sound card compatible with Microsoft Windows
9	MCI and video drivers
10	Printer (optional)
11	Internet access (optional)

accommodate the hardware volatility, targeted at answering the question: have we tested the software on the latest platforms that share the marketplace with the target software product? This test configuration matrix or database should be shared with all partners who share the responsibility for testing of the target software product.

When publishing the software product in a mass consumer market, it is typical to state the basic platform requirements. Table 10.4 gives an example of mass-market platform requirements. The information in this table is not adequate for inclusion in a test configuration matrix. For example, when specifying the operating system for a test configuration, the version and service pack level of the image should be included. Also, the hard disk should be listed with its manufacturer, firmware version, driver version, and any options. Testers should develop negative tests for several configurations that have missing or incompatible components in order to document the way in which the application handles each nonsupported configuration.

Summary

Along with the static testing techniques and tips presented in Chapter 9, Chapter 10 covered the complement set, namely, dynamic testing techniques and tips. Each test engineer should experiment with these techniques and tips to evaluate how each one applies to their testing targets. Writing up your own case studies of utilizing a new technique or tip and adding it to those in this chapter is a great idea. We have learned in this chapter that, even though many practitioners spend a great deal of time testing a target product from the user's-eye-view or GUI, there are a number of very important test cases to be developed around other aspects of a target product other than the GUI. Scalability, robustness, fast tempo, damaged platform environments, and accuracy of the results have been seen as fertile areas to find bugs in a target product. Executing the test cases in parallel requires coordination and, in some cases, a dedicated test coordinator. Using static testing techniques to test results to scrutinize them for possible bugs seems to be a wise expenditure of precious time during the last phase of the development.

Remember this, there is awe and often surprise that flows through the development organization upon hearing that their product has passed the acceptance test. It shouldn't be that way. Everybody on the development team should have taken on enough of the test responsibilities to be confident that the target product is sound, meets user requirements, and will make the enterprise much more successful in the future.

References

IEEE. (1993). IEEE Standard 1044, *IEEE Standard for Software Anomalies,* © 1993 IEEE, New York, NY.

Musa, John D. (1993). "Operational Profiles in Software-Reliability Engineering." *IEEE Software,* 14–19.

McCabe, Thomas J. (1976). "A Complexity Measure." *IEEE Transactions on Software Engineering.*

Myers, Glenford J. (1977). "An Extension to the Cyclomatic Measure of Program Complexity." *SIGPLAN Notices.*

Developing and Using Testing Metrics: Modeling and Forecasting Bugs

Topics Covered in the Chapter

▶ Definition of Metric and Measurement

▶ Using Standard Metrics to Make Improvements

▶ Metrics for Testing

▶ Project-Based Bug Model

▶ Software Error Estimation Program (SWEEP)

▶ Summary

▶ References

In planning a new project, someone always asks, "Where are some measurement data from our prior projects?" You may be asking, "What is the relationship between a plan and measurement data?" A plan is only helpful if it is within +/− 20% accurate in terms of cost to reality. Project measurement data are only helpful if they are applied to a project, which will be run under similar conditions to the previous project that created the measurement data.

Suppose you are the owner of a small ocean-going yacht, and you were planning a trip from Atlantic City, New Jersey, to the Bahamas. You would collect together the navigation maps of the Atlantic coastline, showing the traffic lanes, water depths, harbors, and lighthouses. You would choose your route. You would calculate, using the speed of the yacht and any speed limits that are noted on the navigation maps, how many days of travel will be required to get to the Bahamas. The work of planning requires calculations, using rates of consumption for the various supplies. You would need to decide how many people you plan to take on this trip. Interim results, like the number of days of travel, drives the number of breakfasts, lunches, or dinners that will be required for the number of persons that will be on board. With this plan, you would stock the yacht with a calculated number of gallons of fuel and drinking water, along with the appropriate amount of food and other supplies. This information is documented in a navigation plan, a dining plan, a manifest, and an itinerary.

At sea, the captain of the yacht will refer to the navigation plan, jotting down measurement data, such as the speed and direction that the yacht is traveling, and from this he calculates a time he and other crew should start looking for a particular harbor or lighthouse. This collection of measurement data has, as its purpose, the validation of the navigation plan against known locations. From this tracking against the measurement data and the validation points, the captain can answer the most typical questions, such as "Are we still on course?" and "Are we still on schedule?"

For software development projects, the planning process collects together the selected life cycle and its phases (like navigation maps and the route), the number of functional requirements (like the number of miles to be traversed), measurement data to support the number of lines of code to be generated per staff-hour (like the number of miles per hour estimated for the yacht), the staffing-by-month curve (like the route), and the milestones (like lighthouses and harbors).

When the development starts, the software lead jots down measurement data, for example, the number of use cases designed this week, the number of source lines of code developed this week, the number of bugs reported this week, the number of bugs closed this week, the percentage of total test cases run this week. The software lead also looks at the project plan and its schedule to prepare the answer to the most typical question: "Are we still on schedule?"

Chapter 11 deals with defining metrics and collecting and analyzing measurement data. Chapter 12 deals with estimating the required staffing and schedule for a standard life cycle, using a standard cost estimating model. Software development that uses the rapid testing paradigm is one that uses software metrics to collect and utilize measurement data from prior rapid testing projects in order to continuously improve its processes, quality, cost, and delivery schedule.

Definition of Metric and Measurement

A software metric is a standard way of measuring some attribute of the software development process. A measurement is numerical data that is collected and reported in the units defined by the metric. For example, if the metric is the number of latent bugs per thousand lines of code, then a set of three measurements would be: {Program A: 2.6 bugs/KLOC, Program B: 12.1 bugs/ KLOC, Program C: 5.8 bugs/KLOC}.

The primary benefits of deploying software metrics lie in:

- Sharing benchmark data with other software development projects
- Collecting status data in the same units across an organization to determine progress toward a goal
- Calibrating labor forecasts
- Estimating of development effort or schedule, based upon historical actuals
- Reporting process improvement trend data during formal reviews

Software measurement data must be taken or converted into quantifiable units of measure, as defined by the software metric. This data should relate to attributes of a software process, its products, or the development project's schedule or resources. Table 11.1 contains several example software metrics divided up into industry-standard categories.

One thing to learn early about software metrics is that there are thousands of possible software metrics; most of them take a lot of discipline and staff time to measure, and many of them are not cost-effective to a particular-sized development team. In general, choosing metrics from lists like the one in Table 11.1 can be a real minefield unless you adopt a very pragmatic process for defining and using metrics. Testing metrics are not an exception. The following case study gives a point of view of one of the authors and how he defined software metrics that satisfied the needs of the institution, without being a burden on any project within that institution. The term "institution" is intended to mean a collection of software development projects within the same general management leadership, say within a division of a larger company.

Table 11.1
Categories of Example Software Metrics

Category	Software Metric
Size	Total lines of code written Comment lines Total declarations Total blank lines Number of function points Number of objects
Productivity	Number of work hours spent on the project Number of work hours spent in each object Number of times each object is changed
Maintainability	Number of parameters passed to each object Number of methods per object Number of objects using a method Number of decision points in each object Control flow complexity of each object Lines of code in each object Lines of comment in each object Number of data-declarations in each object Number of direct branches in each object Number of input and output statements in each object
Bug tracking	Severity of each bug Location of each bug Way in which each bug is corrected Person responsible for each bug Number of lines affected by the bug creation Amount of time required to find a bug Amount of time required to fix a bug Number of attempts made to correct each bug Number of new bugs resulting from each bug correction
Quality	Total number of bugs Number of bugs in each object Average bugs per thousand lines of code Mean time between failures Number of compiler-detected bugs

CASE STUDY:

AN INSTITUTION'S METRICS PROGRAM (GARY COBB)

For about six years, the author was the coordinator of software metrics for a software organization with about 450 software engineers. As a member of the Software Engineering Process Group (SEPG), as defined by in the Software Engineering Institute's (SEI) Capability Maturity Model (CMM V1.1), I studied over 400 software metrics that are documented within the research papers of the SEI. Out of this research, I came to realize that there should be very few institutional-standard software metrics. The bulk of the metrics should be team-developed, phase-dependent metrics that are collected, analyzed, and used privately by the software development teams.

In defining a metrics program across several independent software development projects, I set up institutional standards for metrics that would be reported from all projects and analyzed by the SEPG, but also I set up a process for each project to define and tailor their own metrics that were not reported or shared with other projects. The standard set of four software metrics that was proposed, approved, and deployed across all software development projects in an organization is described in Table 11.2.

Measurement data for each of these software metrics are expected to be reported at formal reviews that are held at each major milestone of the development life cycle. These major milestones and their formal reviews follow the primary phases of the waterfall life cycle model, which include Preliminary Design (PD), Detailed Design (DD), Code and Unit Test (CUT), and Integration and System Test (IT). Figure 11.1 shows, as an example, a size metric chart, suitable for presenting at the end of CUT in a formal review. Often the size of a large system will be decomposed into its major subsystems, which are stack-bar charted into a composite bar graph like the one shown. In the example shown in the figure, there is a great deal of volatility in the size graph from phase to phase. Without getting into the details of the project, suffice it to say that the project had a reasonable estimate of size during the proposal

Table 11.2
Institutionwide Set of Software Metrics

Metric Name	Definition
SIZE	Number of thousands of equivalent source lines of code (KESLOC)
EFFORT	The number of nonadministrative staff members on the development project per month
SCHEDULE	The allocation of calendar months to the individual phases of the software development life cycle
QUALITY	The number of bugs per KESLOC

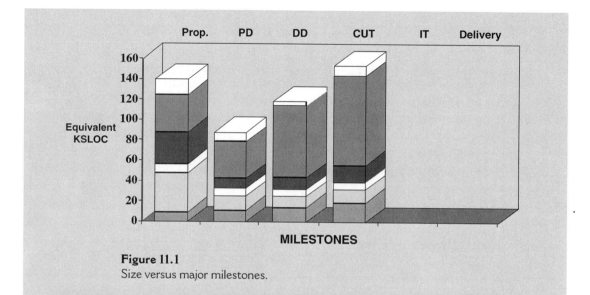

Figure 11.1
Size versus major milestones.

stage of the contract, but was led by management to attempt to reuse over 100,000 lines of code. Later in the project, after the PD phase, it was found that the reuse code was in fact not reusable. New estimates were developed and graphed, starting with the DD phase.

Figure 11.2 is the measurement data for the Effort Metric, showing actual headcount for the first four months (after the 16th week) of a software development plus weekly forecasts through the end of the project. For a large development, the measurement data are decomposed into effort by phase and/or activity, in this case, Preliminary Design (PD), Detailed Design (DD), Programming (Code), Unit Test (UT), System Test (Syst. Test), miscellaneous (Misc.), and the underlying activity of maintaining the software design (SW Des. Lang.). A natural question for the software development manager of the project associated with this Effort Metric graph would be: "What happened in month 4 of the contract when there appeared to be a shortage of staffing?" From the data, it appears that there was a staffing loss in weeks 12, 13, and 14, followed by an aggressive ramping-up of staffing. As a manager, you should challenge the cause of peculiar behavior in a metric such as this to determine whether it's a natural occurrence or an indicator of a problem that needs to be addressed now, rather than later.

Figure 11.3 shows a monthly staffing curve with the phases identified as Requirements (REQ), Preliminary Design (PD), Detailed Design (DD), Code and Unit Test (CUT), and Integration and System Test, combined (IT). Also, the formal reviews are labeled at the top of the graph at the end of the appropriate phase, namely, Award of Contract (AWD), Preliminary Design Review (PDR), Critical Design Review (CDR), Test Readiness Review (TRR), and Acceptance Review (Release). REQ shows negative months because no forecasting can occur until the requirements are known and the Award of Contract is typically the start of the first month of the development contract.

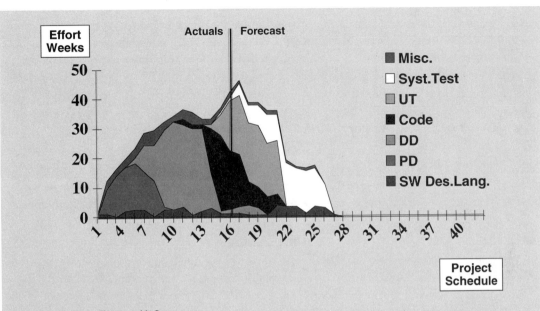

Figure 11.2
Effort (staff size) by week.

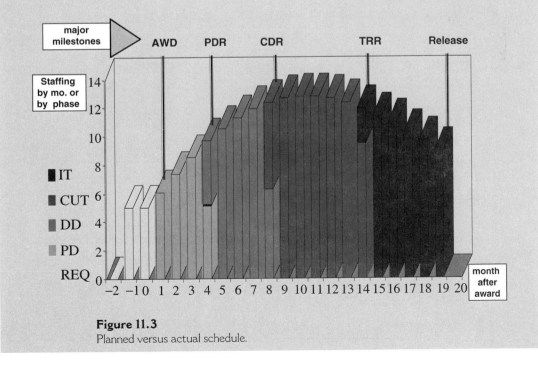

Figure 11.3
Planned versus actual schedule.

To understand the graphical presentation of the "planned date," notice that in month 4 of the graph, there is a transition from the PD to the DD phase about halfway through the month. This is where the planned PDR should take place. If you assume that this graph is made at the end of the project, the location of the major milestones indicate that this project was on schedule (in the same month as the phase-to-phase transition) at each of its milestones, including the release. The schedule metric is shown as an overlay of the staffing graph by shifting the formal review locations to show a rescheduled milestone, and hence a schedule change.

As a rule of thumb, schedule slips or advances can be treated as nominal if they are within 10% of the plan. In a 20-month project plan, it would be nominal for a completion between 18 and 22 months. Individual milestone schedule changes should be calibrated to the nearest half-month. By analogy, if this were a 20-week project plan, it would be nominal for a completion between 18 and 22 weeks, so that the individual milestone changes should be calibrated to the nearest half-week.

Figure 11.4 is an example of a graphic view of measurement data for the Quality metric, namely the number of bugs reported divided by the number of thousands of estimated source lines of code (KESLOC). The number of bugs per KELSOC, found during each phase of the software development life cycle, is reported at the end of each software development phase. In this case the phases are those of the waterfall software development life cycle, namely, Requirements (REQ), Preliminary Design (PD), Detailed Design (DD), Code and Unit Test

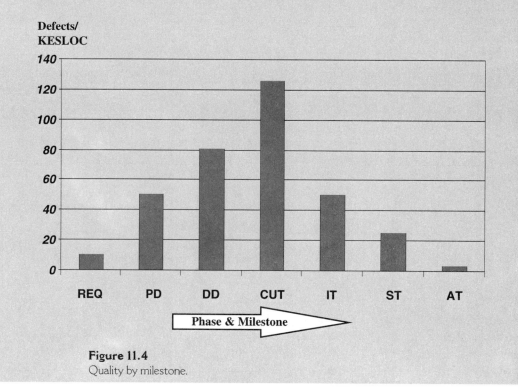

Figure 11.4
Quality by milestone.

(CUT), Integration Test (IT), System Test (ST), and Acceptance Test (AT). Note, for large programs, the bug counts could be charted by severity category and shown as a stack-bar chart. Analysis of the data values of this bar graph indicates that it is a rapid testing project. Why? Out of all the bugs that were found, 41% were found by static testing techniques prior to the start of the CUT phase, 36.3% were discovered during the CUT phase, and 22.7% were discovered by dynamic and static testing techniques after the CUT phase. The majority (77%) of the bugs were found and fixed at the most cost-effective point in the development life cycle, rather than saving them all to be found after the CUT phase.

As a summary for this case study, the SEPG and the institution's management found it extremely helpful to have all projects reporting the same four software metrics (Size, Effort, Schedule, and Quality), using the same definitions and units of measurement, and in a graphical format. The general manager and director-level personnel were able to see comparisons between one project and another and ask better questions of the software development managers.

Figure 11.5 depicts the two-tier metrics collection and reporting program that served this institution for over 5 years. The upper tier has been fully described at this point, with its reporting being done at primary milestones, for example, Preliminary Design Review (PDR), Critical Design Review (CDR), Test Readiness Review (TRR), and at the end of the Final Qualification Testing (FQT). The lower tier represents the project's own private metrics that are collected, analyzed, and reported to meet the special needs of the project.

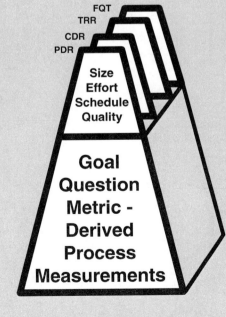

Figure 11.5
Two-tier metrics collection and reporting program.

In the next case study, we look at a technique of establishing a standard process in all software development projects within an institution. It is not a goal to make all the projects use the same units of measurement for their private metrics. Instead, it is a goal to give projects a standard way of going about defining software metrics, making the measurements, and reporting the results within the project's staff.

CASE STUDY:

DEPLOYING GQM FOR PROJECT METRICS (GARY COBB)

The software development teams were coached by the SEPG to use project-specific metrics that were tailored to meet project and customer needs. The teams were taught the Goal-Question-Metric (GQM) process, based on the research of Basili and Weiss (1984) at the University of Maryland. The GQM method consists of identifying the *goals* that stakeholders have for a metric, then asking the *questions* that measurements are intended to answer, and finally defining the normalized *metric* formula that will scale across developments of different sizes. Examples of testing-related questions that may be asked during the GQM process are:

- What is the quality of the software design?
- What is the rework rate being experienced?
- What is the bug report closure rate?
- How does bug rate compare to projections, target, and average?
- Which components will require additional testing?
- What are the predominant problem areas?

Professor Victor Basili from the University of Maryland invented the GQM paradigm along with Dr. David Weiss while working on projects at NASA Goddard Splice Flight Center in the late 1970s. They published their work on the GQM in 1984. Rini van Solingen and Egon Berghout (1999) further developed the GQM concepts and packaged them into a Quality Improvement Paradigm, as shown in Figure 11.6.

In the first step, the SEPG member coached a project team to write down the goals of the institution, the organization managing the project, the project objectives, the decision makers, and any other major stakeholders in the project. Some of the attributes that may be used as goals include profitability, efficiency, product quality, customer satisfaction, software code size, and development productivity.

In the second step, the SEPG member facilitated a meeting in which project staff members brainstormed a set of questions or concerns on what decision makers need to know to effectively guide the software project's plan. Examples of questions that were raised for, say, test schedule risks are as follows:

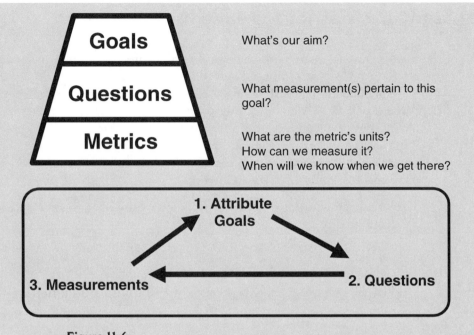

Figure 11.6
The Goal-Question-Metric (GQM) paradigm.

- Is the test schedule impacted by the recent budgeting changes?
- Are we on plan with our test schedule?
- What events are on the critical path in the current test schedule?
- What are the consequences of a schedule overrun?

In the third step, the SEPG member would lead a discussion on what project data is being collected (or is planned to be collected) and whether from this data and its analysis, answers to the questions identified in the second step could be obtained. These measurement data might be collected at the project level or might be external data, such as budgets, actual costs, date for each milestone, product bugs by severity level, or a list of late tasks by build. Table 11.1 contains many of the project-specific metrics related to testing.

To summarize the outcome of these two case studies, the two-tier metrics program was completely accepted by the individual projects, who felt good about having the freedom to create, report internally, and dispose of their project's own ensemble of metrics. The sharing of responsibility between the SEPG (institutional measurement data collection) and the project-specific metrics collection (for the private measurement data collection) was key to the success of the institution, its projects, and its customer base.

Using Standard Metrics to Make Improvements

Simply having many software development projects within an institution working on process improvement does not guarantee a world-class software organization. If each team chooses its own focus for improvement, the process will at best be randomly optimized. Local optimization results in global suboptimization. For a software organization to improve rapidly, the improvement efforts throughout the organization must be aligned with the organization's vision. The successful management of software process improvement is captured in the following:

- Accurately forecast the software functionality by size, effort, schedule, and quality
- Determine the tasks, specifying resource/quality/standards per task
- Ensure the success and performance of each step of the process
- Detect bugs as quickly as possible after the bugs are injected
- Manage the bugs so as to fix important bugs quickly and effectively

A good companion documented strategy for this software metrics program has two parts, as follows:

1. To deploy a standard set of metric definitions and then collect and analyze software measurement data across the institution's software-developing projects.
2. To employ the Goal-Question-Metric (GQM) decision process for project-dependent selection of software measurements.

One of the most helpful activities leading to process improvement is to gain control over the way resource forecasting is done in order to improve its accuracy. Accuracy records can be kept if, at each major milestone of the development process, forecast numbers are plotted and learning curves are best fitted to the data. Figure 11.7, derived from Boehm (1981), gives an example of this technique for effort estimation. Forecast data are normalized by their average, A, and plotted versus time in months on the horizontal axis. The round dots are the normalized forecast, and the last normalized forecast in this example is at the end of the 7th month. A least-squares curve fit of the functions U and L can be overlaid on the graph and the value of the coefficient of the exponent, B, is so determined. The larger the value of B, the faster the forecasting group is converging to the actual.

A software effort/schedule estimation model can be created with reasonable accuracy as a nonlinear function of software size if based on historical

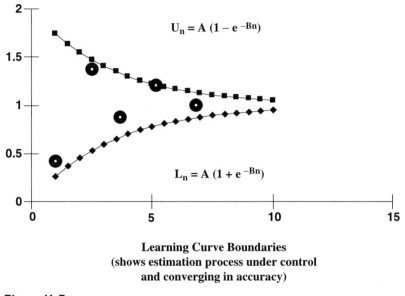

$$U_n = A\,(1 - e^{-Bn})$$

$$L_n = A\,(1 + e^{-Bn})$$

Learning Curve Boundaries
(shows estimation process under control
and converging in accuracy)

Figure 11.7
Fitting learning curves to normalized forecast data.

data. The results of a sound modeling effort can save managers from considerable embarrassment if they are relying on a simple, linear model to predict the effort and time needed for a project. For example, a simple, linear model would predict that, if the new development is about twice the size of a previous development, then the budget should be twice the cost of the previous development. In reality, the relationship between cost and size is nonlinear, and the estimation error can be significant if the wrong model is used.

To start using a nonlinear model of software size, there are four challenges, as follows:

1. Gather historical data from prior projects that are similar to the ones being estimated, including size, financial actual, schedule, and development environment factors.

2. Develop estimates by analogy, comparing the new project to a similar software effort, its financial actual data, its software metrics data, and its development environmental factors.

3. Create the schedule for major milestones, arriving at a schedule of the total effort by month.

4. Complete estimation by allocating the total effort to each task and spread the effort across the appropriate phase of the development schedule.

Having all projects report their measurement data for size, effort, cost, and quality metrics to a central institutional organization, like the SEPG, allows consistency-checking between different projects. In addition, this measurement data supports nonlinear modeling of the institution's development processes that is founded on actual measurement data from prior projects, using a similar development environment. Accurate forecasts of new projects go a long way toward driving chaos out of an organization, and the collection and analysis of measurement data for these standard metrics greatly support this goal. Institutional measurement data management should include each of the five activities shown in Table 11.3.

Software development projects, when supported by these institutional measurement data collection and analysis functions, allow process improvements to be piloted and results to be benchmarked against prior results. This eliminates ad hoc or fad changes from diverting the institution from increasing productivity, improving product quality, or speeding delivery of its software products to the marketplace. Schedule, quality, and costs are the fundamental business metrics, and software processes need to be measured from this business standpoint in order for software businesses to survive. The rapid testing paradigm provides process improvements in the following areas:

- Schedule—by allocating additional resources for testing activities before the CUT phase, thus shrinking the schedule for testing activities after the CUT phase and promoting earlier releases

Table 11.3
Forecast Preparation Activities and Their Definitions

Activities	Definitions
Collecting/organizing data	Direct measurements are collected and derived measurements are calculated and then formatted for the database.
Storing/retrieving data	Direct and derived measurements are stored in the historical database, which is the principle source of decision making.
Analyzing data	Measurements are examined for trends and statistical breakouts (excessive variations from expected norms).
Synthesizing information	Both measurements and analysis data are modeled.
Distributing information	Synthesized reports (status, forecast, risk analyses) are distributed to decision makers.

- Quality—by finding and fixing a greater percentage of bugs, thus reducing the density of latent bugs in the released products
- Costs—by reducing the amount of throwaway effort that is expended on projects that wait until the final stages of the software life cycle to find and fix bugs

Metrics for Testing

If you recall the concept of a two-tier metrics program, you may be wondering how it applies to testing metrics. Do testing metrics lie at the higher, institutional level or the lower, project-specific level of the two-tier program? As we will see in this section, almost all testing metrics fall into the project-specific category. Examples of testing metrics used by the projects are shown in Table 11.4.

Establishment of an effective metrics program calls for strict discipline in taking measurements, performing analyses of these measurements, and reporting trends that result from the analyses. The effort and discipline required can constitute a significant overhead to the development program,

Table 11.4

Categories of Testing Metrics with Examples

Testing Metric Name	Definition
Predicate Logic Bugs	Number of bugs found in the predicates of logical constructs (IF, WHILE, CASE, etc.)/KELOC
Loop Indexing/Limits Bugs	Number of bugs found in the indexing or limits of loop constructs (DO, FOR, etc.)/KELOC
Testing Progress	Number of test cases passed versus tests planned over time (ability to maintain software testing progress)
Change Proposals and Action Item Volatility	Number of mandated product changes and redirections over time (may indicate schedule and cost impacts)
Missing/Incomplete Requirements	Number of bugs found to be from missing or incomplete requirements
Design Progress	Number of requirements documented—planned versus actual (measures an ability to maintain progress during this early phase)

but this overhead is essential to the success of any process improvement initiative. When process improvement changes are being made during the execution of a project, measurements are the only way to determine the value of the process improvements. When comparing one project to another, comparison of the project data is the only way to determine what differences there are between the projects.

Bug Density (Bugs/KSLOC)

The most basic testing metrics are associated with bugs. It is natural for a project to itemize, prioritize, and report status on bugs by category. Prioritization typically follows bug severity (SEV) guidelines, as defined in Table 11.5. Note that the severity (SEV number) is assigned in reverse order so that 1 is assigned to the Catastrophic category while 5 is assigned to the Nuisance category. The severity definitions in Table 11.5 are the same as those used in Table 5.2 in Chapter 5.

Collecting bug data and creating the histogram using the SEV number assigned to each bug allows an analyst to portray the quality of the software build to be reviewed in the formal reviews. Figure 11.8 shows a sample of a histogram of bugs by SEV number. Note that this data has been normalized by the estimated size in KSLOC.

The data in Figure 11.8 shows a large number of bugs found in the early phases of the development life cycle. It is clear from the data that static testing has been used to find bugs in requirements, designs, and code. Note also that more major bugs were found in the DD and Code phases than in IT. This means that thorough testing of the product has started long before the IT phase—a practice that is a hallmark of rapid testing. If you establish a metrics program that counts and reports bugs found in each phase of the

Table 11.5
Severity Code

SEV Number	Guidelines
1	Catastrophic—causes system failure, e.g., blue screen or corrupted data
2	Major—product not usable, e.g., causes erroneous answers, wrong report
3	Moderate—product is usable, bug is customer affecting
4	Minor—product is usable, bug is not customer affecting
5	Nuisance—can be repaired as time permits

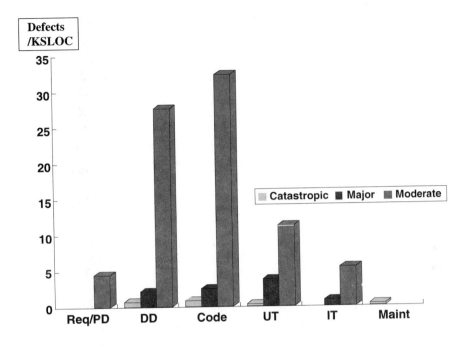

Figure 11.8
Histogram of bug data by selected SEV numbers.

development life cycle, it is possible to evaluate and demonstrate the efficiency of process improvements as you introduce them from project to project.

Project-Based Bug Model

A programming language tends to be susceptible to some types of bugs more than others. For example, one programming language may generate code that is particularly difficult to maintain or reuse. Another language might be easy to maintain or reuse but may lead to poor performance. One way to characterize the susceptibility of a project to various bug types is to create a bug model for that project. Projects using the same programming language can be compared if they use the same bug model. If, when compared to the bug model, a given project is found to have a high incidence of a particular type of bug, there may be a systemic problem in the way the software is being developed. In other words, analysis of the bug data may lead to the finding of a bug in the development process rather than in the product itself.

Table 11.6 defines a set of prominent bug sources. Bugs can be categorized as part of an inspection process, where the inspection team reaches a consensus on the root cause category. For example, if the root cause fell into TR, a traceability bug, and the inspection team determines what phase in the project's life cycle that the TR bug was introduced, for example, the Preliminary Design (PD) phase, these categories can be graphed and analyzed, as shown in Figure 11.9. The histogram of this analysis will lead to a pattern that is characteristic of the programming language and the software life cycle.

Table 11.6
Project's Bug Categories

Code	Bug Category Name	Category Definition
LD	Level of detail	Deviates from proper level of detail: too much, too little, or incomplete
TC	Technical content	Technical contents are incorrect, ambiguous, or substandard
EU	English usage	Spelling, grammar, punctuation, tense, and other language usage bugs
DO	Documentation	Documentation deviates from executing program or other documentation
ST	Standards	Deviates from established standards for formats or procedures; excludes standards for English usage syntax, spelling, or clarity
ID	Inherited	A bug in reuse or legacy code
TR	Traceability	Inconsistent with earlier documents; contradictions, lack of references, wrong references
CM	Completeness	Additional information or functionality is needed in the target product or its documentation
DA	Data	Missing or wrong data input from end-user or from database
IF	Interface	Bug in interface
OT	Other	Bugs that cannot be clearly classified into the above categories
MR	Maintainability and reusability	Difficult to maintain or reuse; there is high complexity or flexibility has been compromised

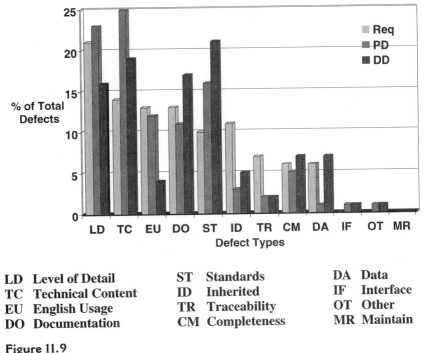

LD   Level of Detail   ST   Standards   DA   Data
TC   Technical Content   ID   Inherited   IF   Interface
EU   English Usage   TR   Traceability   OT   Other
DO   Documentation   CM   Completeness   MR   Maintain

Figure 11.9
Project-based bug model.

Another advantage of analyzing bug data is that a follow-up project can compare itself against the predecessor project. This has two valuable outcomes: being able to focus the inspections around finding bugs with the highest expected value, and being able to know whether a change in the process has a favorable impact on reducing a certain type of bug.

Generally speaking, root cause analysis such as that done in establishing a project's bug model, is a powerful tool for process improvement. Identifying problems in the development process, fixing them, and evaluating the effectiveness of the process fix is the purpose behind establishing a solid testing metrics program.

Software Error Estimation Program (SWEEP)

The Software Error Estimation Program (SWEEP), developed by the Software Productivity Consortium, is a forecasting tool for estimating bug rates, including latent bugs. A latent bug is defined as any bug that remains in a software product; that is, it exists but has not yet been found. The value of the SWEEP model is that it aids in the management and prediction of bugs in software-intensive systems. It supports the establishment of goals for bug detection during software development and helps track progress toward these goals. It monitors and helps control the quality of software products by predicting the number of bugs remaining in a software system. The following is a list of assumptions behind the model:

- All detected bugs should be recorded when they are discovered
- Bugs are fixed when they are discovered, and no bugs are injected during the repair effort
- Bugs should be tracked consistently throughout all phases of the life cycle
- Bugs in software documentation should not be tracked with software bugs
- Data input into SWEEP should be validated and updated on a regular basis
- The accuracy of SWEEP results will improve proportionally as you enter actual bug counts from the other phases of your development process

The three modes of use of SWEEP are shown in Table 11.7.

To the software tester, SWEEP provides a clear graphical representation of the number of bugs discovered and a projection of the remaining bugs. It

Table 11.7
Definitions of Modes of SWEEP

Mode	Name	Features
1	Time-based model	Allows you to estimate and track bugs during system test and integration cycles
2	Phase-based model	Allows you to predict and track bugs for multiple phases and can provide bug information before you execute any code
3	Planning-aid model	Allows the user to set bug discovery objectives in a software project based on experience from previous projects; then it generates a bug discovery profile based on corporate data to guide the software project toward those objectives

also allows users to leverage historical data to produce accurate estimates of the latent bug content for various phases of the life cycle. To the manager or quality assurance personnel, SWEEP enables the accurate prediction of how many more test cycles will be needed to meet a predetermined quality standard. Figure 11.10 is an example of the Phase-Based SWEEP Model. Note that the project has just completed an inspection of the initial source code against its detailed design documentation, finding 3.48 bugs per KSLOC. The best-fit Rayleigh curve for the latest data point, 3.48, and the preceding data points of 3.3 and 7.8, found during the preliminary design and detailed design phases, respectively, pass through the same value: 3.48. This Rayleigh curve tells the team to expect about 2.12 bugs per KSLOC, during the unit testing phase that should occur next. If this data persists, the project should deliver fewer than 0.07 latent bugs per thousand lines of code to the customer(s) of this software product.

The next process maturity step would be to average bugs per KSLOC actuals across a large number of projects with similar environments for each phase (PD, DD, CUT, UT, IT, and ST). A future project should be able to use

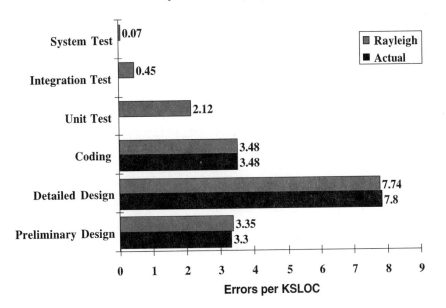

Figure 11.10
SWEEP Mode 2: Phase-Based Model.

this data, which is labeled "Nominal," as graphed in Figure 11.11, as guidance as to how many bugs to expect for the same quality level of its predecessor project, or even a stopping rule for its inspection productivity. Upper and lower control limits are set at, for example, 3 sigma above and below the nominal data.

The Rayleigh curve fitting of bug data is a valuable tool to the system test engineer. During the system test phase, all existing test cases are applied methodically, day after day, in testing new subsystems and in regression testing new builds that fix bugs found in previous builds. Figure 11.12 shows actual bug data collected during a series of system tests of release candidates, where the builds were performed weekly and the bugs that were found were bar-graphed each day. The line-curve fitting is done automatically by SWEEP's Time-Based Model. Note that the testers may confidently use this as a stopping condition for the system test phase if a goal has been set for the number of bugs per thousand lines of code to be shipped to the customer.

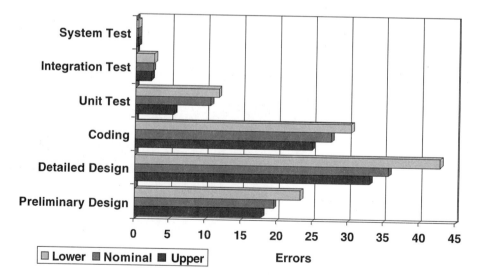

Figure 11.11
SWEEP's Planning-Based Model for Phase-Based Model.

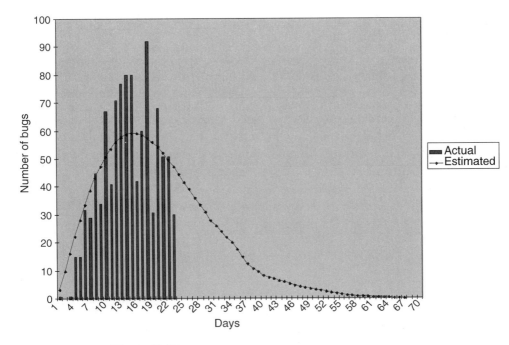

Figure 11.12
SWEEP's Time-Based Model of System Test Bug Data.

Summary

The issues and their solutions that were selected for this chapter dealt with the application of software metrics to testing from a project perspective, as well as for the overall institution. The following gives a review of the points made in this chapter:

- Differentiation between metrics and measurements
- A two-tier approach to collecting and analyzing measurement data
- Useful institutional metrics, namely, size, effort, schedule, and quality
- A paradigm for selecting project-level metrics, called Goal-Quality-Metric (GQM)
- Using metrics to control the software development process and process improvements
- Presentation of a list of testing metrics (all 2nd tier)

- Developing a bug model that can be used for process tracking and quality improvements
- A stopping goal for testing, namely, the application of bug density forecasting, using SWEEP, and working toward a quality goal, namely, the number of latent bugs per KSLOC shipped to the end-user

Many successful projects have used metrics to add visibility and controllability to their schedule, quality, and cost. A few unsuccessful projects have used metrics to destroy trust relationships that are required to develop software. Failures in project metrics programs almost always have a root cause called attribution. Attributing bugs to a person or group of persons that were involved with its development is not the purpose of using metrics to control the software development and quality of the product.

References

Basili, V. R. and D. M. Weiss. (1984). "A Methodology for Collecting Valid Software Engineering Data." *IEEE Transactions on Software Engineering*, SE-10 (6).

Boehm, B. (1981): *Software Engineering Economics*. Englewood Cliffs, NJ: Prentice-Hall.

Software Productivity Consortium (1993). Software Error Estimation Program (SWEEP) User Manual, (SPC-92017-CMC), Version 02.00.10.

van Soligen, Rini, and Egon Berghout. (1999). *The Goal/Question/Metric Method: A practical guide for quality improvement of software development*. Berkshire, England: McGraw-Hill Book Company, UK.

Testing Effort Estimation Techniques and Tips

Topics Covered in the Chapter

- ▶ Using Mathematics To Estimate Software
- ▶ Function Point Technology
- ▶ Summary
- ▶ References

The goal of this chapter is to describe an accurate way of forecasting the staffing by month for test preparation and for test execution, normally called verification and validation (V&V). The approach we take is through a series of case studies that exploit a tool set that was developed by the author.

There are a number of techniques that can be called upon to help generate a schedule and resources schedule for a testing project. The simplest technique is called model forecasting with basis of estimates (BOEs). By-analogy estimation is based on actual resource allocation data from a set of past projects with similar architectures, programming languages, and testing approaches. Estimates of a forthcoming project, when based upon by-analogy estimates, have built in credibility by using experiential facts with incremental improvements, which are based on small decisions that are then consolidated. These incremental improvements increase the accuracy of the forecast. Examples include product size scaling and resource estimation of support groups, for example, quality assurance, configuration management, and program management.

CASE STUDY 1

AN APPROACH TO ESTIMATION (GARY COBB)

One day, I received an email message that read, "Would you have any suggestion as to how we might be able to estimate the size, schedule, and resources needed for an adequate testing effort?" The message went on to say, "Our team has created a scorecard using deliverables that measure our process activities and a forecast of the current status of the overall project, yielding a red, yellow, or green status. In order to get this thing started here, we are assigning some of our test team to be test leads, while others have names like: Product Certification and Quality Assessment (PCQA) consultant. Given the state of our past development efforts, have you any suggestion as to how we might be able to estimate the size, schedule, and resources needed for an adequate testing effort?"

I responded with the following suggestion: a software estimation approach, which I believe could be a repeatable (a quality goal) process for your department is as follows:

1. Categorize all your development staff into defined roles (e.g., requirements definition, architect, designer, coder, tester, manager, configuration controller, product certification, quality assessment, etc.

2. Reverse-engineer a complete schedule for two past projects that were successful, for example, delivered on time and within budget with acceptable quality, and allocate the time and budget back to the roles defined in item 1.

3. Calculate the level of effort (LOE) that was expended for each role LOE (j) for $j = 1, \ldots, n$, where n is the number of roles, expressed in full-time-equivalent (FTE) effort-months.

4. Calculate the sum, S in units of effort-months, of all of these LOEs for each project. Calculate the percents of the total effort that each role took, such as, LOE(j)/S, for $j = 1, \ldots, n$ for each project and compare the two percentage tables.

5. Calculate an average LOE (j)/S for $j = 1, \ldots, n$ across the two projects in order to calibrate a model for LOE (j) values to be used in forecasting LOE (j) for new projects.

6. Estimate size in thousands of estimated source lines of code (KESLOC) for the products from each project by actually counting noncomment lines of executable code, including any released scripts that were developed, or, alternately, count function points (discussed later in this chapter) and, given the Capers Jones conversion table, shown in Table 12.1, convert the function point count to KESLOC.

7. Calculate the Effort Adjustment Factor (EAF) from the equation: EAF = S/(2.4*(KESLOC**1.05)). The following will be your conversion formula between size and effort, going forward: S = EAF*2.4*(KESLOC**1.05), where EAF was derived from the basis-of-estimate and KESLOC is forecasted based upon documented requirements.

	A	B	C
10	Spreadsheet languages	6	50
11	Query languages	16	20
12	SMALLTALK	21	15
13	OBJECTIVE- C	26	12
14	APL	32	10
15	STRATEGEM	35	9
16	Fourth-generation database	40	8
17	LOGO	53	6
18	BASIC	64	5
19	FORTH	64	5
20	LISP	64	5
21	PROLOG	64	5
22	Ada	71	4.5
23	MODULA-2	71	4.5
24	PL/I	80	4
25	RPG	80	4
26	Pascal	81	3.5
27	JOVIAL	106	3
28	FORTRAN	106	3
29	COBOL	106	3
30	CHILL	106	3
31	ALGOL	106	3
32	C	150	2.5
33	Macro Assembler	213	1.5
34	Assembler	320	1

**Lines of Code
Per Function Point**   **Number of Object Instr.
Per Line of Code**

Table 12.1
Conversion from function point count to thousands of equivalent source lines of code (KESLOC)

My first response drew an email reply, as follows: "Thanks for taking your time to answer my questions, but I am more confused than ever. That's why it has taken me so long to respond—I didn't know what was bothering me. Your suggested approach is good, but it presumes that the data is around somewhere. We don't have the effort data available and what would be remembered would be swags. The only suggestion I think is feasible is finding a similar project that has completed, and uses its actual code count as an estimate for this one. Does that sound feasible?"

I responded with a second email, saying, "Yes, that is one way of stabilizing your estimation, for example, with a basis-of-estimate (BOE) from prior code. You can also gather smaller estimates of LOEs from your set of roles and the headcount assigned to each role, such as project lead, programmer, different types of testers, configuration control, quality assurance, build master, promotion to test, production control, and so on. Also, include extended teams, such as software documentation, user trainer, pilot testers, business analysts, subcontracted subsystems, and so on. Once you have this data, divide it by the total headcount in order to turn it into percentage of total effort and then apply it to the new estimate's total effort. It should be accurate to within 30%. By the way, 30% is good, compared to the 2X or 4X that software developments often blow their budgets/estimates. Good luck."

The formulas used in this case study are from the intermediate model of Barry Boehm's COCOMO Model. The seven steps use a reverse engineering approach to determining the EAF factor, rather than Dr. Boehm's approach, which will be presented later in this chapter.

There are some pitfalls of estimating, based upon historical actual data, as follows:

- Previous projects and new projects may use different coding languages, may use different life cycle phases, peer review techniques, and so on. Using historical actual data can lead to inaccurate schedules and costs, due to mismatches in these areas.

- It is tempting to linearly scale time or effort from productivity data calculated on a historical project. For example, the historical project had a coding productivity of 1 line of code per effort-hour on a 5KLOC program, so a 50KLOC program will take 10 times longer with a coding productivity of 1 line of code per effort-hour. This is incorrect, since effort rises exponentially, not linearly, with increased size.

The take-away from this case study is that on a small project everyone knows everything that is going on every day, and team members support one another with brainstorming, help with complex designs, code reading, and often debugging. No one feels the need for a documented process, so no one cares to pack away measurement data. On a small project, each team member needs to take responsibility for the destiny of the project. The person in the case study really felt the need to have a process for estimation of the test effort on the new small-team project. But, there was no process among his historical projects that supported the needs for basis-of-estimate data.

As we go from small projects to large projects, there is an increased need to formalize communications, reporting, leadership, organizational roles, training, and institutional standards; in other words, to define and use a documented process. The next section shows several process flows for modern software developments, concentrating on the testing process and its task identification.

Using Mathematics to Estimate Software

In order to model software developments, one must take into account the different development life cycle models process models that are in use today. Some projects have defined requirements, specified at the beginning of the project and they remain fixed throughout the development phases. The lowest cost software development process is the waterfall. Figure 12.1 depicts a waterfall process. It gets its name from the process flow itself because information flows from top to bottom of the process chart, like water in a waterfall. The arrows that are pointing backwards to an upstream phase are all verification flows; they address questions like: does the source code match what the detailed design documentation stated that it would be.

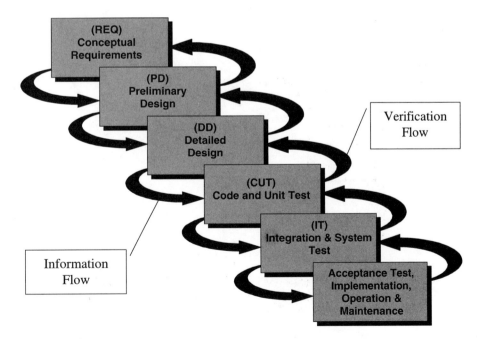

Figure 12.1
Waterfall model.

The test phase seen in the waterfall process chart contains integration, system, and acceptance testing, whereas the implementation phase seen in this chart contains the tasking for unit testing. The developers, prior to their release of code to the independent test organization, perform unit testing. Tasking within the test phase of the waterfall process contains the ensemble of both static and dynamic testing techniques that have been discussed in Chapters 3, 10, and 11.

Another popular software development life cycle model is called the spiral process, which is diagrammed in Figure 12.2 as a prototype development process. This process was first used to accommodate a prototype development to increase confidence in a set of requirements and allow experimentation with the human computer interface, database structure, usability, performance, and installability. Incremental builds are performed in order to provide an executable program to users to play with and give feedback about. These incremental builds are targets of testing, but often the frequency of the incremental builds cause the test team to not be able to finish a complete pass through their test suite. Therefore, finding bugs in the newly added features takes top priority with the test team, but this rushes the development and implementation of brand-new test cases, test scripts, and expected test results. This process can become so fast-paced that it can become chaotic for both developers and testers alike, allowing neither of

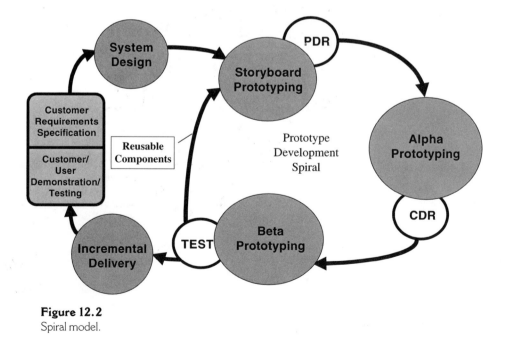

Figure 12.2
Spiral model.

them adequate time to complete and check their work before swapping one build for the next, unless all parts of the work are managed carefully.

The best software development life cycle model for software products that must get to market with limited functionality in order for a business venture to succeed is the spiral model. The spiral model provides a planned set of releases so that redoing some of the user interfaces, database design, or improving the performance of immature algorithms can be accomplished in a later release of the product.

It is also the best process to use when the requirements are fuzzy and there is no precedent product. Supporting the user community with early builds of the future product reduces the overall project risk by winning acceptance by end-users early in the process. The spiral model best accommodates projects that have a high volatility of requirements, since adding, deleting, or changing requirements can easily be worked into the upcoming builds by a parallel effort of maintenance and new development folding into a future build of the product.

You've probably heard "do it right the first time" as a quality slogan. If that applies to the type of software project you are working on, then the low-cost approach for you would be the waterfall model. If the users don't know what they need as a total solution, or if releasing the entire software product some time in the distant future will cause it to fail customer expectations, then the low-risk approach for you would be the spiral model.

There is a modification to a previously discussed software development life cycle that involves outsourcing design, coding, and unit testing phases to a partner. Figure 12.3 shows the hinged waterfall diagram with an overlay of the industry standard responsibility allocation between a prime contractor and one or more subcontractors/partners.

From these examples of the variety of software development life cycle models, it is clear that the requirements for a software cost-estimating model must be modularized. It must be flexible enough to perform subtotals that divide estimates for prime and subcontractor work and flexible enough to divide out the testing effort from, say, the program management or coding estimates. This leads to a design that will be covered in the next series of case studies.

Barry Boehm (1981) identified three clusters in his database of 63 successful software projects, namely, organic, semidetached, and embedded. He developed three software cost estimation models, namely, basic, intermediate, and detailed. Projects that fell in the organic cluster were those that had small teams performing work that they were very familiar with, such as a report being added to a COBOL program. The embedded cluster were those

Industry Standard Responsibility Allocation

Prime: Requirements and Architecture
Subcontractor/Partner: Software Development
Prime: System Test and Acceptance Test

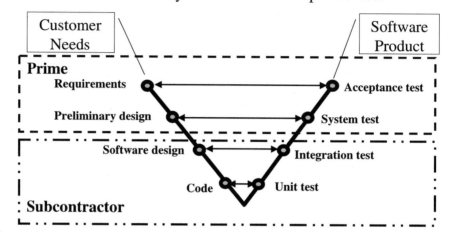

Figure 12.3
Hinged waterfall, showing division of responsibilities between a prime and subcontractor.

projects that had a large development team that assumed risks, such as lack of knowledge of the programming or test environments, requirements volatility, shortened schedule, lack of appropriate tools, tight performance constraints on execution speed, and quality risks. The semidetached cluster was those projects that fell somewhere in between the embedded and organic clusters. These three clusters are called modes in Figure 12.4, which provides a one-sheet summary of Barry Boehm's Constructive Cost Model (COCOMO) equations.

In order to help you visualize the difference between the organic, semidetached, and embedded mode equations, Figure 12.5 shows graphs of the three equations for the same number of thousands of equivalent lines of code (KELOC). It is counterintuitive, to an extent that the higher risk the program is, the sooner it finishes. This is likely caused by managers who staff up to meet the higher-risk projects, as well as possibly starving resources in everyday organic development efforts.

The Intermediate and Detailed COCOMO have a coefficient, called effort adjustment factor (EAF), that is the product of the tabular values, shown in Table 12.2, of software cost drivers.

Basic vs. Intermediate/Detailed COCOMO Equations

Basic COCOMO Model	Intermediate/Detailed COCOMO Model
$MM = 2.4\ (KLOC)^{1.05}$ $TDEV = 2.5\ (MM)^{0.38}$	**Organic Mode** $MM_{Adj} = (EAF)\ 3.2\ (KELOC)^{1.05}$ $TDEV = 2.5\ (MM_{Adj})^{0.38}$

$MM_{Maint} = (Annual\ Change\ Traffic)\ MM_{Adj}$ for maintenance effort

Semidetached Mode
$MM_{Adj} = (EAF)\ 3.0\ (KELOC)^{1.12}$
$TDEV = 2.5\ (MM_{Adj})^{0.35}$

Embedded Mode
$MM_{Adj} = (EAF)\ 2.8\ (KELOC)^{1.20}$
$TDEV = 2.5\ (MM_{Adj})^{0.32}$

ELOC	Equivalent LOC
MM	Staff-Months
EAF	Effort Adjustment Factor
MM_{Adj}	Adjusted MM
TDEV	Time to DEVelop
MM_{Maint}	Annual Maintenance MM

$ELOC = (Adapted\ LOC)\ (1/100)$
$(.4*Percent\ of\ design\ modified +$
$.3*Percent\ of\ code\ modified +$
$.3*Percent\ of\ integration\ modified)$

Figure 12.4
COCOMO model equations for organic, semidetached, and embedded modes.

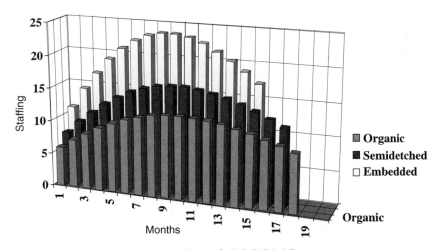

Variation between modes of COCOMO
The relative slower, low-level start and the higher peak staffing requirement of the embedded mode is clearly evident from the taller graph in the back of the semidetached and organic (front) graphs shown below.

Figure 12.5
Modes of COCOMO: organic, semidetached, and embedded.

Table 12.2
Cost Driver Values that are Multiplied Together to Yield the Effort Adjustment Factor
[From Boehm (1981)]

Cost Drivers	Ratings					
	Very Low	**Low**	**Nominal**	**High**	**Very High**	**Extra High**
Product Attributes						
RELY Required software reliability	.75	.88	1.00	1.15	1.40	—
DATA database size	—	.94	1.00	1.08	1.16	—
CPLX Product complexity	.70	.85	1.00	1.15	1.30	1.65
Computer Attributes						
TIME Execution time constraint	—	—	1.00	1.11	1.30	1.66
STOR Main storage constraint	—	—	1.00	1.06	1.21	1.56
VIRT Virtual machine volatility	—	.87	1.00	1.15	1.30	—
TURN Computer turnaround time	—	.87	1.00	1.07	1.15	—
Personal Attributes						
ACAP Analyst capability	1.46	1.19	1.00	.86	.71	—
AEXP Analyst experience	1.29	1.13	1.00	.91	.82	—
PCAP Programmer capability	1.42	1.17	1.00	.86	.70	—
VEXP Virtual machine experience	1.21	1.10	1.00	.90	—	—
LEXP Programming language experience	1.14	1.07	1.00	.95	—	—
Project Attributes						
MODP Modern programming practices	1.24	1.10	1.00	.91	.82	—
TOOL Use of software tools	1.24	1.10	1.00	.91	.83	—
SCED Required development schedule	1.23	1.08	1.00	1.04	1.10	—

The Basic COCOMO doesn't have an effort adjustment factor (EAF). The only difference between the Intermediate and Detailed COCOMO is that one EAF factor is applied to all phases in the Intermediate COCOMO, whereas in the Detailed COCOMO, a different set of cost drivers are multiplied together to arrive at a phase-dependent EAF, which is applied to the appropriate phase in the calculation of effort. The only difference between the COCOMO and Revised and Improved COCOMO (REVIC) models is the coefficients and exponents used in the equations for person months (MM_{Adj}) and time to develop (TDEV).

In Figure 12.6, TDEV is the time-axis length of the graph, in this case 18 months, and (MM_{Adj}) is the area under the curve, which is the sum of the headcount per month for each of the 18 months. The primary cost driver of the COCOMO/REVIC model is the number of thousands of lines of code (KLOC), which is depicted as a coin slot in the center of the diagram. The remaining cost drivers are shown as dials with pointers that point to the selected attribute of the cost driver. The EAF is then the product of the values associated (from a table look-up) to each of the dial settings. This GUI design makes it easy for a modeler to understand the sequence of this process. First

COCOMO/REVIC Object

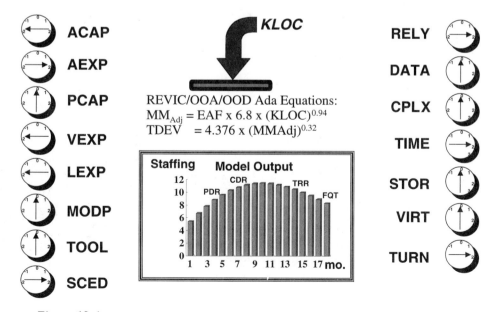

Figure 12.6
COCOMO/REVIC graphical user interface depicts the calculation process.

you set the dials, then you drop the KLOC value into the slot, press go, and out comes the finished product. The graph lays out the staff-months and the area under the graph is the total effort that will be required to perform all software development activities. The time-to-develop (TDEV) is the horizontal length of the graph. The process is repeatable by varying cost drivers and pressing go or entering new size estimates and pressing go.

It is worth pointing out that there is a direct relationship between effort (MM_{Adj}) and the time-to-develop (TDEV) in that, reducing the KLOC, reduces the effort, which in turn reduces the time to deliver. Vice versa, if the modeler is told that the project will be losing its key systems engineer who was developing the architecture and its software design, the ACAP and AEXP dials need to be adjusted, which may raise the effort (MM_{Adj}), which in turn will lengthen the time-to-develop (TDEV). Finally, if you use an average cost of software development staff members, then cost tracks linearly with calculated effort.

As we said earlier, one requirement for a software cost-estimating model is that it be modular. At a minimum, the modeler must be able to slice the effort into the development phase, by developer roles and by build. Figure

COCOMO Staffing Curves From Detailed COCOMO Spreadsheet

- Rayleigh Curve:

    Staffing(t) = MM * [(0.15 * TDEV + 0.7 * t)/(0.25 * (TDEV)^2] * e$^{-\{[(0.15 * TDEV + 0.7 * t)**2] / [.05 * (TDEV)**2)]\}}$,

    for 0 <= t <= TDEV

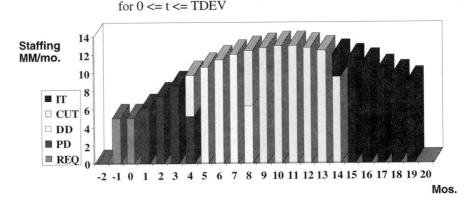

Figure 12.7
Graphical layout of the COCOMO effort by development phase.

12.7 shows the Rayleigh Curve equation, as well as the effort (headcount) by month of the staffing curve. This curve has an added feature in that it is separated into the typical development phases of REQ (requirements documentation), PD (preliminary design), DD (detailed design), CUT (code and unit test), IT (integration and system test). The project estimate cannot be made until the REQ phase is completed, so the convention for labeling the axis is to place a 1 for the first month of PD, where 0 and –1 are labels for two months prior to PD when the REQ work is done. For spiral processes, the REQ phase should develop the overall requirements for all builds, so you may see the REQ separated from PD by a delay factor. TDEV, time to develop, and MM, staff months, are the calculations whose equations are shown in Figure 12.6. Staffing(t) is the project's headcount, shown for each month, t from –1 through 19 in Figure 12.7.

Although the COCOMO model was not intended for estimating maintenance efforts for legacy systems, this option, shown in Figure 12.8, is a pretty accurate method. The maintenance effort, MM_{Maint}, for the first three years after the legacy system is released can be estimated, based upon an annual change traffic (ACT), which as a rule of thumb, averages 15%, 10%, and 5%, respectively, of the effort expended to produce the legacy system.

Modeling Software Maintenance

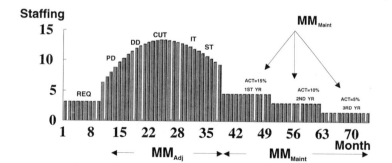

$MM_{Maint} = ACT \times MM_{Adj}$

e.g., $MM_{Adj} = 362$ staff-months
  ACT = 15%, makes
  $MM_{Maint} = 4.525$ staff-month
  for a 50,000 LOC embedded
  development

- Fixing latent bugs in a product can be estimated based upon Annual Change Traffic (ACT), which is the expected percent change in the product per year
  — e.g., 15%, 10%, 5% for each of the first three years after release

Figure 12.8
Maintenance level-of-effort, based upon area under development staffing curve.

An example is shown in the picture of a 50 KLOC program that took 362 staff-months to develop, taking 4.525 staff-months for the first 12 months to sustain the legacy system.

This approach is also applicable to the case where a contractor is given the same amount (50 KLOC) of new commercial-off-the-shelf (COTS) software. Say the contractor bids on adding new functionality to the COTS that would take two years to complete. This contractor should bid the new development as X KLOC integrated into a build of size X + 50 KLOC and add to it 4.525 staff-months for the first year and 3.017 staff-months for the second year, dedicated to the maintenance of the COTS software. For a $55/staff-hour average pay, or $8,305/staff-month, use an average of 151 billable-hours/month. This amounts to $8,305 * 7.542 = $62,636 for the two-year effort. Note there is no regard as to what was originally spent on the legacy COTS software by its vendor, since the 362 staff-months was calculated using your company's EAF, which is tailored to your company's software development processes.

Suppose you heard that a competitor of your company took four years to complete the 50 KLOC COTS that was legacy for your company's new-enhancement contract. Could you gain some competitive information from this? By having the mathematical model equations, you could reverse engineer the (MM_{Adj}) value from the TDEV equation. Then, using this value of (MM_{Adj}), and given that the COTS was 50 KLOC, the only unknown in the (MM_{Adj}) equation is EAF. Knowing your competitor's EAF for the COTS would tell you how they might bid the next project that had, say, 75 KLOC. By continuously improving your company's cost drivers used in the calculation of its EAF value, your company can surpass your competition in an effort to produce lower-cost software. By carefully managing to the mathematical model, your company will be able to say "we can deliver in a shorter time for less money," a true win–win proposition in today's marketplace.

CASE STUDY 2

COCOREV MODELING (GARY COBB)

The mathematical modeling of the software development life cycles have always intrigued me. What follows is a brief overview of the uses I have found of these cost estimating models and some of their flexibility. I selected a spreadsheet design from the very beginning, since it had the modularity and graphical interface that were required. I decided to program for the most complex case, the Detailed COCOMO with its phase-dependent EAF multipliers. CO-COREV has parameterized coefficients and exponents used in the computation of MM_{Adj}

and TDEV equations, so that the same spreadsheet serves to model the REVIC equations. We have elected to call this spreadsheet model the COCOREV spreadsheet model. COCOREV will provide examples of how one could use a mathematical model to estimate software developments. Uniformly, Barry Boehm's Semidetached (Mode = 2) equations will be used and the Intermediate model will assume that a 0.5 EAF factor is uniformly applied to all phases of the development.

There are three parts to this case study, as follows:

- Spiral life cycle with five 15 KLOC builds integrating with legacy code and performed sequentially
- Waterfall life cycle with one 75 KLOC build performed once
- Stacked spiral life cycle with five 15 KLOC builds integrating with legacy code and kicking off one spiral every two months.

A summary of the results of this trade-off analysis will be presented after the third part's data is presented. Figure 12.9 displays the first part's assumptions.

The COCOREV model is a workbook containing multiple worksheets. The top sheet, labeled Cover Sheet, contains all inputs to the model and the summation of all the results data from the five sheets that apply the COCOREV equations to the individual builds of the development, labeled Build 1, Build 2, Build 3, Build 4, and Build 5. One other worksheet, labeled Tables, contains the fixed constants of the model.

Case Study - Part 1

- Assumptions
    - 5 builds
    - 15 KDSI each
    - Each build is integrated with previous build's deliverables
    - All builds use C++ programming language
    - Zoom in on one build
        - Test Planning
        - Verification & Validation

Figure 12.9
Case Study 1 list of assumptions.

Figure 12.10 shows the input portion of the Cover Sheet, which elaborates each of the 15 KELOC builds, integrated with itself or with preceding legacy builds, each written in C++ with an EAF value of .5 for all phases of the development. We set the mode to 2, which stands for semidetached COCOMO. The thousands of delivered instructions (KDSI) column of the Cover Sheet is filled with an incremental increase of 15 KDSI, starting with the first 15 KDSI build. The starting delay was picked to start at 0 and increment by 10 months per build. This was done after the first try with no delays, showing that all builds would be completed in less than 10 months.

Figure 12.11 is part of the combined outputs on the Cover Sheet of COCOREV. Since Build 1 was not delayed, it starts in month 1, whereas Build 2 was delayed by 10 months, so it starts in month 11, and so on. The requirements (REQ) phase for all five builds combined show up in the two months numbered −1 and 0, and all five builds are finished before month 50. While all five staffing curves peak at the start of the CUT phase, you will note the peak staffing increases monotonically from Build 1 through Build 5, which is due to the increase in the amount of integration and system testing that is required with increasing sizes of KDSI. In short, this is not five identical builds, performed in tandem.

If you are wondering "how much is these four years of software development going to set you back," the answer is $1.593 million, assuming a fixed $55/hour average for software developers throughout the period of work. This is another answer that is rolled up on the Cover

COCOREV   Version 1.02

Developed Software

Build Number	Language	KELOC	KDSI	Starting Delay
Build 1	C++	15.000	15.000	0.0
Build 2	C++	15.000	30.000	10.0
Build 3	C++	15.000	45.000	20.0
Build 4	C++	15.000	60.000	30.0
Build 5	C++	15.000	75.000	40.0

Developed Software

Build Number	EAF: REQ	EAF: PD	EAF: DD	EAF: CUT	EAF: IT
Build 1	0.500	0.500	0.500	0.500	0.500
Build 2	0.500	0.500	0.500	0.500	0.500
Build 3	0.500	0.500	0.500	0.500	0.500
Build 4	0.500	0.500	0.500	0.500	0.500
Build 5	0.500	0.500	0.500	0.500	0.500

KELOC	**Thousands of Equivalent Lines of Code**
KDSI	**Thousands of Delivered Source Instructions**
Starting Delay	**Number of months before start of development**
EAF	**Effort Adjustment Factor**

Figure 12.10
Snapshot of COCOREV Cover Sheet's input value: (Name of build, language, KLOC, KDSI, starting delay, mode, and EAF by phase by build).

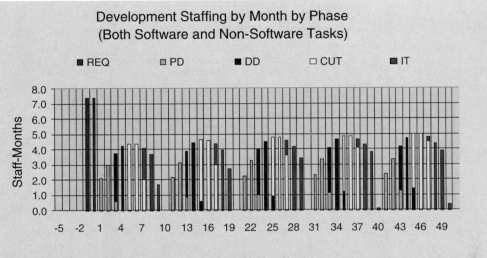

Figure 12.11
Cover sheet of COCOREV, showing five incrementally larger builds, following unified REQ phase.

Build 1
Totals by Phase

###########	###########	###########	###########	###########	###########	###########
34.18	2.75	5.73	7.45	10.76	7.48	31.43
	REQ	PD	DD	CUT	IT	0.92%
Build 1						

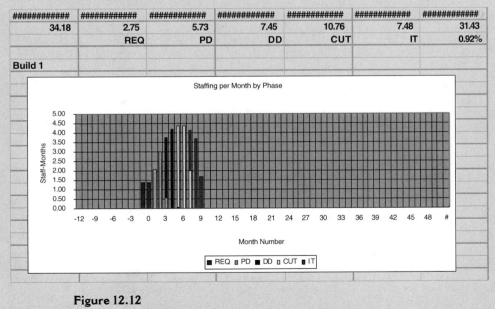

Figure 12.12
COCOREV's build 1 spreadsheet isolates build 1 information.

Sheet. Also, 28,968 staff-hours are in the Cover Sheet summary, broken out in units of staff-months by phase, as follows: REQ = 14.83, PD = 32.50, DD = 41.92, CUT = 60.54, IT = 42.05, totaling 191.94 staff-months.

Figure 12.12 focuses only on the resources allocated to the development of Build 1. Notice that the REQ = 2.75 staff-months and this is the rightful portion of the total REQ = 14.83 staff-months spent on the documentation of all of the multibuild software development. The overall development cost after the requirements is the left total of 34.18 minus 2.75 for REQ, which amounts to 31.43 staff-months, which agrees with the total in the right column. It appears from this COCOREV staff-loading graph that the software lead for this project will have to grow headcount from 2 people to 4.5 people at the peak and back to 1.5 people during the last month.

A companion to Build 1, namely, Build 2, is shown in Figure 12.13. What is the difference between Build 1 and Build 2? Well, for one, before Build 2 can ship, it has to be integrated with Build 1 and the two builds must be tested together. For another difference, Build 2 is delayed for 10 months, which means it starts at the beginning of month 11, about 1.5 months after Build 1 is released. This means that the requirements for Build 2 have been on the shelf for 10 months, which is time for them to have some degree of volatility at no cost, as long as someone maintains the requirements documents. This "at no cost" is the proof that the spiral

Build 2
Totals by Phase

###########	###########	###########	###########	###########	###########	###########
37.10	2.90	6.27	8.10	11.70	8.13	34.20
	REQ	PD	DD	CUT	IT	1.06%

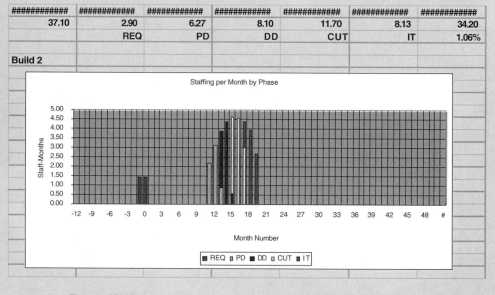

Figure 12.13
COCOREV's build 2 spreadsheet isolates build 2 information.

enthusiasts use to support their statement that the spiral process reduces risks of requirements volatility. Why would the model's allotment for the requirements for Build 2 be larger than the allotment for Build 1 (2.9 staff-months versus 2.75 staff-months, respectively)? The answer lies with the higher complexity of Build 2's requirements for integration with Build 1.

In order to save space, we will skip showing the graphs for Build 3 and Build 4. Figure 12.14 shows the staffing curve for the last of the five builds. Comparing this staffing curve with that of Build 1, we will notice that the difference in total staffing, excluding requirements documentation, is 38.22 – 31.33 = 6.89 staff-months. For a project taking a little over 9 months, Build 5 averages almost one staff person (headcount) more than Build 1. Again, this emphasizes the increased time and staffing needed to accommodate the larger legacy code incoming to Build 5, compared to none coming into Build 1.

At the beginning of this chapter, a goal was set to describe an accurate way of forecasting the staffing by month for test preparation and for test execution, normally called verification and validation (V&V). After the preliminary introductions of the general capabilities of the COCOREV model, we will continue with the case study of the five-build series, seeking to focus now on these two test functions. Let us return to Build 1 and isolate the testing work into two categories: test planning (Figure 12.15) and verification and validation (Figure 12.16). This data is found on the Build 1 spreadsheet of the COCOREV workbook. The term *test*

Build 5
Totals by Phase

############	############	############	############	############	############	############
41.34	3.12	7.05	9.06	13.07	9.05	38.22
	REQ	PD	DD	CUT	IT	1.19%

Build 5

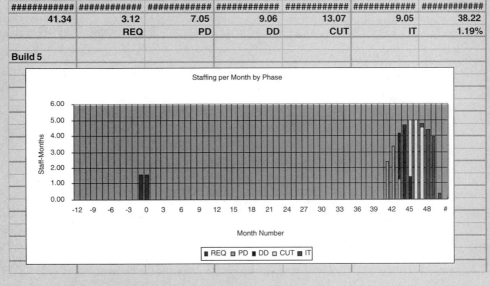

Figure 12.14
COCOREV's build 5 spreadsheet isolates build 5 information.

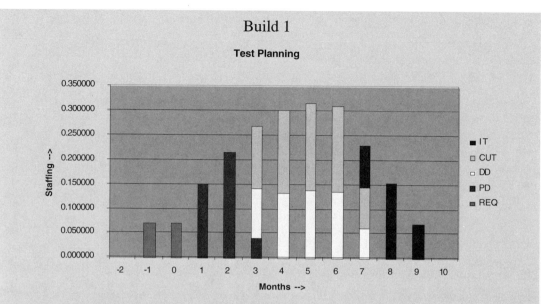

Figure 12.15
COCOREV build 1 test planning staffing curve.

staff will mean the combined test planning staffs and V&V staffs, for example, a combined headcount from both graphs in Figures 12.15 and 12.16.

What's this, a test staff involved with the requirements team? COCOREV allocates test staff a limited number of hours to participate in the requirements documentation in months −1 and 0, leading up to the start of the Build 1 development in month 1. The test staff prompts the requirements authors to state what the requirements are for testing each major function, thus laying the groundwork for the test staff to develop the appropriate test plans, test cases, and test results. It is also helpful for the software design phases to see the test requirements, so that they can incorporate test hooks into their design and implement them into the software.

Examples of test hooks would include transaction logging, undo-like reversals for all database transactions, history files in which to stack change histories of data, path sequences through the exercised code, or shopping cart exit-before-checkout locations for e-commerce Web sites. With their "find the bugs" mentality, the participants from the test staff should read through the storyboards and ancillary documentation to find and document requirements bugs. After all, this is the most cost-effective place to catch bugs—when a pencil and eraser are all the gear required to fix them!

Comparing the graphs, you will note that the phases are the same months in both graphs and the weighting of resources favors planning early and then V&V later in the IT phase. This is consistent with the missions for each of these tasks, for example, planning to find

Build 1

Verification & Validation

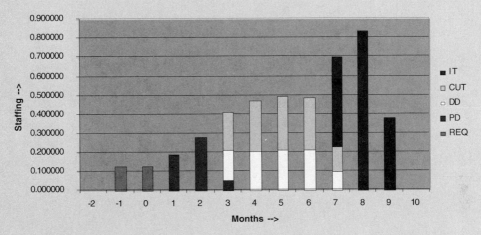

Figure 12.16
COCOREV build 1 verification and validation staffing curve.

bugs, while using static testing techniques during the REQ, PD, DD, and CUT phases, then executing the test plans, finding and documenting bugs, using dynamic testing techniques during IT and acceptance phases. COCOREV does not support the view of a few managers that say, after the developers code the executable deliverable, you can start up an independent test team to find all the bugs. No, successful projects are those that integrate the test planning and execution tests effort throughout all phases of the project. Vigilance in finding and fixing bugs using static means in the first three phases of the development is what is advocated in a rapid testing project.

The assumptions of Case Study 2 are as shown in Figure 12.17. Everything is about the same as the assumptions of Case Study 1, but this time we want to vary one important thing in order to research the risk/pay-off of using waterfall instead of spiral as a life cycle. To do this, we place all 75 KLOC as Build 1 to be integrated with itself (75 KDSI) and turn off using the other four builds in COCOREV.

The results of the COCOREV for Build 1 broken by phase in units of staff-months are as follows: REQ = 11.84, PD = 38.50, DD = 42.85, CUT = 58.86, IT = 51.54 for a total of 204.59. This translates to 30,983.7 staff-hours, assuming 151 billable staff-hours per month. This translates to $1.699 million, assuming $55/staff-hour. The cost for the five-build spiral life cycle, you might recall, was $1.593 million. The graph in Figure 12.18 shows the just over 16-month time to develop, starting the project after the completion of three months of requirements definitions. The peak in the staffing curve comes during the CUT phase at just under 15 person-months per month for three months.

Case Study - Part 2

- ## Assumptions
  - 1 build
  - 75 KDSI
  - Uses C++ programming language
  - Zoom in on:
    - Test planning
    - Verification and validation

Figure 12.17
Assumptions for Case Study 2.

Figures 12.19 and 12.20 shows the test planning and V&V staffing curves, respectively. Most of the test planning occurs in the PD, DD, and CUT phases, where over 0.8 staff-months per months are required for nine consecutive months. Most of the V&V staffing is expended in the IT phase, requiring over 2.5 staff-months per month for three consecutive months.

This ends part 2 of the case study. Figure 12.21 shows the assumptions for part 3.

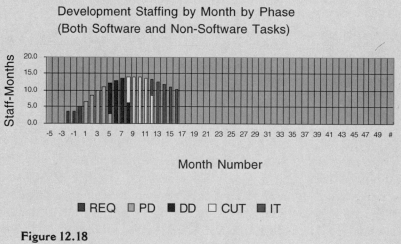

Figure 12.18
COCOREV's waterfall modeling of 75 KLOC of C++.

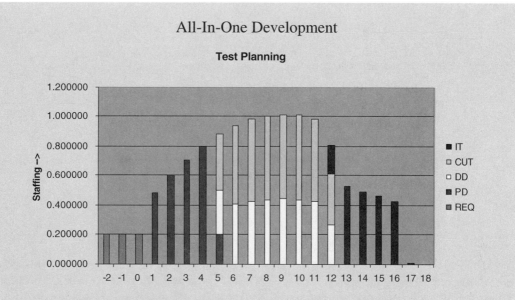

Figure 12.19
Test planning staffing curve for waterfall model of 75 KLOC.

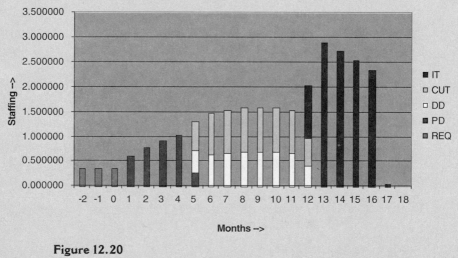

Figure 12.20
Verification and validation staffing curve for waterfall model of 75 KLOC.

Case Study — Part 3

- Assumptions
  - 5 builds, one starting every 2 months
  - 15 KDSI each
  - Each build is integrated with previous build's deliverables
  - Uses C++ programming language

Figure 12.21
Assumptions for part 3 of the case study.

The results of this part are graphed in Figure 12.22. The staffing of each of the phases is as follows: REQ = 14.83, PD = 32.50, DD = 41.94, CUT = 60.54, IT = 42.05, and a grand total of 191.86 staff-months. This amounts to 28,971.1 staff-hours, assuming 151 billable staff-hours per staff-month, costing $1.593 million, assuming $55 per staff-month.

Since each software development phase, namely, PD, DD, CUT, IT, has a staff that is trained/certified to perform all tasks that would be required by that phase of the life cycle, the value of the stacked spiral life cycle is that the staff can complete their phase of one build and transition to the same phase of the next build, so that everyone has job continuity for one year. Another value of the stacked spiral life cycle is that the users begin using the first part of the new system about halfway through the stacked spiral life cycle and continue to receive regular releases of additional functionality throughout the remaining 10 months of the life cycle.

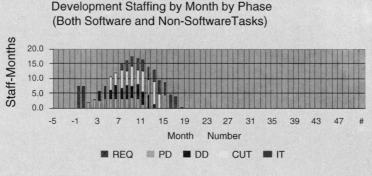

Figure 12.22
A stacked spiral life cycle.

From the point of view of the test planning and V&V staffs, a new release can be managed to closure every 2 months for the last 10 months of the life cycle. From a financial point of view, the five-build spiral approach wins over the waterfall. Table 12.3 demonstrates the vital statistics from each of the parts of this case study.

Stacked spiral life cycle is the most efficient model for this case study, since it gets this application into the hands of the end-users earlier, works staff in each phase constantly for about a year as their part of the development, costs less than the waterfall, and has the opportunity of taking advantage of process improvements within each phase as the staff moves through the five builds.

Table 12.3
Trade-off Matrix for Three-Part Case Study

Part	Description	$ (M)	Peak Headcount	TDEV
1	5 Builds, 15 KLOC, tandem	1.593	5	49
2	1 Build, 75 KLOC	1.699	14	15
3	5 Builds, 15 KLOC, stacked	1.593	18	17

Function Point Technology

In Albrecht (1979), a methodology of sizing software is presented that is built upon the premise that software development productivity is related to functionality. The areas of functionality that are to be counted, called the information domain values, include those in the following list:

- Number of user inputs—the count of the number of user inputs. Each user input that provides distinct application-oriented information to the user is counted. Inputs should be distinguished from inquiries that are counted separately.

- Number of user outputs—the count of the number of user outputs. Each user output that provides application-oriented information to the user is counted. In this context output refers to reports, screens, error messages, and so on. Individual data items within a report are not counted separately.

- Number of user inquiries—an inquiry is defined as an online input that results in the generation of some immediate software response in the form of an online output.

- Number of files—each logical master file (i.e., a logical grouping of data that may be one part of a large database of separate files) is counted.

- Number of external interfaces—all machine-readable interfaces (e.g., data files on some media that are used to transmit to another system are counted.

Enter these counts into the column marked Count in Figure 12.24.

Figure 12.23 provides the first of a two-step process to counting function points (FP). Step 1 begins by a person trained in function point replying to the questionnaire, using the appropriate numbers that are defined at the top of the questionnaire. After answering the 14 questions, add up the numbers you have chosen for your answers to these questions and carry this sum forward to the next step.

In Step 2, remember to multiply the counts by the weights, shown under the appropriate column, marked simple, average, or complex, and add up these products into the Count-totals box, as instructed earlier in this section. Finally, apply the formula shown at the bottom of Figure 12.24, bringing the

Step 1

- **Once the data has been collected, a complexity adjustment scale Fi, i = 1 ... 14, is associated with each count. Rate each factor on a scale of 0 to 5:**

  (0 = no influence; 1 = incidental; 2 = moderate; 3 = average; 4 = significant; 5 = essential)

_____1. Does the system require reliable backup and recovery?
_____2. Are data communications required?
_____3. Are there distributed processing functions?
_____4. Is performance critical?
_____5. Will the system run in an existing, heavily utilized operational environment?
_____6. Does the system require online data entry?
_____7. Does the online data entry require the input transaction to be built over multiple operational screens?
_____8. Are the master files updated online?
_____9. Are the inputs, outputs, files, or inquiries complex?
___10. Is the internal processing complex?
___11. Is the code designed to be reusable?
___12. Are conversion and installation included in the design?
___13. Is the system designed for multiple installations in different organizations?
___14. Is the application designed to facilitate change and ease of use by the user?

Figure 12.23
Function point complexity adjustment factors.

Step 2

Measurement parameter	Count	Weighting factors		
		Simple	Average	Complex
Number of user inputs		x 3	4	6 =
Number of user outputs		x 4	5	7 =
Number of user inquiries		x 3	4	6 =
Number of files		x 7	10	15 =
Number of external interfaces		x 5	7	10 =
Count - total				

FP = count-total x [.65 + .01 x SUM(F$_i$)]

Figure 12.24
Step 2 of the function point calculator.

sum of the complexity adjustment factors from Step 1 into the Sum (F$_i$) factor of this formula.

A function point is a weighted index-type of metric for measuring the quantity of functionality of a software package as seen by an end-user. Allan Albrecht invented the concept of a function point while working at IBM in the early 1970s. He felt that the functionality of a software application is a more significant determinant of application size than LOC, which has been the tradition metric for software size. Function points align with the information-processing functions delivered to the user. Function points provide a size measurement that is independent of development technique, technology, or programming language. As a size metric, function point counts are more reliable and can be determined earlier in the life cycle of the development.

The function-point metric, like line-of-code (LOC) count, is somewhat controversial. Those that are opposed to using function points claim that there is some slight-of-hand since the computations are based on subjective, rather than objective, data. These data are also said to be difficult to tie back to the actual counts taken at the end of the project. Also, function points do not have the physical connotation like LOC does. Proponents claim that function points have the advantage that they are independent from programming language, which make it of higher value than LOC for fourth-generation languages that are nonprocedural and do not have code lines. Function points can be estimated directly from the requirements, whereas only through analogy can LOC estimates be made at concept definition time.

Today, there is an International Function Point Users Group (IFPUG) that was formed over a decade ago to standardize the definitions and usage of the technology. Several other software development organizations already use function-point technology, while most of our projects estimate software sizes in units of number of lines of code, although a couple of our projects have successfully used function points in estimating size. Capers Jones's conversion table, shown in Table 12.1, can be used to translate function-point counts to LOC count, for several applicable programming languages.

Summary

When planning for a software development project, the following tasks should be fulfilled:

- Select of the software development life cycle.
- Understand the preliminary requirements and main limitations.
- Forecast the effort and schedule that will be needed, performing sizing and costing based on historical actuals as a basis of estimate.
- Use a divide-and-conquer approach to laying out software tasking for the skill set to be applied.

The appropriate estimation process is as follows:

- Gather input information, including the software size estimation matrix, and the decisions made concerning the software development life cycle.
- Generate the estimated total effort (in hours), based upon historical actuals.
- Spread the estimated total effort across each of the software tasks and schedule, in agreement with the major phase boundaries, and, if applicable, across the multiple builds in a spiral life cycle.
- Document each task, its effort, and schedule on a spreadsheet, including the basis-of-estimate information, listing the development life cycle assumptions that apply.
- Review the estimates for management and make suggested adjustments, as required.

References

Albrecht, Allan J. (1979). "Measuring Application Development Productivity." *Proceedings of the IBM Application Development Symposium*, 83–92.

Boehm, Barry. (1981). *Software Engineering Economics*. Englewood Cliffs, NJ: Prentice Hall.

Jones, Capers. (1986). *Programming Productivity*. New York: McGraw-Hill.

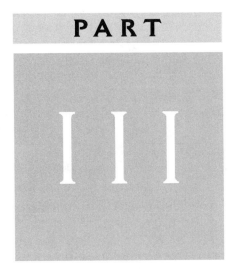

PART

III

Rapid Testing Examples

Example Requirements

13

Chapter 2 was devoted to the requirements definition process. A diagram of the requirements process, which was originally presented in Chapter 2, is repeated for convenience as Figure 13.1.

The requirements definition document captures all the system requirements in natural language so that it is easy to understand by customers and by those involved in product development. The input to the requirements definition document is the set of requirements that have been elicited from customers during informal interviews and from more structured sessions such as a Joint Application Requirements (JAR) session, as described in Chapter 8.

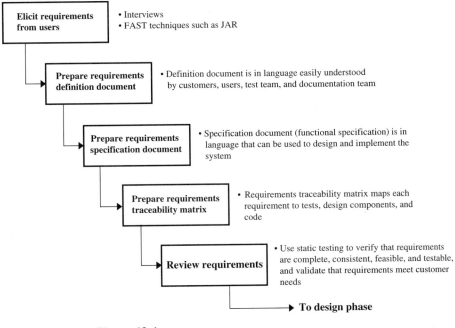

Figure 13.1
The requirements process.

As we discussed in Chapter 2, the requirements definitions should have the following characteristics:

- Each requirement should be uniquely identified so that we can refer to it unambiguously when we plan for test coverage, design test cases, and report test results.

- The requirements should be presented from a system user's viewpoint. System and acceptance tests will need to be designed based on the requirement definitions, so the definitions must be stated from a system-level perspective. This explicitly precludes requirements that deal with system internal details, which would require detailed knowledge of the code in order to perform testing. Such requirements should be derived in later phases of development, and should be covered by unit testing.

- Both *functional* and *nonfunctional* requirements should be included. Functional requirements are those that describe the services or features that the system is to perform. Nonfunctional requirements describe constraints that apply to system operation, such as the number of concurrent users and standards with which the system must comply. We need to test both types of requirements.

- The requirements definition document needs to be placed under configuration management. This means at a minimum that the document should be under version control, and that all versions of the document should be placed in a safe repository such as a directory that is routinely backed up. As the requirements change, we need to be able to track the changes and make corresponding changes to the systems and acceptance test cases.

An outline for the requirements definition document can be based on *IEEE Standard 830: The IEEE Guide to Software Requirements Specifications* (see Chapter 2 for discussion and reference).

In the remainder of this chapter, we present an example requirements definition document that has been prepared for the fictitious Test Management Toolkit (TMT) product. The Test Management Toolkit is an application that will allow test managers and engineers to manage test plans, bug reports, test results, and other information related to software testing. It is a Web-based application that permits several users, even when geographically dispersed, to support one or more test projects simultaneously. The TMT development project will provide examples throughout Part III. In the next chapter, an example test plan will be presented that is based on the TMT requirements that are defined here.

Document Identifier: TMT-RD-10
Revision: 0.8
Author: Chris Brown

Test Management Toolkit

Release 1.0

Requirements Definition

Revision History

Version	Date	Author	Description
0.1	08/31/2001	Chris Brown	TMT Requirements Draft
0.2	09/02/2001	Chris Brown	Project Management Added, Cleanup
0.3	09/02/2001	Chris Brown	Data Structure Expanded, Cleanup
0.4	09/03/2001	Chris Brown	Added the Create Trace Matrix Option
0.5	09/03/2001	Chris Brown	Added Help Screens
0.6	09/03/2001	Chris Brown	Added Project Name Field to Data Structure
0.7	09/07/2001	Chris Brown	Added Multi-User Requirement
0.8	09/07/2001	Chris Brown	Added Multi-User to Index Section 3

Approvals

Department	Name	Approval Date
Marketing	Chuck D. Klout, Director Marketing	09/07/2001
Development	Suzanna Perl, Manager Software Engineering	09/09/2001
Testing	Bret Gater, Manager Software Testing	09/09/2001

Table of Contents

1   Introduction

1.1   Purpose

The purpose of this document is to define requirements for the Test Management Toolkit (TMT) software product. The target audience is the marketing team, the software development team, the test team, and technical support personnel. The document is organized so that individual requirements can be separately identified and retrieved. The requirements are explained to a level of detail that will allow developers to design the product and testers to validate the product. The TMT product can be used to facilitate hardware, software, and systems testing. For simplicity, all examples of product use will be limited to software testing. This document is intended for internal use only.

1.2 Scope

The Test Management Toolkit is an application that will allow test managers and engineers to manage test plans, bug reports, test results, and other information related to software testing. It is a Web-based application that will allow several users, even when geographically dispersed, to support one or more test projects simultaneously.

1.3 Overview

This document will first provide a general description of the TMT application and will then list detailed requirements for the product. Each requirement will be tagged with a unique identifier to allow the engineering teams to trace their development and test efforts back to the requirements. The requirement tags take the form of section headings. For example, Section 2.2.1 is a requirement for how the TMT application handles test plan documents. The tag "2.2.1" can be used in subsequent project documentation to ensure that later references to this requirement can be traced back to its original statement in this document.

2 General Description

2.1 Product Perspective

The TMT application was developed to facilitate software testing. TMT will assist in the development, execution, and tracking of test programs. This requirements document will address features required to make this a commercial product for application in the development and test space.

2.2 Product Functions

This section describes the high-level functionality of the TMT product. More detailed requirements are given in Section 3.0.

2.2.1 Test Plans

The TMT product shall provide a means for creating, modifying, viewing, storing, and retrieving test plan documents.

2.2.2 Run List

The TMT product shall provide a means for creating, modifying, viewing, storing, and retrieving a list of tests to be executed. This list will be referred to in this document as "run list."

2.2.3 Tests

The TMT product shall provide a means for creating, modifying, viewing, storing, and retrieving individual tests, which may consist of components such as setup procedures, equipment lists, test procedures, test data, and test cleanup procedures.

2.2.4 Test Execution

The TMT product shall provide a means for executing tests from the run list in such a way that test results and log files can be created for each test.

2.2.5   Bug Reports

The TMT product shall provide a means for creating, modifying, viewing, sorting, storing, and retrieving bug reports.

2.2.6   Summary Reports

The TMT product shall provide a means for producing reports that summarize testing status, test results, and bug reports.

2.2.7   Backup and Restore

The TMT product shall provide a means for backing up and restoring tests and test results.

2.2.8   Security

The TMT product shall provide a means for creating users and assigning passwords. The TMT product will require user authentication to run tests and log results.

2.2.9   Remote Administration

The TMT product will have a module that allows for remote administration. The manager, lead, or systems administrator will have the ability to log in remotely to perform administrative functions on the database, and to create or modify user information.

2.2.10   Requirements Traceability Matrix

The TMT product will have a module that creates a requirements traceabilty matrix. This will be the framework or placeholder for the final trace matrix and will be filled in with the actual requirement numbers and description.

2.3   User Characteristics

The intended users of this product are managers, team leads, engineers, and technicians who test software products.

2.4   General Constraints

None of the following items are expected to limit the development team's options for designing the product.

- Regulatory policies
- Hardware limitations
- Interfaces to other applications
- Higher-order language requirements
- Protocols
- Criticality of the product

2.5   Assumptions and Dependencies

This section describes assumptions and dependencies for the TMT product. Each assumption or dependency is tagged with an identifier (section heading) for reference in later documents. These assumptions should be used when designing system configurations for testing the TMT product.

2.5.1   Operating Systems

It is assumed that the user will run the client application on a machine that is running one of the following operating systems:

Microsoft
- Windows 95
- Windows 98
- Windows Millennium Edition
- Windows XP
- Windows NT 3.51 or higher
- Windows 2000

Apple
- MAC OS 9.x or higher

It is assumed that the server application will be run on a machine that is running one of the following operating systems:

Microsoft
- Windows NT 3.51 or higher

UNIX
- Sun Solaris 2.6 or higher
- HPUX 10.x or higher
- Open BSD
- AIX 2.4.1 or higher
- SCO Open Desktop
- Linux Red Hat 6.x or higher

2.5.2   Browsers

It is assumed that the user will use one of the following browsers on the client machine: Netscape 4.0 or higher, or Internet Explorer 5.0 or higher.

2.5.3   Relational Database

It is assumed the host computer (server) is running a relational database capable of having multiple indexes loaded. It is also assumed that this database is capable of record locking. It is assumed that this relational database has an API that is compatible with standard SQL queries. The Oracle database application will be targeted for use with the initial release of TMT. Other database systems will be used with later releases as determined by customer response to the initial release.

2.5.4   Web Page Server

It is assumed the host computer (server) is running a Web page server application such as Apache or Microsoft Internet Information Server.

2.5.5   Processor Dependence

The application is not dependent on the type of processor used. The assumed operating systems can be used for x86, RISC, SPARC, Motorola, or PPC.

3   Specific Requirements

This section presents detailed requirements for the TMT product.

3.1   *Functional Requirements*

3.1.1   User Interface

The user interface for the TMT client will be created using HTML and displayed using a Web browser. The use of HTML will reduce the dependencies on a particular browser.

3.1.2   Navigation

The main menu for the Test Management Toolkit will include the following inventory:

Current Projects

Completed Projects

Project Maintenance

> *Create New Project*
> *Modify Project*
> *Remove Project*
> *Help*

Test Case Maintenance

> *Create Test Case or Suite*
> *Modify Test Case or Suite*
> *Remove Test Case or Suite*
> *Display Test*
> *Display Suite*
> *Help*

Test Case Execution

> *Run Single Test*
> *Run Suite*
> *Create Run List*
> *Execute Run List*

Test Results

> *Bug Summary*
> *Single Test*
> *Suite or Run List*
> *Help*

Utilities

> ***Create Trace Matrix***

Backup
Test Cases
Test Suites
Test Results
Help

Restore
Test Cases
Test Suites
Test Results
Help

Export
Test Cases
Test Suites
Test Results
Help

3.1.3   User Authentication—Client

The client session is established by logging into the host system by way of the Internet or company intranet. The users must enter their user name and password to run tests and log results. The user name and password will be unique, will be assigned by the administrator, and cannot be changed by the user.

3.1.4   User Authentication—Administrator

The manager, lead, or administrator shall be required to enter a user name and password to access user information or to administer the database. The user name and password will be unique and can be changed only by the administrator.

3.1.5   Current Projects

Once logged into the system the user will have the option to view active or current projects. Once the user selects this option from the main menu, a list of active projects will be displayed. By the project name will be the total number of tests or suites for the project. Next to the total number of tests/suites will be displayed the percent complete. Next to the percent complete will be displayed the number of passed tests. Next to the passed tests will be the passed tests as a percentage of the total number of tests. Next to the percent passed will be displayed the number of failed tests. Next to the failed tests will be the failed tests as a percentage of the total number of tests. Next to the failed percentage will be the total number of blocked tests. Next to the total number of blocked tests will be the number of blocked tests as a percentage of the total number of tests. Next to the blocked test percentage will be the time remaining for the project.

The time remaining will display "Not Known" or an actual number display as hours and minutes. The time taken for each test was determined the last time the test was executed. The time remaining will be the total time (aggregate of all tests) minus the time taken for the test already run.

3.1.6   Completed Projects

Once logged into the system the user will have the option to view completed projects. Once the user selects this option from the main menu, a list of completed projects will be displayed. Next to the project name will be the total number of tests or suites for the project. Next to the total number of tests/suites will be displayed the percent complete. Next to the percent complete will be displayed the number of passed tests. Next to the passed test will be the passed tests as a percentage of the total number of tests. Next to the percent passed will be displayed the number of failed tests. Next to the failed tests will be the failed tests as a percentage of the total number of tests. Next to the failed percentage will be the total number of blocked tests. Next to the total number of blocked tests will be the number of blocked tests as a percentage of the total number of tests. Next to the blocked test percentage will be the time required to run all tests for the project.

3.1.7 Create New Project

Once logged into the system the user will have the ability to create a new project. The creation process is started when the user selects "Create New Project" from the "Project Maintenance" menu. The user will be prompted for a name for this project. Once the user provides a name for the project a list of all available test cases and suites will be displayed.

Once the user has selected the test cases and/or suites for the project, the user will have the option to save the project or cancel the action and return to the main menu. If the user selects save, then the list of test cases and/or suites will be saved as a project.

3.1.8 Modify Project

Once logged into the system the user will have the ability to modify an existing project. The modification process is started when the user selects modify project from the "Project Maintenance" menu. The user will be prompted for a name for this project and will be displayed a list of available projects to choose from. The user will have the option to enter the name of the project they wish to modify or can simply double-click on the project name from the list displayed.

If there are no projects created, the message "No Projects Have Been Created" will be displayed. The user will have only one choice at this point and that is to acknowledge the message by clicking "OK" and returning to the main menu.

3.1.9 Remove Project

The removal process is initiated when the user selects "Remove Project" from the "Project Maintenance" menu. The user will be prompted for the name of the project they wish to remove and will be presented a list of available projects from which to choose. The user will have the option to enter the name of the project they wish to remove or can simply double-click on the project name from the list displayed.

If there are no projects created the message "No Projects Have Been Created" will be displayed. The user will have only one choice at this point and that is to acknowledge the message by clicking "OK" and returning to the main menu.

3.1.10 Create Test Case or Suite

Once logged into the system the user will have the ability to create new test cases or suites of tests. The creation process is started when the user selects "Create Test Case or Suite Test" from the "Test Case Maintenance" menu.

If there is a project already identified, then the user will be prompted to either enter the name or se-lect it from the list. If there are no projects or suites identified the user will be asked if this is a single test case or part of a suite. If the user selects single then the user will be prompted for a name for this test. If the user selects suite then the user will be prompted for a name for this suite.

Test Case:

The user will be presented with a form-type interface with predetermined fields requiring data of a pre-determined type to be entered. This form will be referred to as a "bucket" at this stage, which is a repre-sentation of the data structure of the record about to be created. Once the data is entered for this record, the user will have the option to save the test or cancel the action. Once the user selects save, the data record is appended to the database. The user is given an option to send the test case to a printer.

Suite:

If the user selects suite there will be a prompt to enter the name of the suite. Then a list of available (al-ready created) test cases will be displayed. The user simply selects the test cases by clicking the check box by the test case that is to be included. Once the selections are complete, the user will have the op-tion to save the suite or cancel the action. Once the user selects save the suite is created and is ap-pended to the database. The user is given an option to send the test suite to a printer.

3.1.11   Modify Test Case or Suite

Once logged into the system the user will have the ability to modify existing test cases or suites of tests. The modification process is started when the user selects "Modify Test Case or Suite" from the "Test Case Maintenance" menu.

The user will be prompted to either enter the name of the test or suite. The user will have the option to select it from a list. If there are no tests or suites then the user will see the message "There are no Test Cases or Suites to Modify."

Test Case:

The user will be presented with the test in the same format as with creation. The user will be presented with a form-type interface with the fields containing data of the type predetermined for the field. Once changes are made to the test case, the user will have the option to save the changed test or cancel the action. Once the user selects save, the data record is appended to the database. The user is then given an option to send the test case to a printer.

Suite:

If the user selects a suite to modify, all of the available tests will be displayed with the ones already se-lected for the suite identified with the check boxes.

The user will have the option to select additional tests or deselect the ones already checked. Once the user has completed the selection or deselection process, there will be three options available. The modified suite can be saved with the same name as before or saved as a new suite. Once save is se-lected, the suite is closed and the changes are appended to the database. The user will also have the option to cancel the action and abandon all changes. The user is given an option to send the test suite to a printer.

3.1.12   Remove Test Case or Suite

The removal process is initiated when the user selects "Remove Test Case or Suite" from the "Test Case Maintenance" menu. The user will have the option of removing a single test case or an entire test suite. Upon selection, a list of suites or test cases will be displayed. Each entry will have a check box associated with it. The user simply selects or deselects the items to be removed.

The user then has the option to delete the selected files or cancel the action. If the user selects delete there will be one additional prompt, "Are you sure?" The user will have the option to select "Yes, Delete the selected files" or cancel the action. If the user selects the option to continue the removal process then the records will be removed from the system. The user is given an option to send the removed file list to a printer.

3.1.13   Display Test

This option will give the user the ability to view the detail of a test case. When the user selects "Display Test" from the "Test Case Maintenance" menu, there will be a list of all available tests. The user simply double-clicks on the test they wish to view. The test case will be displayed in the same format as when the data was entered during the creation phase. The displayed data is strictly read-only from this screen. The user is given an option to send the test case to a printer.

3.1.14   Display Suite

This option will give the user the ability to view the contents of a test suite. When the user selects "Display Suite" from the "Test Case Maintenance" menu, there will be a list of all available suites. The user simply double-clicks on the suite they wish to view. The contents of the test suite will be displayed as a list of test cases. Only the test cases that were checked during the creation phase will be displayed. No changes to the contents of the suite can be made on the screen, as this option is read-only. The user is given an option to send the test suite to a printer.

3.1.15   Run Single Test

This option is initiated when the user selects "Run Single Test" from the "Test Case Execution" menu. The user will be presented with a list of all available tests. The user simply double-clicks on the test case they wish to run. Both manual and automated tests can be run, as explained below.

Manual Testing:

The test case is displayed in read-only mode with several options at the bottom. It is assumed that the tester will perform actions detailed in the test case and observe the results. The user selects "Pass," "Fail," or "Blocked." If "Fail" or "Blocked" are selected the tester will be prompted for details. A text box is opened and the user enters details of the fail if they are available. The user would enter details for a "Blocked" test as well. Once the user has entered the details of the nonpassed test then the user selects "Finish" and the result is logged.

Automated Testing:

If the test is automated, then double-clicking will initiate the script, which can be written in Perl, TCL, or another scripting language. The test will run and the results will automatically be logged.

3.1.16　Run Suite

This option is initiated when the user selects "Run Suite" from the Test Execution menu. A list of available suites will be displayed. The user double-clicks the suite that they wish to run. This will cause one of two actions. The tests could all be manual, in which case they would be displayed one at a time, giving the user time to go through the manual steps and enter the pass/fail results. The next test would then be displayed, and so on.

If the tests are automated, then all of the tests in the suite would be run and the results logged.

It is also be possible to have a combination of manual and automated tests. This depends on the details of the individual tests that are selected during the creation phase of the suite.

3.1.17　Create Run List

This option allows the user to generate a list of tests that can be selected from any test cases contained in any test suite. Each run list is given a name and can be saved for later execution.

3.1.18　Execute Run List

This option allows the user to select and execute any run list that has been previously created and saved.

3.1.19　Bug Summary

This option will prompt the user to choose current or completed projects to analyze. It is selected from the Test Results menu. If the user chooses current, then a list of current projects will be displayed. If the user selects completed, then a list of completed projects will be displayed. The user will double-click the name of the project they wish to analyze. A detailed display of the bugs found will be displayed by severity. This is useful when looking for trends or gauging product readiness or stability.

3.1.20　Test Results—Single Test

This option will display a list of test case results. It is selected from the Test Results menu. The display can be sorted by test identifier, date of test, and time of test, or on the status of the test, these being pass, fail, or blocked. Ranges can be selected and totals generated.

3.1.21　Test Results—Suite or Run List

This option will produce a list of suites or run lists that have been executed or are in progress. The option is selected from the Test Results menu. Totals for pass, fail, blocked, and percent complete will be displayed.

3.1.22　Create Trace Matrix

This option will generate the Requirements Traceabilty Matrix for use during the test planning, test executions phase. This option is initiated when the user selects "Create Trace Matrix" from the "Utilities" menu. The user will be prompted for the name of a project to use for this generation. The users have the option to enter the name of the project they wish to map or can simply double-click on the name of the project displayed on the same screen. A screen report will be created with the defined requirements on one axis and placeholders for the corresponding test case information. This screen will also give the user the option to send the matrix to a printer or output it to an Excel-compatible spreadsheet.

If there are no projects created the message "No Projects Have Been Created" will be displayed. The user will have only one choice at this point and that is to acknowledge the message by clicking "OK" and returning to the main menu.

3.1.23   Backup—Test Cases

This option will allow the user to create archival backups of test cases. This action is initiated when the user selects the "Backup Test Cases" option from the "Utilities" menu. The user will be prompted for a name of the backup and a target media. This will differ from system to system. In a Windows environment the standard list of physical, logical, or mapped network drives will be displayed. On a UNIX system, you may have a list of aliased mounts from which to choose. Depending on the size of the files to be backed up it may be impractical to send this to a floppy. On some systems with CDR or CDRW, you can simply point to this device and it will write to it without the need to use CD-burning software.

3.1.24   Backup—Test Suites

This option will allow the user to create archival backups of test suites. This action is initiated when the user selects the "Backup Test Suites" option from the "Utilities" menu. The user will be prompted for a name of the backup and a target media. This will differ from system to system. In a Windows environment the standard list of physical, logical, or mapped network drives will be displayed. On a UNIX system, you may have a list of aliased mounts from which to choose. Depending on the size of the files to be backed up it may be impractical to send this to a floppy. On some systems with CDR or CDRW, you can simply point to this device and it will write to it without the need to use CD-burning software.

3.1.25   Backup Test Results

This option will allow the user to create archival backups of the test results. This action is initiated when the user selects the "Backup Test Results" option from the "Utilities" menu. The user will be prompted for a name of the backup and a target media. This will differ from system to system. In a Windows environment the standard list of physical, logical, or mapped network drives will be displayed. On a UNIX system, you may have a list of aliased mounts from which to choose. Depending on the size of the files to be backed up it may be impractical to send this to a floppy. On some systems with CDR or CDRW, you can simply point to this device and it will write to it without the need to use CD-burning software.

3.1.26   Restore Test Cases

This option allows the user to restore test cases that were previously backed up. This action is initiated by selecting the "Restore Test Cases" option from the "Utilities" menu. You will be prompted for a source location and file name to restore.

3.1.27   Restore Test Suites

This option allows the user to restore test suites that were previously backed up. This action is initiated by selecting the "Restore Test Suites" option from the "Utilities" menu. You will be prompted for a source location and file name to restore.

3.1.28   Restore Test Results

This option allows the user to restore test results that were previously backed up. This action is initiated by selecting the "Restore Test Results" option from the "Utilities" menu. You will be prompted for a source location and file name to restore.

3.1.29 Export Test Cases

This option will export the selected test cases in a comma delimited ASCII format. This action is initiated by selecting the "Export Test Cases" option from the "Utilities" menu. A list of all available test cases will be displayed. The user simply double-clicks the test case they wish to export. They will then be prompted for a target location and target file name. The user will be given the option to send this to a printer.

3.1.30 Export—Test Suites

This option will export the selected test suite, broken into individual test cases in a comma delimited ASCII format. This action is initiated by selecting the "Export Test Suites" option from the "Utilities" menu. A list of all available test suites will be displayed. The user simply double-clicks the test suite they wish to export. They will then be prompted for a target location and target file name. The user will be given the option to send this to a printer.

3.1.31 Export—Test Results

This option will export the selected test results in a comma delimited ASCII format. This action is initiated by selecting the "Export Test Results" option from the "Utilities" menu. A list of all available test results will be displayed. The user simply double-clicks the test case they wish to export. They will then be prompted for a target location and target file name. The user will be given the option to send this to a printer.

3.1.32 Help

This will be a feature-specific help screen for each menu. The contents of this help screen will be specific to the menu on which it is located.

3.1.33 Multiuser Functionality

The product will be used in a commercial, networked environment and will likely have more then one user testing one or more projects simultaneously. We need to ensure that the product does not suffer too great a performance hit when more than one tester is on the system. Based on input from marketing, the ability to have as many as five testers on at the same time would be greatly desired.

3.2 External Interface Requirements

There are no external hardware or software interface dependencies.

3.3 Performance Requirement

This section describes a performance requirement on the TMT product.

3.3.1 Multiple User Ability

The Test Management Toolkit is designed to be multiuser. Since it is primarily a design as well as an internal tool, the stress loads of commercial Web applications will not be met. It is important, however, to make sure that as many as five client sessions coexist without intolerable degradation of performance.

Testing should examine performance with one to five users performing similar and dissimilar activities simultaneously.

3.4 Design Constraints

The initial release of the TMT product will use the Oracle database application. Design and implementation of the product should be compatible with Oracle.

3.5 Data Structure

The design of the data structure for the test case is shown in Table 3.1 and the active indices are shown in Table 3.2.

3.6 Attributes

There are no dependencies on maintainability and portability.

3.7 Other Requirements

No other requirements are stated at this time.

Field Description	Field Label	Field Type	Field Size
Project Name	PRJNAM	Character	20
Requirement Satisfied	REQSAT	Numeric	8
Requirement Name	REQNAM	Character	20
Test Identifier	TSTID	Character	20
Test Name	TSTNAM	Character	20
Expected Result	XRSLT	Character	50
Hardware Required	HWREQ	Character	256
Test Setup	TSTSUP	Character	256
Configuration Name	CFGNAM	Character	20
Test 1 Name	TST1NAM	Character	20
Test 1 Steps	TST1STP	Character	256
Test 2 Name	TST2NAM	Character	20
Test 2 Steps	TST2STP	Character	256
Test 3 Name	TST3NAM	Character	20
Test 3 Steps	TST3STP	Character	256
Test 4 Name	TST4NAM	Character	20
Test 4 Steps	TST4STP	Character	256
Test 5 Name	TST5NAM	Character	20
Test 5 Steps	TST5STP	Character	256
User ID	UID	Character	20
Date	DATRUN	Date	8
Time Start	START	Time	4
Time Stop	STOP	Time	4
Time Needed	TIMREQ	Numeric	4
Pass	PASS	Logical	T/F
Fail	FAIL	Logical	T/F
Fail Detail	FLDTL	Character	256
Blocked	BLCKD	Logical	T/F
Blocked Detail	BLKDTL	Character	256
Post Test Cleanup	CLNUP	Character	50

Table 3.1   Test Case Data Structure

Index Description	Index Name
Requirement Satisfied	REQSAT.IDX
Test Identifier	TSTID.IDX
User ID	UID.IDX
Pass	PASS.IDX
Fail	FAIL.IDX
Blocked	BLCKD.IDX

Table 3.2 Test Case Indices

References

No references.

Appendix 1—Acronyms

API—Application Programming Interface
ASCII—American Standard Code for Information Interchange
CDR—Compact Disc Recordable
CDRW—Compact Disc Rewriteable
HTML—Hypertext Markup Language
ISO—International Organization for Standardization
PPC—Power PC
RISC—Reduced Instruction Set Computing
SQL—Structured Query Language
SPARC—Scalable Processor Architecture
TCL—Tool Command Language
TMT—Test Management Toolkit
X86—Refers to the Intel line of processors

Appendix 2—Definition of terms

Not applicable.

Appendix 3—Email approvals

From: Chuck D. Klout [cdklout@tmtco]

Sent: Wed 9/7/01 2:23 PM

To: Chris Brown [cbrown@tmtco]; test@tmtco; development@tmtco

Cc: marketing@tmtco; customersupport@tmtco

Subject: TMT 1.0 Requirements Definition

Team,

I have reviewed the requirements definition for the first release of TMT and find that this document very much addresses the requirements as laid out by our customers. I approve the requirements definition TMT-RD-10 Rev 8 as written.

I am meeting with our customers next week to refine the must-have hardware list and should have an answer in time to review the test plan.

Thanks,

Chuck

Chuck D. Klout

Director, Marketing

TMTCO

cdklout@tmtco.com

From: Suzie Perl [sperl@tmtco.com]

Sent: Thurs 9/9/2001 09:30 AM

To: Chris Brown [cbrown@tmtco]; test@tmtco; development@tmtco

Cc: marketing@tmtco; customersupport@tmtco

Subject: TMT 1.0 Requirements Definition

All,

Good job! I have reviewed the requirements definition TMT-RD-10 Revision 8 for the first release of TMT and approve it for use by development as written.

Regards,

Suzie

Suzanna Perl

Manager, Software Engineering

TMTCO

From: Bret Gater [bgater@tmtco.com]

Sent: Thurs 9/9/2001 07:30 AM

To: Chris Brown [cbrown@tmtco]; test@tmtco; development@tmtco

Cc: marketing@tmtco; customersupport@tmtco

Subject: TMT 1.0 Requirements Definition

Team,

I have reviewed the requirements definition TMT-RD-10 Rev 8 and approve it for use by the test team as written.

Regards,

Bret

Bret Gater

Manager, Software Engineering

TMTCO

Example Test Plan

14

In Chapter 3 we emphasized the importance of effectiveness of test planning as being a major factor of success for the project in terms of meeting the budget and schedule. A diagram of test planning activities, which was originally presented in Chapter 3, is repeated for convenience as Figure 14.1.

The inputs to the planning process are the requirements documents that were described in Chapter 2. An example of a requirements definition document was given in Chapter 13. The output of the test planning activities is a test plan, which is a document or set of documents that should be reviewed by the test team, the development team, and program management. The test plan identifies the resources that will be needed to test the product, defines what will be tested, how the testing will be done, and what outputs or deliverables will result from testing. The contents and format of the test plan were discussed in Chapter 3, and an example of a test plan is given in this chapter.

A useful guideline for developing a test plan may be found in *IEEE Standard 829, IEEE Standard for Software Test Documentation* (see discussion and reference in Chapter 3). You may choose to use an alternate format, but you should consider including all the material in the IEEE standard in whatever format you choose. In this chapter we'll use IEEE Standard 829 as the basis for the example test plan.

The outline of a test plan is defined in the standard to have 16 components:

1. Test-plan identifier
2. Introduction
3. Test items
4. Features to be tested
5. Features not to be tested
6. Approach

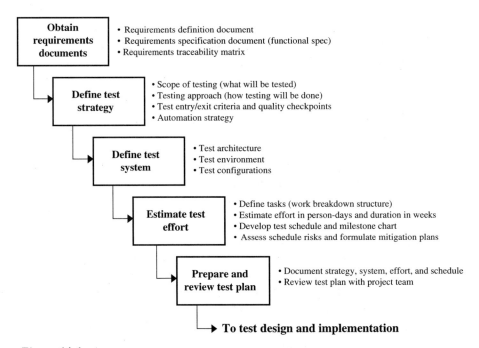

Figure 14.1
Test planning activities.

7. Item pass/fail criteria

8. Suspension criteria and resumption requirements

9. Test deliverables

10. Testing tasks

11. Environmental needs (or test configuration information)

12. Responsibilities

13. Staffing and training needs

14. Schedule

15. Risks and contingencies

16. Approvals

If you consider the list above, you'll see two things that the standard test plan is *not*—it is not a detailed specification of how the tests are to be performed, and it is not a place where test results are recorded. Some test organizations combine one or more of these items with the contents of a test plan in order to keep the test documentation all in one place. That can work very well, but in this book we will go for the more modular set of documentation that is set forth in the standard.

In the remainder of this chapter, we present an example test plan that has been prepared for the fictitious Test Management Toolkit (TMT) product. The test plan uses the TMT Requirements Definition document presented in Chapter 13 as its input.

Document Identifier: TMT-TP-10
Revision: 0.8
Authors: C. Brown
             J. Barnes

Test Management Toolkit

Release 1.0

Test Plan

Revision History

Version	Date	Author	Description
0.1	09/02/2001	Chris Brown	Test plan draft for requirements doc: TMT-RS-05
0.2	09/03/2001	Chris Brown	Clean up and sync to: TMT-RS-05
0.3	09/03/2001	Chris Brown	Started building detailed test cases
0.4	09/05/2001	Chris Brown	Completed test cases. Last scrub
0.5	09/06/2001	Chris Brown	Major cleanup, more test cases, final format
0.6	09/07/2001	Chris Brown	Final Sync with TMT-RS-07 added MU Tests
0.7	09/09/2001	Chris Brown	Added MU Test Case to section 2
0.8	09/10/2001	J. Barnes	Test configurations, effort estimate, and schedule

Approvals

Department	Name and Title	Approval Date
Marketing	Chuck D. Klout, Director Marketing	09/11/2001
Development	Suzanna Perl, Manager Software Engineering	09/12/2001
Testing	Bret Gater, Manager Software Testing	09/12/2001

Table of Contents

1   Introduction

The purpose of this document is to detail the test procedures designed to validate the functionality of the Test Management Toolkit. The features addressed in this document are derived from the requirements document entitled: Test Management Toolkit, Requirements Definition. The requirements document is identified as: TMT-RD-10, which is located under document control at:

   http://www.tmtcointernal.com/usr/www/docstores/design/requirements/TMT-RD-10.doc

2   Test Items

The following is a high-level list of the product components that are addressed by this test plan:

- **Release to be tested**—This test effort will address the feature functionality of the Test Management Toolkit, release 1.0.
- **Bug fixes**—This is the first release of this product so there are no fixes of bugs found in previous releases that require testing. All bugs that are found and fixed during this test effort will be verified as fixed.

- **Distribution media**—The initial release of the product will be downloadable from the developer's Web site. Customers who have been approved by marketing can also obtain the product on CD. Both forms of distribution will be tested.
- **End-user documents**—The client and server are presumed to be in different locations so there will be two separate modules, each with its own installer. End-user documents such as user guides, installation guides, and release notes will be downloadable separately so that the customer can review the system requirements and installation procedures. The installation and packaging will be tested and the documentation reviewed for accuracy.

3   Features To Be Tested

The following features will be tested to ensure that the Test Management Toolkit satisfies the requirements specified in the TMT Requirements Specification:

- Requirement 3.1.1 User Interface
- Requirement 3.1.2 Navigation
- Requirement 3.1.3 User Authentication—Client
- Requirement 3.1.4 User Authentication—Administrator
- Requirement 3.1.5 Current Projects
- Requirement 3.1.6 Completed Projects
- Requirement 3.1.7 Create Project
- Requirement 3.1.8 Modify Project
- Requirement 3.1.9 Remove Project
- Requirement 3.1.10 Create Test Case or Suite
- Requirement 3.1.11 Modify Test Case or Suite
- Requirement 3.1.12 Remove Test Case or Suite
- Requirement 3.1.13 Display Test
- Requirement 3.1.14 Display Suite
- Requirement 3.1.15 Run Single Test
- Requirement 3.1.16 Run Suite
- Requirement 3.1.17 Create Run List
- Requirement 3.1.18 Execute Run List
- Requirement 3.1.19 Bug Summary
- Requirement 3.1.20 Test Results – Single Test
- Requirement 3.1.21 Test Results – Suite or Run List
- Requirement 3.1.22 Create Requirements Traceability Matrix
- Requirement 3.1.23 Backup—Test Cases
- Requirement 3.1.24 Backup—Test Suites
- Requirement 3.1.25 Backup Results
- Requirement 3.1.26 Restore Test Cases
- Requirement 3.1.27 Restore Test Suites
- Requirement 3.1.28 Restore Test Results
- Requirement 3.1.29 Export Test Cases
- Requirement 3.1.30 Export—Test Suites

- Requirement 3.1.31 Export—Test Results
- Requirement 3.1.32 Help
- Requirement 3.1.33 Multiuser Functionality

4 Features Not To Be Tested

The following is a list of functionality and/or system configurations that will not be tested.

- Installation and functionality of the relational database will not be addressed by this test plan. It is assumed that the database is installed and is operational. It is also assumed the data structure is accurate and contains the required fields of the type and size defined in the requirements specification. These requirements are detailed in the preparation and installation documentation guides.
- The Web Server (Apache or IIS) will not be tested directly by this plan.
- Expansive client/server stress testing will not be addressed by this test plan. Multi-user functionality will be tested with five real users, which was specified as a minimal multi-user configuration.

5 Approach

The overall testing approach includes feature testing, regression testing, product installation testing, backup and restore testing, and GUI testing. Each type of testing is described in more detail in this section.

5.1 Feature testing

All features described in the requirements definition TMT-RD-10 will be tested on the selected combinations of client/server configurations that will be described in Section 10. Feature testing will include both functional testing and negative testing (performing operations or using data not intended by the designers).

5.2 Regression testing

Since this is the first product release, there is no need to verify that bugs fixed in previous releases are not broken. The concern in this release is that bug fixes made during the system test phase do not break previously working functionality.

The following approach will be taken to provide regression testing of the first release.

- Bugs are to be fixed as they are found. For each software build that is released to the test team, tests will be run to verify that the bugs fixed in that build do not reoccur. In other words, each bug fix will be verified in the build in which it is fixed.
- Once the product is stable and test cases proven, there will be one final regression pass before the readiness review. For this release, the regression pass will include all test cases.

5.3 Product installation

Each software build released to the test team will be installed in accordance with the installation procedure that will be used by the customer. However, for each build, the client and server modules will only be installed on a subset of all possible combinations of platforms and operating systems defined in the requirements specification. It will be assumed that successful installation on one UNIX platform implies success on all other UNIX platforms, and the same will be assumed for the different flavors of Windows. This approach meets with customer approval (see approval email from marketing).

5.4   Backup and restore

Backup and restore will be tested on projects, test cases, test suites, and test results. We will backup physical and logical devices both locally and across a network. Backup across a network is the most likely scenario for the customer, and will therefore receive the most attention.

5.5   GUI testing

The following approach will be taken to test the TMT GUI:
- The graphical user interface will be tested using Netscape Navigator and Microsoft Internet Explorer. A complete inventory will be performed as well as test of the navigation with both browsers.
- All testing will be performed manually.
- All defects will be tracked to closure using the corporate defect tracking system. This point is intended to address shortfalls in GUI testing identified in various recent post-project assessments.

6   Pass/Fail Criteria

The pass/fail criterion for each test case is described by its expected result. If the expected result is obtained when a test case runs, the test passes. If the expected result is not obtained when the test is run, the test fails. If a test cannot be run due to a blocking bug in the build, the result of the test can be called "blocked."

In order for the TMT product to successfully exit the system test phase, 100% of the tests defined in this test plan will need to be run on at least one build of software. 100% of all tests run will need to pass, and there can be no bugs of catastrophic severity that remain unfixed at the end of testing.

7   Suspension Criteria and Resumption Requirements

If fundamental functionality, such as the ability to install and run the program, does not work, testing will be suspended until the functionality is available. Attempts will be made to continue in the face of catastrophic bugs unless the bugs are so severe that 50% or more of the test cases are blocked. If testing is suspended, the development and test teams will meet daily to assess progress until they agree that testing can resume.

8   Test Deliverables

The following items are work products that will be outputs of the testing process:
- This test plan
- A requirements traceabilty matrix

- Test specification document
- Test result reports
- Daily test status updates to test and development managers
- Defect (bug) reports

Release notes will be the responsibility of development; however, the release notes will be reviewed and approved by the test team before the readiness review.

9   Testing Tasks

The tasks to be performed in testing the TMT application are listed below:

- Perform product installation testing
- Run feature tests and report bugs
- Verify bug fixes
- Run backup and restore tests
- Perform GUI testing
- Conduct bug reviews
- Prepare test status reports
- Write test results report

In this section an estimate will be made of the time (in person-hours) that will be required to perform the tasks listed above. These effort estimates are based on a Wideband Delphi session held on 9/1/2001. The factor that has the most impact on the amount of time and resources needed to test the TMT product is the number of client/server operating systems called for in the requirements definition. A summary of the operating systems is shown in Table 9.1.

It can be seen from Table 9.1 that there are seven client operating systems and seven server operating systems called out in the requirements definition, assuming that only one of the various versions of Windows NT, Solaris 2.6, OS9.x, and Linux 6.x are used. This means there are a total of 49 possible combinations of client and server operating systems. If it takes an average of 5 hours to install each combination of client/server system, then the total time that would be required for product installation testing alone is 5 x 49 = 245 hours, or about 30 working days. Note that installation includes installing

Client Operating System	Server Operating System
Microsoft Windows	Microsoft Windows
- Windows 95	- Windows NT 3.51 or higher
- Windows 98	UNIX
- Windows ME	- Sun Solaris 2.6 or higher
- Windows XP	- HPUX 10.x or higher
- Windows NT 3.51 or higher	- Open BSD
- Windows 2000	- AIX 2.4.1 or higher
Apple	- SCO Open Desktop
- MAC OS 9.x or higher	- Linux Red Hat 6.x or higher

Table 9.1   Client and Server Operating Systems

an operating system, a relational database application, and the TMT application on client and server, as well as installation of a browser on the client. If all feature tests and backup tests are run on all 49 combinations, the time required to test TMT would be prohibitive.

Due to the excessive time required to test all possible combinations, the subset of client/server combinations that will be used for product installation testing is shown in Table 9.2.

The reduced number of combinations is expected to lower the effort required for product testing to 35 person-hours, which is significantly reduced from the 245 hours needed for all combinations. The number of combinations listed in Table 9.2 is still excessive for running the feature tests and for the backup/restore testing. For this testing, the number of client/server combinations is further reduced to the two configurations shown in Table 9.3.

Assuming that the selected client/server combinations shown in Tables 9.2 and 9.3 are used, the estimated effort for each test cycle of the TMT application is given in Table 9.4. Note that a single test cycle includes running a complete set of planned tests against a candidate software build. It is assumed that three test cycles will be required to test the TMT application, so the total test effort will be three times the effort estimated in Table 9.4.

Combination	Client Operating System	Server Operating System
1	- Windows 95	- Windows NT 3.51
2	- Windows 98	- Sun Solaris 2.6
3	- Windows ME	- HPUX 10.1
4	- Windows XP	- Open BSD
5	- Windows NT 3.51	- AIX 2.4.1 or higher
6	- Windows 2000	- Linux 6.5
7	- MAC OS 9.0	- SCO Open Desktop

Table 9.2   Selected Client/Server Combinations for Product Installation Testing

Combination	Client Operating System	Server Operating System
1	- Windows 98	- Sun Solaris 2.6
2	- Windows 2000	- Linux 6.5

Table 9.3   Selected Client/Server Combinations for Feature and Backup/Restore Testing

Task	Time (hrs)
Product installation testing	35
Run feature tests & report bugs	16
Verify bug fixes	24
Backup and restore tests	24
GUI testing	16
Report test status	16
Conduct bug reviews	8
Total	139

Table 9.4   Estimated Effort for Each Test Cycle

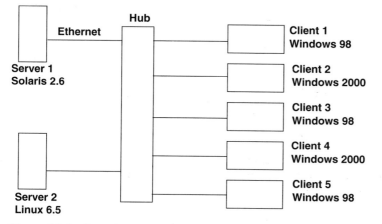

Figure 10.1   Test Setup #1.

10   Test Configuration Information

A diagram of Test Setup #1, which will be used for feature testing, backup/restore testing, and GUI testing, is shown in Figure 10.1. There are two servers and five clients in the test setup, with the servers and clients all connected to a common network. Test Setup #1 is based on the selected combinations of client/server operating systems given in Table 9.3. It is anticipated that Test Setup #1 will be the primary configuration used for bug verification.

Although it is not shown explicitly in Figure 10.1, the servers, and clients will all be running the Oracle database application as the relational database system used by TMT. This limitation in testing configuration needs to be included in the release notes. It is expected that other database systems will be used in future testing.

Also not shown explicitly in the figure is the use of Internet Explorer as the browser application on Clients 1, 3, and 5, and the use of Netscape Navigator as the browser application on Clients 2 and 4. A diagram of Test Setup #2 is shown in Figure 10.2. This test setup is designed for the product installation tests, but can be used for other testing if needed. Note that Test Setup #2 is the only setup that supports testing with an Apple Macintosh platform.

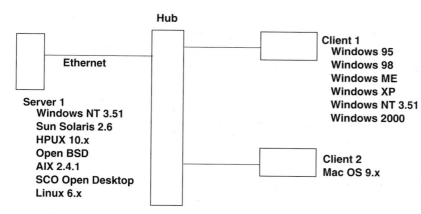

Figure 10.2   Test Setup #2.

11   Responsibilities

This section discusses testing responsibilities at an organizational level; it does not cover the roles and responsibilities of individual test engineers, which is discussed in the next section.

Development Team Responsibilities
- Unit test features as they are developed
- Perform integration testing on features before they are packaged in a build for the test team
- Prepare software builds for the test team at times to be determined in weekly meetings held with the development and test teams
- Assist test engineers in assessing test results and characterizing bugs as needed so that accurate reports can be entered into the defect tracking system
- Fix bugs entered into the defect tracking system
- Prepare release notes for bugs that are not fixed in a release that is shipped to a customer
- Engineer "low customer impact" workarounds for bugs that are not fixed but that are included in the release notes

Test Team Responsibilities
- Run planned tests and enter bug reports into the defect tracking system for anomalous results
- Assist the development engineer in reproducing bugs
- Conduct regular bug reviews during the system test phase; the reviews will be conducted on a weekly basis, unless the test and development teams decide that more frequent reviews are needed
- Test bug fixes to verify that the repaired software demonstrates expected behavior (satisfies the specified requirements)
- Prepare weekly status reports on test progress and bugs found
- Prepare a test results report at the end of the system test phase; a summary of this report will be presented at the product readiness review; the summary will include a determination of whether the test exit criteria specified in Section 6 have been met

12   Staffing and Training Needs

The staffing roles and responsibilities for testing the TMT application are shown in Table 12.1.

D. Nguyen will require training on Oracle database administration, and C. Taylor, who is new to the company, will require the internal training program, "Software Testing 101," which will include mentoring by J. Barnes. All training will be completed prior to delivery of the first software build to the test team by development.

Person	Position	Responsibility	Availability
J. Barnes	Test Lead	Test coordination, reporting, & feature tests	100%
D. Nguyen	Tester	Product installation and testbed setup	100%
S. Scafidi	Tester	Backup/restore tests	50%
C. Taylor	Tester	GUI tests	50%
B. Wheeler	Developer	Unit and integration testing, bug fixes	100%

Table 12.1   Test Staffing

13   Schedule

The schedule for system testing the TMT application is shown in Table 13.1. The smoke test shown in the schedule is intended as an early look at the software, and will allow major blocking bugs in the application as well as bugs in the test configuration and test cases to be found. The smoke test will consist of a subset of the installation and feature test cases.

Task	Start Date	End Date
Configure & debug test setups #1 and #2	10/1	10/12
Smoke test on preliminary build	10/15	10/19
Test cycle #1	10/22	11/2
Test cycle #2	11/5	11/16
Test cycle #3	11/19	11/30
Readiness review	12/3	12/3

Table 13.1   Schedule for TMT System Testing

It is assumed that all unit and integration testing done by the development team will occur prior to the start of Test Setup #1, and that all catastrophic bugs found in that testing will be fixed prior to start of system testing.

14   Risks and Contingencies

Table 14.1 shows the risks associated with testing TMT, the estimated probability that the risk will occur, the impact that would result from the risk, and a brief description of the mitigation plan for each risk.

Risk	Likelihood	Impact	Mitigation
Development of backup test cases are likely to be delayed because backup subsystem design has not been finalized, and prototyping has revealed major problems.	75%	Major	Test lead will attend development design meetings and revise test cases as information becomes available.
C. Taylor may be on leave during the month of November due to a family illness. Her absence would cause schedule slip of 2 days per test cycle.	50%	Minor	One of the GUI developers, R. Carini, has agreed to run the GUI tests, and S. Scafidi will review the test results, if Taylor is absent.
The service contract on the networking system has expired, and contract renewal is under negotiation. If the contract is not renewed by start of test, schedule delays could occur in the event of networking problems.	20%	Minor	Monitor the status of the service contract and advise upper management of the risk if an agreement has not been reached by start of the smoke test.

Table 14.1   Risk Identification and Mitigation

References

Chris Brown, *Test Management Toolkit, Requirements Definition*. Document TMT-RD-10, which is located under document control at:

> http://www.tmtcointernal.com/usr/www/docstores/design/requirements/TMT-RD-10.doc

Appendix 1—Acronyms

API—Application Programming Interface
ASCII—American Standard Code for Information Interchange
CDR—Compact Disc Recordable
CDRW—Compact Disc Rewriteable
HTML—Hypertext Markup Language
ISO—International Organization for Standardization
PPC—Power PC
RISC—Reduced Instruction Set Computing
SQL—Structured Query Language
SPARC—Scalable Processor Architecture
TCL—Tool Command Language
TMT—Test Management Toolkit
X86—Refers to the Intel line of processors

Appendix 2—Definition of Terms

Not applicable.

Appendix 3—Email Approvals

From: Chuck D. Klout [cklout@tmtco.com]

Sent: Wed 9/11/01 4:40 PM

To: Chris Brown [cbrown@tmtco]; test@tmtco; development@tmtco

Cc: marketing@tmtco; customersupport@tmtco

Subject: TMT 1.0 Test Plan

Team,

First, I would like to thank the team for working so hard to produce the requirements and test plan for this release. I approve the test plan TMT-TP-10 Rev 8 as written.

I have met with our customers to define a must-have list of certified hardware for this release. The assertions made in the test plan regarding assumed compatibility with a limited test matrix makes good sense to our customers so we should proceed with the short list of systems and operating systems referred to in sections 9 and 10 regarding Test Configuration Information. This combination of hardware and operating systems will cover actual configurations in use and planned by our customers.

Thanks,

Chuck

Chuck D. Klout
Director, Marketing
TMTCO

From: Suzie Perl [sperl@tmtco]

Sent: Thurs 9/12/2001 09:30 AM

To: Chris Brown [cbrown@tmtco]; test@tmtco; development@tmtco

Cc: marketing@tmtco; customersupport@tmtco

Subject: TMT 1.0 Test Plan

All,

Great job! I have reviewed the test plan TMT-TP-10, Revision 8, for the first release of TMT and approve it for use by development as written.

Regards,

Suzie

Suzanna Perl

Manager, Software Engineering

TMTCO

From: Bret Gater [bgater@tmtco]

Sent: Thurs 9/12/2001 07:30 AM

To: Chris Brown [cbrown@tmtco]; test@tmtco; development@tmtco

Cc: marketing@tmtco; customersupport@tmtco

Subject: TMT 1.0 Test Plan

Team,

I have reviewed the test plan TMT-TP-10 Rev. 8 and approve it for use by the test team as written.

Regards,

Bret

Bret Gater

Manager, Software Engineering

TMTCO

Test Design and Development Examples

15

Writing effective test cases consists of two parts, as we saw in Chapter 4. Assuming that a solid requirements definition and a test plan addressing those requirements have been prepared, the development of the test cases consists of:

- Test design
- Development of detailed test procedures
- Verification and debugging of test procedures

This general approach holds true for both manual tests and automated tests; in fact, it is a good idea to develop and debug manual procedures before automating them.

A diagram of the activities that make up test design and development is shown in Figure 15.1. The primary input to the process is the set of test plan documents that were described in Chapter 3. The test plan should give the approach that will be used and the scope of the test effort. It should have defined the test architecture, meaning that at least the test suites should be defined. It should have also defined a set of test configurations around which the tests can be designed. An example of a test plan was presented in the previous chapter.

The output of the design and development activities is a set of reviewed and debugged test cases that are ready to be used in system and acceptance testing. The test cases should map back to the customer requirements. They should provide good coverage by testing at least all of the high priority requirements, and ideally all of the customer requirements. The test cases should provide good code coverage by exercising most if not all the logic paths in the code.

Once a test engineer has the necessary requirements specification and test plan, test design can begin. The test design consists of preparing the following activities:

- Define the test objectives
- Define the inputs needed for each test
- Define the test configuration needed for each test
- Conducting a review of the designs to ensure technical accuracy and that all requirements are tested

More detail about each of these steps is covered in Chapter 4. There are two work products that come from the test design process: a test design document and a test specification document. These two documents can be combined, as they are in the example presented in this chapter.

The purpose of the test design document is to capture the information generated by the test design activities. The test design document could take the form of a spreadsheet, a table generated by a word processor, or a database. It could be an output from an automated tool used to manage requirements and the tests that are generated based on requirements. In the example test procedure specification document presented later in this chapter, the test designs are generated using Microsoft Excel, then put into the specification document using cut-and-paste.

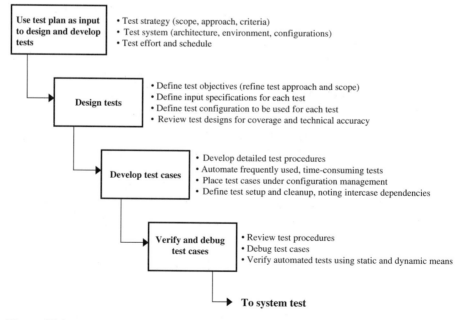

Figure 15.1

Test design and implementation.

The test designs in the example follow closely the format that was specified in Chapter 4, which is repeated here for convenience as Figure 15.2.

The table bears some resemblance to the Requirements Traceability Matrix (RTM) discussed in Chapter 2 (see Figure 2.5). The first two columns in the table should correspond to entries in the RTM, and the remaining columns correspond to the data described in the preceding three sections of this chapter. Due to the similarity in the design tables to the RTM, an example of the RTM has not been included.

Once the test design document has been produced, it needs to be reviewed in the context of its related material: the requirements definition document, the test input definitions, and the test configuration. As mentioned in Chapter 4, the purpose of the review is to perform the following verifications:

- Verify that all requirements are taken into account by the test design document. If a requirement is not being tested, an entry should be present in the RTM or in the test design document stating why the requirement is not covered.
- Verify that each test case has an appropriate set of input test data.
- Verify that each test case has a suitable test configuration, and that the test configurations being used are not redundant.

The test design document serves as a basis for developing detailed test procedures. Following its review, tests can be assigned to engineers on the team for detailed development. Examples of detailed test procedures are included in the Test Procedure Specification document that constitutes the remainder of this chapter.

Requirement Definition ID	System Test Case ID	Test Input	Test Configuration	Test Objective
RD2.2.1	ST2.2.4	TP_Input1.doc	TC2.0	TO2.2.4 Verify that a qualified user can retrieve and view any test plan document that has been created and stored.

Figure 15.2
Example of an entry in the test design document.

The detailed test procedures in the example are written in the form of "action/expected result" pairs. That is, the test engineer is told to take some action, such as clicking on a selection of a menu, and comparing the result of that action to the expected result. If the expected result is obtained, the test passes; otherwise, it fails. To conserve space, the test cases were not written in the test case template format described in Chapter 4. However, to be sure that the ideas behind the test case template are conserved, it is repeated for convenience as Figure 15.3.

The main elements of the test case template are:

- Test case ID—include the version number.

- Owner of test—name or initials of the person that maintains the test (may be different from the original author of the test).

- Date of last revision—this helps you see if the test is current.

- Name of test—a descriptive name of the test that makes it easy to find the test and understand its objective. Nondescriptive names like "xxxLLL0123.tst" are not recommended.

- Location of test—his is the complete path name, including the server.

- Requirement tested—this should be a unique ID that maps to the requirements documents.

- Test objective—a brief, clear statement of what the test should achieve. See "Define Test Objectives" in Chapter 4 for more discussion.

- Test configuration—input specs, output specs, test environment.

- Test setup—this would be similar to the test procedure; describe the action taken by the tester and the expected result. If the setups are automated, the setup might be a statement like: run setupSC03.pl.

- Test procedure—description of the action taken by the tester and the expected result.

- Test case interdependencies—identify any test cases that must be run prior to this one so that the test will begin with a known initial condition.

- Test cleanup—if you have placed the system into an unstable state or corrupted data, here is a chance to undo the damage.

Test Case Information

Test Case ID	SC03 ver3.0
Owner of Test	Jean Douglas
Test Name	Shipping Cost Range
Test Location (path)	TestServer: D:\TestProject\TestSuite\SC03.doc
Date of Last Revision	mm/dd/yy
Requirement Tested	SC101
Test Configuration	ST02
Test Interdependencies	Run test SC01 and its setup before this test.
Test Objective	Verify that valid entries of shipping weight give valid shipping costs and that invalid values of shipping weight give error messages.

Test Procedure

Test Setup	None	N/A

Step	Action	Expected Result	Pass (✓)
1	Click "Shipping Cost" in Main Menu.	Shipping Cost menu is displayed.	✓
2	Enter "101" in shipping weight field.	Error message "Invalid shipping weight" is displayed.	✓
3	Enter "0" in shipping weight field.	Error message "Invalid shipping weight" is displayed.	X
4	Enter "100" in shipping weight field.	Shipping weight is displayed as "100 oz."	✓
5	Enter "1" in shipping weight field.	Shipping weight is displayed as "1 oz."	✓

Test Cleanup	None	N/A

Test Result

Tester: JD	Date of test: mm/dd/yy	Test Result (P/F/B):	F

Notes:

- Test failed in step 3. No error message displayed.
- Bug report BR1011 entered against problem.

Document Identifier: TMT-TPS-10

Figure 15.3
Example test case.

Document Identifier: TMP-TPS-10
Revision: 0.5
Authors: C. Brown
              J. Barnes

Test Management Toolkit

Release 1.0

Test Procedure Specification

Revision History

Version	Date	Author	Description
0.1	08/29/2001	J. Barnes	Test designs
0.2	09/03/2001	Chris Brown	Started building detailed test cases
0.3	09/05/2001	Chris Brown	Completed test cases
0.4	09/06/2001	Chris Brown	Major cleanup based on test case review
0.5	09/10/2001	J. Barnes	Discussion of GUI and Installation tests

Approvals

Department	Name and Title	Approval Date
Development	Suzanna Perl, Manager Software Engineering	09/11/2001
Marketing	Chuck D. Klout, Marketing	09/12/2001
Testing	Bret Gater, Manager Software Testing	09/12/2001

Table of Contents

1 Introduction

The purpose of this document is to detail the test procedures designed to validate the functionality of the Test Management Toolkit. The features addressed in this document are derived from the requirements document entitled Test Management Toolkit, Requirements Definition. The requirements document is identified as: TMT-RD-08, which is located under document control at:

http://www.tmtcointernal.com/usr/www/docstores/design/requirements/TMT-RD-08.doc

Design of the tests are based on the TMT test plan, document TMT-TP-08, which is located at:

http://www.tmtcointernal.com/usr/www/docstores/design/plans/TMT-TP-08.doc

Design of the tests is described in Section 3, and the test procedures are presented in Section 5.

2 Features To Be Tested

The following features will be tested to ensure that the Test Management Toolkit satisfies the requirements specified in the TMT Requirements Definition:

- Requirement 3.1.1 User Interface
- Requirement 3.1.2 Navigation
- Requirement 3.1.3 User Authentication—Client
- Requirement 3.1.4 User Authentication—Administrator
- Requirement 3.1.5 Current Projects
- Requirement 3.1.6 Completed Projects
- Requirement 3.1.7 Create Project
- Requirement 3.1.8 Modify Project
- Requirement 3.1.9 Remove Project
- Requirement 3.1.10 Create Test Case or Suite
- Requirement 3.1.11 Modify Test Case or Suite
- Requirement 3.1.12 Remove Test Case or Suite
- Requirement 3.1.13 Display Test
- Requirement 3.1.14 Display Suite
- Requirement 3.1.15 Run Single Test
- Requirement 3.1.16 Run Suite
- Requirement 3.1.17 Create Run List
- Requirement 3.1.18 Execute Run List
- Requirement 3.1.19 Bug Summary
- Requirement 3.1.20 Test Results—Single Test
- Requirement 3.1.21 Test Results—Suite or Run List

- Requirement 3.1.22 Create Requirements Traceability Matrix
- Requirement 3.1.23 Backup—Test Cases
- Requirement 3.1.24 Backup—Test Suites
- Requirement 3.1.25 Backup Results
- Requirement 3.1.26 Restore Test Cases
- Requirement 3.1.27 Restore Test Suites
- Requirement 3.1.28 Restore Test Results
- Requirement 3.1.29 Export Test Cases
- Requirement 3.1.30 Export—Test Suites
- Requirement 3.1.31 Export—Test Results
- Requirement 3.1.32 Help
- Requirement 3.1.33 Multiuser functionality

3 Test Design

The testing approach includes feature, regression, product installation, backup and restore, and GUI testing. Each type of testing is described in more detail in this section.

The design of the feature tests is shown in Table 3.1. The table shows the requirements numbers, the test Ids, the test data and configuration required to run the test, and states the objective of each test. Some features such as the ability to export data and user help screens have been separated from

Requirement Definition ID	System Test Case ID	Test Input	Test Configuration	Test Objective
RD3.1.1	TC3.1.1	NA	Test Setup #1	Verify that TMT user interface can be accessed by displaying the TMT Main Menu.
RD3.1.2	TC3.1.2	NA	Test Setup #1	Verify that TMT user interface can be accessed by navigating the menu system.
RD3.1.3	TC3.1.3	User accounts	Test Setup #1	Verify user access security on the client with valid and invalid users.
RD3.1.4	TC3.1.4	Admin accounts	Test Setup #1	Verify administration security on the server with valid and invalid administrators.
RD3.1.5	TC3.1.5	Sample project data	Test Setup #1	Verify that an authenticated user can view current projects.
RD3.1.6	TC3.1.6	Sample project data	Test Setup #1	Verify that an authenticated user can view completed projects.
RD3.1.7	TC3.1.7	Sample test info data	Test Setup #1	Verify that an authenticated user can create new projects with the option to select existing tests and test suites.

(continued)

Requirement Definition ID	System Test Case ID	Test Input	Test Configuration	Test Objective
RD3.1.8	TC3.1.8	Sample project data	Test Setup #1	Verify that an authenticated user can modify projects.
RD3.1.9	TC3.1.9	Sample project data	Test Setup #1	Verify that an authenticated user can remove projects.
RD3.1.10	TC3.1.10	Sample project data	Test Setup #1	Verify that an authenticated user can create single test cases or test suites for a project.
RD3.1.11	TC3.1.11	Sample project data	Test Setup #1	Verify that an authenticated user can modify single test cases or test suites for a project.
RD3.1.12	TC3.1.12	Sample project data	Test Setup #1	Verify that an authenticated user can remove single test cases or test suites for a project.
RD3.1.13	TC3.1.13	Sample project data	Test Setup #1	Verify that an authenticated user can display (view) single test cases for a project.
RD3.1.14	TC3.1.14	Sample project data	Test Setup #1	Verify that an authenticated user can display (view) test suites for a project.
RD3.1.15	TC3.1.15	Sample project data	Test Setup #1	Verify that an authenticated user can run (execute) single test cases for a project.
RD3.1.16	TC3.1.16	Sample project data	Test Setup #1	Verify that an authenticated user can run (execute) a suite of test cases for a project.
RD3.1.17	TC3.1.17	Sample project data	Test Setup #1	Verify that a run list can be created for a project.
RD3.1.18	TC3.1.18	Sample project data	Test Setup #1	Verify that a run list can be executed for a project.
RD3.1.19	TC3.1.19	Sample bug data	Test Setup #1	Verify that an authenticated user can display (view) all bugs for a project.
RD3.1.120	TC3.1.20	Sample test results	Test Setup #1	Verify that an authenticated user can display (view) the results of running a test case.
RD3.1.21	TC3.1.21	Sample test results	Test Setup #1	Verify that an authenticated user can display the results of running a suite or run list.
RD3.1.22	TC3.1.22	Sample requirement data	Test Setup #1	Verify that an authenticated user That can create a requirements trace ability matrix for a project containing proper requirements data.

Table 3.1   Feature Test Design

the main body of feature tests because these features may not be available in the first build. These additional features are covered in the section "Additional Features."

3.1 Regression Testing

Since this is the first product release, there is no need to verify that bugs fixed in previous releases are not broken. The concern in this release is that bug fixes made during the system test phase do not break previously working functionality. The regression testing for this test effort will include all test cases.

3.2 Backup and Restore

Backup and restore will be tested on projects, test cases, test suites, and test results. We will backup to physical and logical devices both locally and across a network. Backup across a network is the most likely scenario for the customer, and will therefore receive the most attention.

The design of the backup and restore tests is shown in Table 3.2. The table shows the requirements numbers, the test Ids, the test data and configuration required to run the test, and states the objective of each test.

Requirement Definition ID	System Test Case ID	Test Input	Test Configuration	Test Objective
RD3.1.23	TC3.1.23	Sample test data	Test Setup #1	Verify that an authenticated user can back up a single test case.
RD3.1.24	TC3.1.24	Sample test data	Test Setup #1	Verify that an authenticated user can back up a suite of test cases.
RD3.1.25	TC3.1.25	Sample test data	Test Setup #1	Verify that an authenticated user can back up the results from an individual test.
RD3.1.26	TC3.1.26	Sample backup data	Test Setup #1	Verify that an authenticated user can restore a single test case.
RD3.1.27	TC3.1.27	Sample backup data	Test Setup #1	Verify that an authenticated user can restore a suite of test cases.
RD3.1.28	TC3.1.28	Sample backup data	Test Setup #1	Verify that an authenticated user can restore test results.

Table 3.2   Backup/Restore Test Design

3.3 Additional Features

The design of tests for additional features such as data exporting and help functions as well as testing of multiuser functionality are shown in Table 3.3.

Requirement Definition ID	System Test Case ID	Test Input	Test Configuration	Test Objective
RD3.1.29	TC3.1.29	Sample test data	Test Setup #1	Verify that an authenticated user can export an individual test case.
RD3.1.30	TC3.1.30	Sample test data	Test Setup #1	Verify that an authenticated user can export a suite of tests to an external application.
RD3.1.31	TC3.1.31	Sample test data	Test Setup #1	Verify that an authenticated user can export test results.
RD3.1.32	TC3.1.32	NA	Test Setup #1	Verify that each screen has an assciated help screen that can be opened.
RD3.1.33	TC3.1.33	Sample project and test data	Test Setup #1	Verify that five users can simultaneously exercise TMT features.

Table 3.3   Additional Features Test Design

3.4   Product Installation

Each software build released to the test team will be installed in accordance with the installation procedure that will be used by the customer. However, for each build, the client and server modules will only be installed on a subset of all possible combinations of platforms and operating systems defined in the requirements specification. It will be assumed that successful installation on one UNIX platform implies success on all other UNIX platforms, and the same will be assumed for the different Windows platforms. This approach meets with customer approval (see approval email from marketing).

Specific test cases have not been written for product installation. This is because the test will follow the product installation document that will be supplied to the customer. If the product installs successfully, the feature tests specified in Table 3.1 can be run.

3.5   GUI Testing

The following approach will be taken to test the TMT GUI:
- The graphical user interface will be tested using Netscape Navigator and Microsoft Internet Explorer. A complete inventory will be performed as well as a test of the navigation with both browsers.
- All testing will be performed manually.
- All defects will be tracked to closure using the corporate defect tracking system. This point is intended to address shortfalls in GUI testing identified in various recent post-project assessments.

Specific GUI tests have not been written. This is because the GUI is implicitly used in all the feature tests and backup/restore tests described by Tables 3.1, 3.2, and 3.3. If any of these tests fails, it will be determined if the failure is associated with the GUI or with the functionality presented by the GUI.

4   Test Configuration Information

The test designs in Tables 3.1, 3.2, and 3.3 refer to specific test configurations. Diagrams of Test Setup #1 and Test Setup #2 are given in the TMT Test Plan, document TMT-TP-08.

5   Test Cases

This section presents test procedures for each of the tests designed in Tables 3.1, 3.2, and 3.3. Each test case should be run with Netscape Navigator and then repeated with Microsoft Internet Explorer.

5.1   TC 3.1.1 User Interface

The application server will have a name and an IP address. The application together with the server will be aliased and for the purpose of the test will be called "TMT."

Case 1

Launch Netscape Navigator. Enter the URL "TMT" and press enter.

Expected result:

The Test Management Toolkit Main Menu should be displayed.

5.2   TC 3.1.2 Navigation

Case 1

Launch Netscape Navigator. Enter the URL "TMT" and press enter.

Expected result:

The Test Management Toolkit Main Menu should be displayed.

Case 2

The Menu should contain "buttons" or links to other pages. The main menu should have the following links:

> **Current Projects**
> **Completed Projects**
> **Project Maintenance**
> **Test Case Maintenance**
> **Test Case Execution**
> **Test Results**
> **Utilities**
> **Help**

Expected result: The menu has the labels described above.

Case 3

Select "Current Projects" from the main menu.

Expected result 1:

A screen titled "Current Projects" with the project or projects displayed.

Expected result 2:

An error message indicating there are no current projects (when this test is performed before the creation of projects).
Select the Back Arrow on the browser to go back to the main menu.

Expected result 3:

The user should be returned to the main menu.

Case 4

Select "Completed Projects" from the main menu.

Expected result 1:

A screen titled "Completed Projects" with the project or projects displayed.

Expected result 2:

An error message indicating there are no current projects (when this test is performed before the creation of projects).
Select the Back Arrow on the browser to go back to the Main Menu.

Expected result 3:

The user should be returned to the Main Menu.

Case 5

Select "Project Maintenance" from the main menu.

Expected result 1:

A screen titled Project Maintenance should be displayed.

Expected result 2:

The following options should be available:

Create New Project
Modify Project
Remove Project
Help

Case 6

Select "Create New Project" from the Project Maintenance Menu.

Expected result 1:

A screen prompting the user for the name of the project you wish to create.
Select the Back Arrow on the browser to go back to the Project Maintenance Menu.

Expected result 2:

The user should be taken back to the Project Maintenance Menu.

Case 7

Select "Modify Project" from the Project Maintenance Menu.

Expected result 1:

A screen prompting the user for the name of the project you wish to modify and a list of all available projects.

Expected result 2:

An error message indicating that there are no projects to modify (when this test is performed before the creation of projects).
Select the Back Arrow on the browser to go back to the Project Maintenance Menu.

Expected result 3:

The user should be taken back to the Project Maintenance Menu.

Case 8

Select "Remove Project" from the Project Maintenance Menu.

Expected result 1:

A screen prompting the user for the name of the project you wish to remove and a list of all available projects.

Expected result 2:

An error message indicating that there are no projects to remove (when this test is performed before the creation of projects).
Select the Back Arrow on the browser to go back to the Project Maintenance Menu.

Expected result 3:

The user should be taken back to the Project Maintenance Menu.

Case 9

Select "Help" from the Project Maintenance Menu.

Expected result 1:

A screen detailing all of the Project Maintenance options (future releases will contain context sensitive help with index and search).
Select the Back Arrow on the browser to go back to the Project Maintenance Menu.

Expected result 2:

The user should be taken back to the Project Maintenance Menu.

Case 10

Select "Test Case Maintenance" from the main menu.

Expected result 1:

A screen titled Test Case Maintenance should be displayed.

Expected result 2:

The following options should be available:

> **Create Test Case or Suite**
> **Modify Test Case or Suite**
> **Remove Test Case or Suite**
> **Display Test**
> **Display Suite**
> **Help**

Case 11

Select "Create Test Case or Suite."

Expected result 1:

A screen prompting the user for the name of the project for which you wish to create a new test case or suite. The user can double-click the name of an existing project.

Expected result 2:

The user will be prompted to choose Test or Suite. If the user selected Suite, they will be prompted for the name of the suite. If the user selects Test, then they will be prompted for the name of the test. At this point, the data-entry screen for the particulars of the test will be presented.

Case 12

Select "Modify Test Case or Suite."

Expected result 1:

A screen prompting the user for the name of the project that contains the test case or suite they wish to modify. The user can double-click the name of an existing project.

Expected result 2:

Once the project is identified, the user will be prompted to choose the Test or Suite contained in the project that they which to modify.
If the user selects a Suite, they will be prompted for the name of the suite. The user may double-click on the name of the suite they wish to modify.

Expected result 3:

A screen indicating that there are no suites to modify (when this test is performed before the creation of test suites).

Expected result 4:

If the user selects Test, then they will be prompted for the name of the test they wish to modify. At this point, the data-entry screen for the particulars of the test will be presented.

Expected result 5:

A screen indicating that there are no tests to modify (when this test is performed before the creation of test cases).

Select the Back Arrow on the browser to go back to the Test Case Maintenance Main Menu.

Expected result 6:

The user should be taken back to the Test Case Maintenance Main Menu.

Case 13

Select "Remove Test Case or Suite."

Expected result 1:

A screen prompting the user for the name of the project that contains the test case or suite they wish to remove. The user can double-click the name of an existing project.

Expected result 2:

Once the project is identified, the user will be prompted to choose the test case or suite contained in the project that they which to remove.

If the user selects a suite, they will be prompted for the name of the suite. The user may double-click on the name of the suite they wish to remove.

Expected result 3:

A screen indicating that there are no suites to remove (when this test is performed before the creation of test suites).

Expected result 4:

If the user selects test, then they will be prompted for the name of the test they wish to remove. The user may double-click on the name of the test they wish to remove.

Expected result 5:

A screen indicating that there are no tests to remove (when this test is performed before the creation of test cases).

Select the Back Arrow on the browser to go back to the Test Case Maintenance Menu.

Expected result 6:

The user should be taken back to the Test Case Maintenance Menu.

Case 14

Select Help from the Test Case Maintenance Menu.

Expected result 1:

A screen detailing all available Test Case Maintenance options (future releases will contain context-sensitive help with index and search).

Select the Back Arrow on the browser to go back to the Test Case Maintenance Main Menu.

Case 15

Select Display Test from the Test Case Maintenance Main Menu.

Expected result 1:

The user will be prompted to enter the name of the test they wish to display (view). Below this prompt there will be a list of all available tests. The user will have the option to double-click on the name of the test Case they wish to display.

Expected result 2:

A screen indicating that there are no test cases to display (when this test is performed before the creation of test cases).

Case 16

Select Display Suite from the Test Case Maintenance Main Menu.

Expected result 1:

The user will be prompted to enter the name of the suite they wish to display (view). Below this prompt there will be a list of all available suites. The user will have the option to double-click on the name of the suite they wish to display.

Expected result 2:

A screen indicating that there are no suites to display (when this test is performed before the creation of suites).

Case 17

Select Help from the Test Case Maintenance Menu.

Expected result 1:

A screen detailing all available Test Case Maintenance options (future releases will contain context-sensitive help with index and search).
Select the Back Arrow on the browser to go back to the Test Case Maintenance Main Menu.

Expected result 2:

The user should be taken back to the Test Management Toolkit Main Menu.

Case 18

Select Test Execution from the Test Management Toolkit Main Menu.

Expected result:

A screen titled Test Execution Menu should be displayed. The inventory items for this screen are as follows:

Run Single Test
Create Run List
Execute run List
Help

Case 19

Select Run Single Test from the Test Case Execution Menu.

Expected result 1:

The user will be prompted for the name of the test case they wish to execute. Below this prompt will be a list of all available test cases. The user will have the option of entering the name of the test case they wish to execute or can simply double-click on the name of the test case they want.

Expected result 2:

A screen indicating that there are no test cases created (when this test is performed before the creation of test cases).
Select the back arrow on the browser.

Expected result 3:

The user should be taken back to the Test Execution Main Menu.

Case 20

Select Run Suite from the Test Case Execution Menu.
The user will be prompted for the name of the test suite they wish to execute. Below this prompt will be a list of all available test suites. The user will have the option of entering the name of the test suite they wish to execute or can simply double-click on the name of the test suite they want.

Expected result 2:

A screen indicating that there are no test suites created (when this test is performed before the creation of test suites).
Select the back arrow on the browser.

Expected result 3:

The user should be taken back to the Test Case Execution Menu.

Case 21

Select Create Run List from the Test Case Execution Menu.

Expected result 1:

The user is prompted for the name of the run list they wish to create. Below this prompt will appear a list of available run lists.
Select the back arrow on the browser.

Expected result 2:

The user is returned to the Test Case Execution Menu.

Case 22

Select Execute Run List from the Text Case Execution Menu.

Expected result 1:

The user is prompted for the name of the run list they wish to execute. Below this prompt will appear a list of available run lists.

Select the back arrow on the browser.

Expected result 2:

The user is returned to the Test Case Execution Menu.

Case 23

Select Help from the Test Case Execution Menu.

Expected result 1:

A screen detailing all available Test Execution options will be displayed (future releases will contain context-sensitive help with index and search).
Select the Back Arrow on the browser to go back to the Test Execution Main Menu.
Select the Back Arrow on the browser once again.

Expected result 2:

The user should be taken back to the Test Management Toolkit Main Menu.

Case 24

Select Test Results from the Test Management Toolkit Main Menu.

Expected results:

The user will be taken to a screen titled Test Results Menu.

Case 25

Select Bug Summary from the Test Results Menu.

Expected results 1:

This is a higher-level bug view so the user will be prompted for the name of the project they wish to examine. Below this prompt will be displayed a list of all available projects both current and completed.
The user will have the option to enter the name of the project they wish to examine or can simply double-click on the name of the project they want.
If the user selects a past or present project they will be taken to a screen that will show the number of tests, passes, fails, blocked and times taken and the date run.

Expected results 2:

A screen indicating that there are no test results available (when this test is performed before the execution or completion of a project).
Select the Back Arrow on the browser to go back to the Test Results Menu.

Expected results 3:

The user should be taken back to the Test Results Menu.

Case 26

Select Single Test from the Test Results Menu.

Expected results 1:

The user will be prompted for the name of the test case they wish to examine. Below this prompt will be a list of all available test cases that have been run. The user will have the option to enter the name of the test or can simply double-click on the test case they wish to examine.

Expected results 2:

A screen indicating that there are no test results available (when this test is performed before the execution or completion of a test case).
Select the Back Arrow on the browser to go back to the Test Results Menu.

Expected results 3:

The user should be taken back to the Test Results Menu.

Case 27

Select Test Results Suite from the Test Results Menu.

Expected results 1:

The user will be prompted for the name of the test suite they wish to examine. Below this prompt will be a list of all available test suites that have been run. The user will have the option to enter the name of the suite or can simply double-click on the test suite they wish to examine.

Expected results 2:

A screen indicating that there are no test results available (when this test is performed before the execution or completion of a test suite).
Select the Back Arrow on the browser to go back to the Test Results Menu.

Expected results 3:

The user should be taken back to the Test Results Menu.
Select the Back Arrow once again to be taken back to the Test Management Toolkit Main Menu.

Expected result 4:

The user should be taken back to the Test Management Toolkit Main Menu.

Case 28

Select Utilities from the Test Management Toolkit Main Menu.

Expected result:

The user should be taken to a screen titled Utilities Main Menu with the following contents:

Create Trace Matrix
Backup Project
Backup Test Suite
Backup Test Case
Backup Test Results
Restore Project
Restore Test Suite

> **Restore Test Case**
> **Restore Test Results**
> **Export Project**
> **Export Test Suite**
> **Export Test Case**
> **Export Test Results**
> **Help**

Case 29

Select Create Trace Matrix from the Utilities Main Menu.

Expected result 1:

The user will be prompted for the name of a requirements document to parse. Below this prompt, the user will be presented with a list of all available requirements documents. The user will have the option to enter the name of the requirements document or can simply double-click on the name of the document they wish to process. Once the user selects the documents the traceabilty matrix will be created on the screen. This can be sent to a printer or exported as a spreadsheet.

Expected result 2:

The user will be given an error message indicating that there are no requirement documents in the default directory. This would be the case if no documents have been created in or moved to the required directory.
Select the Back Arrow on the browser to return to the Utilities Main Menu.

Expected result 3:

The user should be taken back to the Utilities Main Menu.

Case 30

Select Backup Project from the Utilities Main Menu.

Expected result 1:

The user will be taken to a screen titled Project Backup. The user will be prompted for the name of the project they wish to back up. Below this prompt will be a list of all available projects. The user will have the option to enter the name of the project they wish to back up or can simply double-click on the name of the project they want. Once the project is selected the user will be asked where they want the backup placed.

Expected result 2:

An error will be displayed indicating that there are no projects to back up. This would be the case if no projects had yet been created.
Select the Back Arrow in the browser to return to the Utilities Main Menu.

Expected result 3:

The user should be taken back to the Utilities Main Menu.

Case 31

<u>Select Backup Suite from the Utilities Main Menu.</u>

Expected result 1:

The user will be taken to a screen titled Suite Backup. The user will be prompted for the name of the Suite they wish to back up. Below this prompt will be a list of all available suites. The user will have the option to enter the name of the suite they wish to back up or can simply double-click on the name of the suite they want. Once the project is selected the user will be asked where they want the backup placed.

Expected result 2:

An error will be displayed indicating that there are no suites to back up. This would be the case if no suites had yet been created.
Select the Back Arrow in the browser to return to the Utilities Main Menu.

Expected result 3:

The user should be taken back to the Utilities Main Menu.

Case 32

<u>Select Backup Test Case from the Utilities Main Menu.</u>

Expected result 1:

The user will be taken to a screen titled Test Case Backup. The user will be prompted for the name of the test case they wish to back up. Below this prompt will be a list of all available test cases. The user will have the option to enter the name of the test case they wish to back up or can simply double-click on the name of the test case they want. Once the test case is selected the user will be asked where they want the backup placed.

Expected result 2:

An error will be displayed indicating that there are no test cases to back up. This would be the case if no test cases had yet been created.
Select the Back Arrow in the browser to return to the Utilities Main Menu.

Expected result 3:

The user should be taken back to the Utilities Main Menu.

Case 33

<u>Select Backup Test Results from the Utilities Main Menu.</u>

Expected result 1:

The user will be taken to a screen titled Test Results Backup. The user will be prompted for the name of the test results they wish to back up. Below this prompt will be a list of all available test results. The user will have the option to enter the name of the test results they wish to back up or can simply double-click on the name of the test results they want. Once the Test Results is selected, the user will be asked where they want the backup placed.

Expected result 2:

An error will be displayed indicating that there are no test results to back up. This would be the case if no test results had yet been created. This would indicate either the project was never run or no results had yet been posted.

Select the Back Arrow in the browser to return to the Utilities Main Menu.

Expected result 3:

The user should be taken back to the Utilities Main Menu.

Case 34

Select Restore Project from the Utilities Main Menu.

Expected result 1:

The user will be taken to a screen titled Restore Project. The user will be prompted for the name of the backup to restore. Once the backup is selected the user will be asked where they want the backup restored. A default will be provided.

Select the Back Arrow in the browser to return to the Utilities Main Menu.

Expected result 2:

The user should be taken back the Utilities Main Menu.

Case 35

Select Restore Suite from the Utilities Main Menu.

Expected result 1:

The user will be taken to a screen titled Restore Suite. The user will be prompted for the name of the backup to restore. Once the backup is selected the user will be asked where they want the backup restored. A default will be provided.

Select the Back Arrow in the browser to return to the Utilities Main Menu.

Expected result 2:

The user should be taken back to the Utilities Main Menu.

Case 36

Select Restore Test Case from the Utilities Main Menu.

Expected result 1:

The user will be taken to a screen titled Restore Test Case. The user will be prompted for the name of the backup to restore. Once the backup is selected the user will be asked where they want the backup restored. A default will be provided.

Select the Back Arrow in the browser to return to the Utilities Main Menu.

Expected result 2:

The user should be taken back to the Utilities Main Menu.

Case 37

Select Restore Test Results from the Utilities Main Menu.

Expected result 1:

The user will be taken to a screen titled Restore Test Results. The user will be prompted for the name of the backup to restore. Once the backup is selected the user will be asked where they want the backup restored. A default will be provided.
Select the Back Arrow in the browser to return to the Utilities Main Menu.

Expected result 2:

The user should be taken back to the Utilities Main Menu.

Case 38

Select Export Project from the Utilities Main Menu.

Expected result 1:

The user will be taken to a screen titled Export Project. The user will be prompted for the name of the project they wish to export. Below this prompt will be a list of all available projects. The user will have the option to enter the name of the project they wish to export can simply double-click on the name of the project they want. Once the project is selected, the user will be asked where they want the exported project placed.

Expected result 2:

An error will be displayed indicating that there are no projects to export. This would be the case if no projects had yet been created.
Select the Back Arrow in the browser to return to the Utilities Main Menu.

Expected result 3:

The user should be taken back to the Utilities Main Menu.

Case 39

Select Export Test Case from the Utilities Main Menu.

Expected result 1:

The user will be taken to a screen titled Export Test Case. The user will be prompted for the name of the test case they wish to export. Below this prompt will be a list of all available test cases. The user will have the option to enter the name of the test case they wish to export can simply double-click on the name of the test case they want. Once the project is selected, the user will be asked where they want the exported project placed.

Expected result 2:

An error will be displayed indicating that there are no test cases to export. This would be the case if no test cases had yet been created.
Select the Back Arrow in the browser to return to the Utilities Main Menu.

Expected result 3:

The user should be taken back to the Utilities Main Menu.

Case 40

Select Export Test Suite from the Utilities Main Menu.

Expected result 1:

The user will be taken to a screen titled Export Test Suite. The user will be prompted for the name of the test suite they wish to export. Below this prompt will be a list of all available test suites. The user will have the option to enter the name of the test suite they wish to export can simply double-click on the name of the test suite they want. Once the test suite is selected, the user will be asked where they want the exported test suite placed.

Expected result 2:

An error will be displayed indicating that there is no test suite to export. This would be the case if no test suites had yet been created.
Select the Back Arrow in the browser to return to the Utilities Main Menu.

Expected result 3:

The user should be taken back to the Utilities Main Menu.

Case 41

Select Export Test Results from the Utilities Main Menu.

Expected result 1:

The user will be taken to a screen titled Export Test Results. The user will be prompted for the name of the test results they wish to export. Below this prompt will be a list of all available test results. The user will have the option to enter the name of the test results they wish to export can simply double-click on the name of the test results they want. Once the test results are selected, the user will be asked where they want the exported test results placed.

Expected result 2:

An error will be displayed indicating that there are no test results to export. This would be the case if no test results had yet been created.
Select the Back Arrow in the browser to return to the Utilities Main Menu.

Expected result 3:

The user should be taken back to the Utilities Main Menu.

Case 42

Select Help from the Utilities Main Menu.

Expected result 1:

A screen detailing all available Utilities options will be displayed (future releases will contain context-sensitive help with index and search).

Select the Back Arrow on the browser to go back to the Utilities Main Menu.
Select the Back Arrow on the browser once again to return to the Test Management Toolkit Main Menu.

Expected result 2:

The user should be taken back to the Test Management Toolkit Main Menu.

5.3 TC 3.1.3 User Authentication—Client

For the purpose of this test the following accounts have been created:

User ID	Password
Admin	Admin
User1	password
User2	password
User3	password
User4	password
User5	password

Case 1

When the user enters TMT in the URL bar of the browser and hits enter, they will be challenged to enter their user name and password. Initiate the login process by entering the alias TMT in the URL and press enter.

Expected result 1:

A box will open in the center of the screen requesting User Name and Password.
Enter "User9" and press enter with no password.

Expected result 2:

The error message "You entered an invalid Username or Password" will be displayed.
Enter "User9" for the user name and for the password enter "password".

Expected result 3:

The error message "You entered an invalid Username or Password" will be displayed.
Enter "User1" for the user name and "pickle" for the password.

Expected result 4:

The error message "You entered an invalid Username or Password" will be displayed.
Enter "User1" for the user name and "password" for the password.

Expected result 5:

The Test Management Toolkit Main Menu will be displayed.

5.4 TC 3.1.4 User Authentication—Administrator

Client Side
Case 1

When the user enters TMT in the URL bar of the browser and hits enter, they will be challenged to enter their user name and password. Initiate the login process by entering the alias TMT in the URL and press enter.

Expected result 1:

A box will open in the center of the screen requesting Username and Password.
<u>Enter "User9" and press enter with no password.</u>

Expected result 2:

The error message "You entered an invalid Username or Password" will be displayed.
<u>Enter "User9" for the user name and for the password enter "password".</u>

Expected result 3:

The error message "You entered an invalid Username or Password" will be displayed.
<u>Enter "User1" for the user name and "pickle" for the password.</u>

Expected result 4:

The error message "You entered an invalid Username or Password" will be displayed.
<u>Enter "Admin" for the user name and "Admin" for the password.</u>

Expected result 5:

The Test Management Toolkit Main Menu will be displayed.

Server Side

Case 2

When the user enters TMTADMIN in the URL bar of the browser and hits enter, they will be challenged to enter their user name and password. Initiate the login process by entering the alias TMTADMIN in the URL and press enter.

Expected result 1:

A box will open in the center of the screen requesting Username and Password.
<u>Enter "User9" and press enter with no password.</u>

Expected result 2:

The error message "You entered an invalid Username or Password" will be displayed.
<u>Enter "User9" for the user name and for the password enter "password".</u>

Expected result 3:

The error message "You entered an invalid Username or Password" will be displayed.
<u>Enter "User1" for the user name and "pickle" for the password.</u>

Expected result 4:

The error message "You entered an invalid Username or Password" will be displayed.
<u>Enter "Admin" for the user name and "Admin" for the password.</u>

Expected result 5:

The Test Management Toolkit Administration Menu will be displayed.

5.5   TC 3.1.5 Current Projects

Once logged in to the system the user will have the option to view current projects. This is initiated by selecting Current Project from the Test Management Toolkit Main Menu.

Case 1

Select Current Project from the Test Management Toolkit Main Menu.

Expected result:

A screen titled Current Projects will be displayed. The project names will be associated with the total numbers of tests, passes, and fails, blocked and completed tests. The time remaining and total time will be displayed if the tests have been run before and the data collected.

5.6   TC 3.1.6 Completed Projects

Once logged in to the system the user will have the option to view completed projects. This is initiated by selected Completed Project from the Test Management Toolkit Main Menu.

Case 1

Select Completed Projects from the Test Management Toolkit Main Menu.

Expected result:

A screen titled Completed Projects will be displayed. The project names will be associated with the total numbers of tests, passes, and fails, blocked and completed tests. The total time will be displayed in hours and minutes.

5.7   TC 3.1.7 Create Project

Once logged in to the system the user will have the option to create new projects. This is initiated by selecting Create Project from the Project Maintenance menu.

Case 1

Select Project Maintenance from the Test Management Toolkit Main Menu.

Expected result 1:

A screen titled Project Maintenance menu will be displayed.
Select Create Project from the Project Maintenance menu.

Expected result 2:

The user will be prompted for a name for the new project. Once the user enters the name for the new project, the user will then be prompted to add individual test cases or test suites.
The user will see a list of all available test cases and test suites.
The user will have the option to select any or all of the test cases or suites.
Once the user has finished the selection process, they will have the option to Save the project or Cancel the action.
The user will be returned to the Project Maintenance menu no matter which option they choose.

5.8   TC 3.1.8 Modify Project

Once logged into the system the user will have the option to modify projects. This is initiated by selecting Modify Project from the Project Maintenance menu.

Case 1

Select Project Maintenance from the Test Management Toolkit Main Menu.

Expected result 1:

A screen titled Project Maintenance menu will be displayed.
Select Modify Project from the Project Maintenance menu.

Expected result 2:

The user will be prompted for the name of the project they wish to modify.
The user will also be presented a list of all available projects.
The user will have the option to enter the name of the project they wish to modify or can simply double-click on the name of the project they wish to modify.
Once the user has made changes to the project they will have the option to Save the changes or Cancel the action.
The user will be returned to the Project Maintenance menu no matter which option they choose.

5.9   TC 3.1.9 Remove Project

Once logged into the system the user will have the option to remove projects. This is initiated by selecting Remove Project from the Project Maintenance menu.

Case 1

Select Project Maintenance from the Test Management Toolkit Main Menu.

Expected result 1:

A screen titled Project Maintenance menu will be displayed.
Select Remove Project from the Project Maintenance menu.

Expected result 2:

The user will be prompted for the name of the project they wish to remove.
The user will also be presented a list of all available projects.
The user will have the option to enter the name of the project they wish to remove or can simply double-click on the name of the project they wish to remove.
Once the user has made changes to the project, they will have the option to Save the changes or Cancel the action.
The user will be returned to the Project Maintenance menu no matter which option they choose.

5.10   TC 3.1.10 Create Test Case or Suite

Once logged into the system the user will have the option to create test cases. This is initiated by selecting Create Test Case or Suite from the Test Case Maintenance menu.

Case 1

Select Test Case Maintenance from the Test Management Toolkit Main Menu.

Expected result 1:

A screen titled Test Case Maintenance will be displayed.
Select Create Test Case or Suite

Expected result 2:

The user will be prompted to choose to create a Test Case or Test Suite.
Once the user has decided which to create they will be prompted for a name for the test. Once the user supplies the name for the test or suite they will be taken to the data-entry screen.

Expected result 3:

The data entry form will be displayed.
Once the user fills in all of the test information they will have the option to Save the information or Cancel the action.
They will be taken back to the Test Case Maintenance menu regardless of which option they choose.

5.11 TC 3.1.11 Modify Test Case or Suite

Once logged into the system the user will have the option to modify test cases. This is initiated by selecting Modify Test Case or Suite from the Test Case Maintenance menu.

Case 1

Select Test Case Maintenance from the Test Management Toolkit Main Menu.

Expected result 1:

A screen titled Test Case Maintenance will be displayed.
Select Modify Test Case or Suite

Expected result 2:

The user will be prompted for a name of the Test Case or Suite they wish to modify. A list of all available Test Cases and Suites will be displayed. The user will have the option of entering the name of the test case or suite they wish to modify or can simply double-click on the name of the test they wish to modify.

Expected result 3:

Once the user makes the desired changes, they will have the option to Save the information or Cancel the action.
They will be taken back to the Test Case Maintenance menu regardless of which option they choose.

5.12 TC 3.1.12 Remove Test Case or Suite

Once logged into the system the user will have the option to remove test cases. This is initiated by selecting Remove Test Case or Suite from the Test Case Maintenance menu.

Case 1

Select Test Case Maintenance from the Test Management Toolkit Main menu.

Expected result 1:

A screen titled Test Case Maintenance will be displayed.
Select Remove Test Case or Suite

Expected result 2:

The user will be prompted for a name of the test case or suite they wish to remove. A list of all available test cases and suites will be displayed. The user will have the option of entering the name of the test case or suite they wish to remove or can simply double-click on the name of the test they wish to remove.

Expected result 3:

Once the user makes the desired changes, they will have the option to Save the information or Cancel the action.
They will be taken back to the Test Case Maintenance menu regardless of which option they choose.

5.13   TC 3.1.13 Display Test

Once logged into the system the user will have the option to display (view) test cases. This is initiated by selecting Display Test Case or Suite from the Test Case Maintenance menu.

Case 1

Select Test Case Maintenance from the Test Management Toolkit Main Menu.

Expected result 1:

A screen titled Test Case Maintenance will be displayed.
Select Display Test Case or Suite

Expected result 2:

The user will be prompted for a name of the test case or suite they wish to display. A list of all available test cases and suites will be displayed. The user will have the option of entering the name of the test case or suite they wish to display or can simply double-click on the name of the test they wish to display.
The test case details will be displayed (read-only) in the same format as the data was entered.
When the user is finished, they will have the option to return to the Test Case Maintenance menu.

5.14   TC 3.1.14 Display Suite

Once logged into the system the user will have the option to display (view) test suites. This is initiated by selecting Display Test Case or Suite from the Test Case Maintenance menu.

Case 1

Select Test Case Maintenance from the Test Management Toolkit Main menu.

Expected result 1:

A screen titled Test Case Maintenance will be displayed.
Select Display Test Case or Suite

Expected result 2:

The user will be prompted for a name of the test suite they wish to display. A list of all available test suites will be displayed. The user will have the option of entering the name of the test case or suite they wish to display or can simply double-click on the name of the suite they wish to display.
The test cases that make up the suite will be displayed. The user will have the option of double-clicking on the test cases and viewing the details for that test case.
When the user is finished, they will have the option to return to the Test Case Maintenance menu.

5.15   TC 3.1.15 Run Single Test

Once logged into the system the user will have the option to run test cases. This is initiated by selecting Run Single Test from the Test Execution menu.

Case 1

Select Test Case Execution from the Test Management Toolkit Main Menu.

Expected result 1:

A screen titled Test Case Execution will be displayed.
Select Run Single Test

Expected result 2:

The user will be prompted for a name of the test case they wish to run. A list of all available test cases will be displayed. The user will have the option of entering the name of the test case or suite they wish to run or can simply double-click on the name of the test they wish to run.

Expected result 3:

The detailed steps to the test case will be displayed. The user will perform the tasks as described in the test details. The user will select one of the following:
The test passed, failed, or is blocked and cannot be run.
Once the user selects one of the results they will be taken back to the Test Execution menu.

5.16   TC 3.1.16 Run Suite

Once logged into the system the user will have the option to run test suites. This is initiated by selecting Run Suite from the Test Execution menu.

Case 1

Select Test Case Execution from the Test Management Toolkit Main Menu.

Expected result 1:

A screen titled Test Case Execution will be displayed.
Select Run Suite

Expected result 2:

The user will be prompted for a name of the test suite they wish to run. A list of all available test suites will be displayed. The user will have the option of entering the name of the test suite they wish to run or can simply double-click on the name of the suite they wish to run.

Expected result 3:

The detailed steps of the test cases contained in the suite will be displayed. The user will perform the tasks as described in the test details. The user will select one of the following for each test:
The test passed, failed, or is blocked and cannot be run.
Suite results are cumulative. All of the tests in the suite must pass for the suite to pass. If one test fails then the suite fails.
Once the user selects one of the results they will be taken back to the Test Execution menu.

5.17   TC 3.1.17 Bug Summary

This is a project-level view of the status of the test effort. Once the user is logged into the system, they have the option to view the Bug Summary. This is initiated by selecting Test Results from the Test Management Toolkit Main Menu.

Case 1

Select Test Results from the Test Management Toolkit Main Menu.

Expected results 1:

A screen titled Test Results will be displayed.
Select Bug Summary from the Test Results menu.

Expected results 2:

The user will be prompted for the name of the project they wish to examine. A list of all current and completed projects will be displayed. The user will have the option of entering the name of the project they wish to examine or can simply double-click the name of the project they want.
The project name and the total number for tests passes, fails, and blocked will be displayed. Each will be displayed as a percentage of the total number for each.
The user will have the option to return to the Test Results menu when finished.

5.18   TC 3.1.18 Test Results—Single Test

This is a test case-level view of the status of the test effort. Once the user is logged into the system, they have the option to view test results for a single test. This is initiated by selecting Test Results from the Test Management Toolkit Main Menu.

Case 1

Select Test Results from the Test Management Toolkit Main Menu.

Expected results 1:

A screen titled Test Results will be displayed.
Select Single Test from the Test Results menu.

Expected results 2:

The user will be prompted for the name of the test case they wish to examine. A list of all available test case results will be displayed. The user will have the option of entering the name of the test case they wish to examine or can simply double-click the name(s) of the test case they want.

The test case name and the result as pass, fail, and blocked will be displayed. The user will have the option to return to the Test Results menu when finished.

5.19   TC 3.1.19 Test Results—Suite or Run List

This is a suite-level view of the status of the test effort. Once the user is logged into the system, they have the option to view test results for a suite or run list. This is initiated by selecting Test Results from the Test Management Toolkit Main Menu.

Case 1

Select Test Results from the Test Management Toolkit Main Menu.

Expected results 1:

A screen titled Test Results will be displayed.
Select Suite or Run List from the Test Results menu.

Expected results 2:

The user will be prompted for the name of the test suite or run list they wish to examine. A list of all available test suite and run list results will be displayed. The user will have the option of entering the name of the test suite or run list they wish to examine or can simply double-click the name of the test suite or run list they want.

The test suite or run list name and the result as pass, fail, and blocked will be displayed. The user will have the option to return to the Test Results menu when finished.

5.20   TC 3.1.20 Create Requirements Traceability Matrix

Once the user is logged into the system, they will have the option to produce a Requirements Traceabilty Matrix. This is initiated by selecting the Create Requirements Traceabilty Matrix option from the Utility menu.

Case 1

Select Utility from the Test Management Toolkit Main Menu.

Expected result 1:

A screen titled Utility Menu will be displayed.
Select Create Requirements Traceabilty Matrix from the Utilities menu.

Expected result 2:

The user will be prompted for the name of a requirements document to parse.
The location for these documents is hard-coded. On the same screen that prompts the user for the name of the document, there will be a list of all available requirement documents. The user has the

option to enter the name of the document they want or can simply double-click on the name of the file they want.

Expected result 3:

Once the user has selected the file they want a new window will open that contains the requirements for the product/project in a column. There will be rows of columns for the placement of the corresponding test cases that prove the requirement. This is a read-only form suitable for printing and manual entry. The user will have the choice of sending this to the printer or exporting it to a spreadsheet.
Once the user has chosen one or more of these options they will be taken back to the Utilities menu.

5.21   TC 3.1.21 Backup—Test Case

Once the user is logged into the system, they will have the option to back up individual test cases. This is initiated by selecting the Backup Test Case option from the utilities menu.

Case 1

Select Utility from the Test Management Toolkit Main Menu.

Expected result 1:

A screen titled Utility Menu will be displayed.
Select Backup – Test Case from the Utilities Menu.

Expected result 2:

The user will be prompted for the name of the test case they want to back up. There will also be displayed a list of all available test cases. They will have the option to manually enter the name of the test case they want to back up or can simply double-click the name of the test case they want to back up.

Expected result 3:

Once the user has picked the test case they wish to back up, they will be asked for a target location. This will vary by system but could be a floppy disk, local hard drive, network drive, or tape unit. This could also be a CDR or CDRW. They will also have the option to specify a different name for the backup. Default will be the name of the test case.
Once the user has finished, they will be taken back to the Utilities menu.

5.22   TC 3.1.22 Backup—Test Suite

Once the user is logged into the system, they will have the option to back up individual test suites. This is initiated by selecting the Backup Test Suite option from the Utilities Menu.

Case 1

Select Utility from the Test Management Toolkit Main Menu.

Expected result 1:

A screen titled Utility Menu will be displayed.
Select Backup—Test Suite from the Utilities Menu.

Expected result 2:

<u>The user will be prompted for the name of the test suite they want to back up.</u> There will also be displayed a list of all available test suites. They will have the option to manually enter the name of the test suite they want to back up or can simply double-click the name of the test suite they want to back up.

Expected result 3:

Once the user has picked the test suite they wish to back up, they will be asked for a target location. This will vary by system but could be a floppy disk, local hard drive, network drive, or tape unit. This could also be a CDR or CDRW. They will also have the option to specify a different name for the backup. Default will be the name of the test suite.
Once the user has finished, they will be taken back to the Utilities Menu.

5.23   TC 3.1.23 Backup Results

Once the user is logged into the system, they will have the option to back up individual test results. This is initiated by selecting the Backup Results option from the Utilities Menu.

Case 1

<u>Select Utility from the Test Management Toolkit Main Menu.</u>

Expected result 1:

A screen titled Utility Menu will be displayed.
<u>Select Backup—Results from the Utilities Menu.</u>

Expected result 2:

<u>The user will be prompted for the name of the results they want to back up.</u> There will also be displayed a list of all available test results. They will have the option to manually enter the name of the test results they want to back up or can simply double-click the name of the test results they want to back up.

Expected result 3:

Once the user has picked the test results they wish to back up, they will be asked for a target location. This will vary by system but could be a floppy disk, local hard drive, network drive, or tape unit. This could also be a CDR or CDRW. They will also have the option to specify a different name for the backup. Default will be the name of the test results.
Once the user has finished, they will be taken back to the Utilities Menu.

5.24   TC 3.1.24 Restore Test Case

Once the user is logged into the system, they will have the option of restoring test cases back to the original location. This is initiated by selecting Restore Test Case from the Utilities Menu.

Case 1

<u>Select Utility from the Test Management Toolkit Main Menu.</u>

Expected result 1:

A screen titled Utilities Menu will be displayed.

Select Restore Test Case from the Utilities Menu.

Expected result 2:

The user will be prompted for the location from which to restore. This will vary by system but could be a floppy disk, local hard drive, network drive, or tape unit. This could also be a CDR or CDRW. Once the location is established the user will be prompted for the name of the archived test case that the user wishes to restore. A list of all available archived test cases will be displayed. The user will have the option to manually enter the name of the test case they wish to restore or can simply double-click on the name of the archived file they wish to restore.

Once the user has chosen the location and file, the utility will restore the test case to its original location. The user will then be returned to the Utilities Menu.

5.25   TC 3.1.25 Restore Test Suite

Once the user is logged into the system, they will have the option of restoring test suites back to the original location. This is initiated by selecting Restore Test Suite from the Utilities Menu.

Case 1

Select Utility from the Test Management Toolkit Main Menu.

Expected result 1:

A screen titled Utilities Menu will be displayed.
Select Restore Test Suite from the Utilities Menu.

Expected result 2:

The user will be prompted for the location from which to restore.
This will vary by system but could be a floppy disk, local hard drive, network drive, or tape unit. This could also be a CDR or CDRW. Once the location is established the user will be prompted for the name of the archived test case that the user wishes to restore. A list of all available archived test cases will be displayed. The user will have the option to manually enter the name of the test suite they wish to restore or can simply double-click on the name of the archived suite they wish to restore.

Once the user has chosen the location and file, the utility will restore the test suite to its original location. The user will then be returned to the Utilities Menu.

5.26   TC 3.1.26 Restore Test Results

Once the user is logged into the system, they will have the option of restoring test results back to the original location. This is initiated by selecting Restore Test Results from the Utilities Menu.

Case 1

Select Utility from the Test Management Toolkit Main Menu.

Expected result 1:

A screen titled Utilities Menu will be displayed.
Select Restore Test Results from the Utilities Menu.

Expected result 2:

The user will be prompted for the location from which to restore.

This will vary by system but could be a floppy disk, local hard drive, network drive, or tape unit. This could also be a CDR or CDRW. Once the location is established the user will be prompted for the name of the archived test results that the user wishes to restore. A list of all available archived test results will be displayed. The user will have the option to manually enter the name of the test results they wish to restore or can simply double-click on the name of the archived results they wish to restore.

Once the user has chosen the location and file, the utility will restore the test results to its original location. The user will then be returned to the Utilities Menu.

5.27   TC 3.1.27 Export Test Case

Once the user is logged into the system, they will have the option to export a test case for use in other applications. This is initiated by selecting Export Test Case from the Utilities Menu.

Case 1

Select Utility from the Test Management Toolkit Main Menu.

Expected result 1:

A screen titled Utilities Menu will be displayed.

Select Export Test Case from the Utilities Menu.

Expected result 2:

The user will be prompted for the name of the test case they wish to export. Below this there will be displayed all available test cases. The user will have the option of manually entering the name of the test case they wish to export or they can simply double-click on the name of the test case they wish to export.

Once the user has selected the name of the test case they wish to export they will be prompted for a target drive. This will vary by system but could be a floppy disk, local hard drive, network drive, or tape unit. This could also be a CDR or CDRW.

Once the user has provided the name of the test case and the target location they will click "Continue" and the file will be exported. The user will be returned to the Utilities Menu when complete.

5.28   TC 3.1.28 Export—Test Suite

Once the user is logged into the system, they will have the option to export Test Suite for use in other applications. This is initiated by selecting Export Test Suite from the Utilities Menu.

Case 1

Select Utilities from the Test Management Toolkit Main Menu.

Expected result 1:

A screen titled Utilities Menu will be displayed.
Select Export Test Suite from the Utilities Menu.

Expected result 2:

The user will be prompted for the name of the test suite they wish to export. Below this there will be displayed all available test suites. The user will have the option of manually entering the name of the test suite they wish to export or they can simply double-click on the name of the test suite they wish to export.

Once the user has selected the name of the test suite they wish to export they will be prompted for a target drive. This will vary by system but could be a floppy disk, local hard drive, network drive, or tape unit. This could also be a CDR or CDRW.

Once the user has provided the name of the test case and the target location they will click "Continue" and the file will be exported. The user will be returned to the Utilities Menu when complete.

5.29   TC 3.1.29 Export—Test Results

Once the user is logged into the system, they will have the option to export Test Results for use in other applications. This is initiated by selecting Export Test Results from the Utilities Menu.

Case 1

Select Utilities from the Test Management Toolkit Main Menu.

Expected result 1:

A screen titled Utilities Menu will be displayed.
Select Export Test Results from the Utilities Menu.

Expected result 2:

The user will be prompted for the name of the test results they wish to export. Below this there will be displayed all available test results. The user will have the option of manually entering the name of the test results they wish to export or they can simply double-click on the name of the test results they wish to export.

Once the user has selected the name of the test results they wish to export they will be prompted for a target drive. This will vary by system but could be a floppy disk, local hard drive, network drive, or tape unit. This could also be a CDR or CDRW.

Once the user has provided the name of the test results and the target location they will click "Continue" and the file will be exported. The user will be returned to the Utilities Menu when complete.

5.30   TC 3.1.30 Help

Each screen will have its own unique Help screen. The help screen will provide detailed information about all of the options available to the user on each menu. The help will include examples, syntax, warnings, and other useful information. In future versions there will be an integrated Help subsystem that is global for the entire application. This will include context-sensitive help, index, and will be searchable. For now the hard-coded help is what we have.

Case 1

Select Help from any menu.

Expected results:

The screen will have an entry for each menu option. The spelling and syntax will be correct.

5.31   TC 3.1.31 Multiuser Functionality

We will attempt to synchronize the activities to stress certain subsystems. We will follow a carefully choreographed sequence or actions designed to stress certain components. October 8th will be the date of the test. To minimize the impact of work-related network observances we will start the test at 6:00 P.M.

Case 1

6:00 P.M. User1, User2, User3, User4, and User5 will create project, test cases, and test suites in no particular order.

Expected result 1:

It is expected that each user be able to perform the activities without noticeable degradation.

Case 2

6:15 P.M. User1, User2, User3, User4, and User5 will enter test results for test cases and suites in no particular order.

Expected result 2:

It is expected that each user be able to perform the activities without noticeable degradation.

Case 3

6:30 P.M. User1, User2, User3, User4, and User5 will query the system for project level, test suite, and test Case results.

Expected result 3:

It is expected that each user be able to perform the activities without noticeable degradation.

Case 4

6:45 P.M. User1, User2, User3, User4, and User5 will send the results of the queries to the printer.

Expected result 4:

It is expected that each user be able to perform the activities without noticeable degradation.
Pass for this test will be the ability to perform the above activities without crashing the systems. We will add the needed wording to attempt to describe the potential degradation of the system's performance. Fail for this test will be the inability to perform the activities defined. If there is a problem, we will characterize the failure by starting with a single user and adding one at a time until such time that the system fails. It is expected that all of the above activities should be performed with no noticeable degradation.

References

Brown, Chris *Test Management Toolkit, Requirements Definition*. Document TMT-RD-08, which is located under document control at:

http://www.tmtcointernal.com/usr/www/docstores/design/requirements/TMT-RS-08.doc

Brown, Chris, and J. Barnes. *Test Management Toolkit, Test Plan*. Document TMT-TP-08, which is located under document control at:

http://www.tmtcointernal.com/usr/www/docstores/design/plans/TMT-TP-08.doc

Appendix 1—Acronyms

API—Application Programming Interface
ASCII—American Standard Code for Information Interchange
CDR—Compact Disc Recordable
CDRW—Compact Disc Rewriteable
HTML—Hypertext Markup Language
ISO—International Organization for Standardization
PPC—Power PC
RISC—Reduced Instruction Set Computing
SQL—Structured Query Language
SPARC—Scalable Processor Architecture
TCL—Tool Command Language
TMT—Test Management Toolkit
X86—Referring to the Intel line of processors

Appendix 2—Definition of Terms

Not applicable.

Approvals 3—Email Approvals

From: Chuck D. Klout [cdklout@tmtco]

Sent: Wed 9/11/01 2:23 PM

To: Chris Brown [cbrown@tmtco]; test@tmtco; development@tmtco

Cc: marketing@tmtco; customersupport@tmtco

Subject: TMT 1.0 Test Procedures

Team,

I have reviewed the Test Procedures Specification document, TMT-TPS-10 Rev. 5, and believe that it addresses the requirements for testing this release. I approve the document as written. The limited testing of platforms and operating systems has been discussed with several customers and is approved for the first release.

Thanks,

Chuck

Chuck D. Klout
Director, Marketing
TMTCO

From: Suzie Perl [sperl@tmtco]

Sent: Thurs 9/12/2001 09:30 AM

To: Chris Brown [cbrown@tmtco]; test@tmtco; development@tmtco

Cc: marketing@tmtco; customersupport@tmtco

Subject: TMT 1.0 Test Plan

All,

My team and I have reviewed the test procedures TMT-TPS-10 Rev. 5 for the first release of TMT and approve it for use as written.

Regards,

Suzie

Suzanna Perl

Manager, Software Engineering

TMTCO

From: Bret Gater [bgater@tmtco]

Sent: Thurs 9/12/2001 07:30 AM

To: Chris Brown [cbrown@tmtco]; test@tmtco; development@tmtco

Cc: marketing@tmtco; customersupport@tmtco

Subject: TMT 1.0 Test Plan

Team,

I have reviewed the test procedures TMT-TPS-10 Rev. 5 and approve it for use by the test team as written.

Regards,

Bret

Bret Gater

Manager, Software Engineering

TMTCO

Example System Test Summary Report

16

Chapter 5 gave a detailed discussion of the system test phase of product development. It was noted that the system test phase is like game day for an athlete or show time for a stage actor. A lot of planning and preparation has been done, the stage is set, and it's time to produce. An overview of the system test phase is shown in Figure 16.1.

As shown in Figure 16.1, the first task of system testing is to verify that everything is in place and ready to go. This can be accomplished by applying the set of system test entry criteria that was defined in the test plan. If the entry criteria are satisfied, system testing can begin.

Testing consists of running the tests called for in the test plan. As tests are run, bugs are discovered, bug reports are written, and bug-tracking data is entered into a bug-tracking database. A continuous dialog is maintained between the development and test teams by holding bug reviews.

Once testing is underway, it is important to communicate test status to all members of the product development team and to management. This communication is accomplished through periodic test status reports and by preparing a test summary report at the end of the system test phase. This chapter provides an example of a summary report prepared at the end of system testing of the fictitious Test Management Toolkit (TMT) product.

As discussed more fully in Chapter 5, the purpose of the test summary report is to address the following:

- What has been tested
- How the actual test activities deviated from the test plan
- How the schedule and effort compared to the test plan
- What bugs were found
- What bugs remain open at the end of testing and how they will be handled

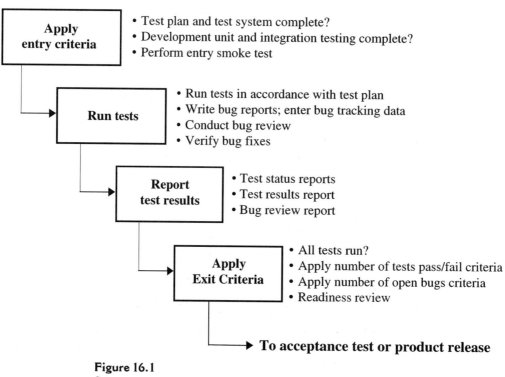

Figure 16.1
System testing overview.

The test summary report does not need to contain the detailed test results for each test run but it can refer to those results if they have been compiled and archived. The collection and archiving of all test results is one of the benefits of having a commercial test management tool. If the tool rolls up all the results into a single document, then that document can be referred to by the test summary report.

The remainder of this chapter consists of an example test summary report. Note that the example contains elements that may be used in other reports. Specifically, the following items may be extracted for other reporting needs:

- Test Status Report
- Open Bugs Report
- Summary of Bugs Found by Severity

Document Identifier: TMT-TSR-10
Revision: 0.2
Authors: J. Barnes

Test Management Toolkit

Release 1.0

Test Summary Report

Revision History

Version	Date	Author	Description
0.1	12/02/2001	J. Barnes	Test results write-up
0.2	12/03/2001	J. Barnes	**Modifications based on review**

Approvals

Department	Name and Title	Approval Date
Testing	Bret Gater, Manager Software Testing	12/03/2001

Table of Contents

1   Introduction

The purpose of this document is to report the results obtained during system test of the Test Management Toolkit Release 1.0 product.

The tests were conducted in accordance with the TMT Test Plan document:

http://www.tmtcointernal.com/usr/www/docstores/design/plans/TMT-TP-10.doc

The features addressed in this document are derived from the requirements document entitled: Test Management Toolkit, Requirements Definition, document:

http://www.tmtcointernal.com/usr/www/docstores/design/requirements/TMT-RD-10.doc

2   Summary of Test Results

Three complete test cycles were run for the TMT product, with composite test coverage of 100%. On the final test run, 95% of the tests run passed, and there were no catastrophic bugs found. On the basis of these results, the test team recommends that the product be approved for release.

A summary of the bugs remaining open at the end of testing is given in Table 2.2.

A cumulative summary of bugs found during the testing of the TMT product is shown in Table 2.3. The bug summary is presented as a bar chart in Figure 3.1.

Test Suite	# Tests	# Pass	# Fail	# Not Run	% Run
3.1.1 User Interface	20	18	2	0	100%
3.1.2 Navigation	25	24	1	0	100%
3.1.3 User Authentication—Client	12	12	0	0	100%
3.1.4 User Authentication— Administrator	12	12	0	0	100%
3.1.5 Current Projects	15	15	0	0	100%
3.1.6 Completed Projects	15	15	0	0	100%
3.1.7 Create Project	12	12	0	0	100%
3.1.8 Modify Project	12	12	0	0	100%
3.1.9 Remove Project	12	12	0	0	100%
3.1.10 Create Test Case or Suite	15	15	0	0	100%
3.1.11 Modify Test Case or Suite	15	15	0	0	100%
3.1.12 Remove Test Cases or Suites	15	15	0	0	100%
3.1.13 Display Test	10	10	0	0	100%
3.1.14 Display Suite	10	10	0	0	100%
3.1.15 Run Single Test	10	10	0	0	100%
3.1.16 Run Suite	10	10	0	0	100%
3.1.17 Bug Summary	12	11	1	0	100%
3.1.18 Test Results – Single	15	15	0	0	100%
3.1.19 Test Results – Suite	15	15	0	0	100%
3.1.20 Create Requirements Traceability Matrix	10	9	1	0	100%
3.1.21 Backup—Test Case	12	12	0	0	100%
3.1.22 Backup—Test Suite	12	12	0	0	100%
3.1.23 Backup Results	12	12	0	0	100%
3.1.24 Restore Test Case	12	12	0	0	100%
3.1.25 Restore Test Suite	12	12	0	0	100%
3.1.26 Restore Test Results	12	12	0	0	100%
3.1.27 Export Test Case	12	11	1	0	100%
3.1.28 Export—Test Suite	12	11	1	0	100%
3.1.29 Export—Test Results	12	11	1	0	100%
3.1.30 Help	18	18	0	0	100%
3.1.31 Multiuser Functionality	10	10	0	0	100%
	408	400	8	0	100%

Table 2.1   Test Status Report

Test Management Toolkit **Open Bugs Summary**						
Date of review: 30-11-01						
Attendees:						
Bug ID	**State**	**Severity**	**Date Found**	**Bug Summary**		**Action**
B3.1.1A	Assigned	Minor	15-10-01	Label for the field "Test Identifier" misspelled. *Tset Identifier		Fix for 1.0
B3.1.1B	Assigned	Minor	16-10-01	Label for the field "Test Name" misspelled. *Test Nnme		Fix for 1.0
B3.1.2	Assigned	Minor	17-10-01	Menu Label "Utility Menu" missing		Fix for 1.0
B3.1.16	Assigned	Minor	20-10-01	Fields Pass and Fail overlap		Fix for 1.0
B3.1.19	Assigned	Minor	22-10-01	When selected creates Trace Matrix in the root directory. Should be in /Trace		Fix for 1.0
B3.1.26	Assigned	Major	01-11-01	When Exporting "Test Case", data is corrupted		Defer to 1.1
B3.1.27	Assigned	Major	01-11-01	When Exporting "Test Suite", data is corrupted		Defer to 1.1
B3.1.28	Assigned	Major	01-11-01	When Exporting "Test Result", data is corrupted		Defer to 1.1
Notes: B3.1.26, B3.1.27, and B3.1.28– This problem will require an architecture change that needs to be deferred to the next release.						

Table 2.2   Open Bugs Report

	Week 1	**Week 2**	**Week 3**	**Week 4**	**Week 5**	**Week 6**
Catastrophic	5	6	4	4	2	0
Major	6	7	5	4	3	0
Minor	25	32	18	7	3	2

Table 2.3   Summary of Bugs Found During Testing

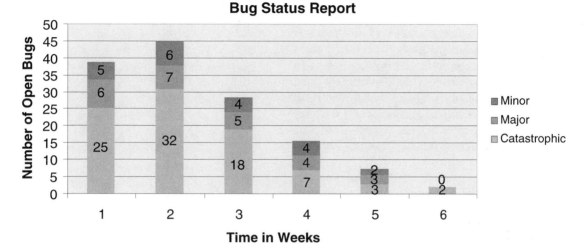

Figure 3.1   Summary of Bugs Found by Severity

3   Features Tested

The following features were tested to ensure that the Test Management Toolkit satisfies the requirements specified in the TMT Requirements Specification:

- Requirement 3.1.1 User Interface
- Requirement 3.1.2 Navigation
- Requirement 3.1.2 User Authentication—Client
- Requirement 3.1.3 User Authentication—Administrator
- Requirement 3.1.4 Current Projects
- Requirement 3.1.5 Completed Projects
- Requirement 3.1.6 Create Project
- Requirement 3.1.7 Modify Project
- Requirement 3.1.8 Remove Project
- Requirement 3.1.9 Create Test Case or Suite
- Requirement 3.1.10 Modify Test Case or Suite
- Requirement 3.1.11 Remove Test Cases or Suites
- Requirement 3.1.12 Display Test
- Requirement 3.1.13 Display Suite
- Requirement 3.1.14 Run Single Test
- Requirement 3.1.15 Run Suite
- Requirement 3.1.16 Bug Summary
- Requirement 3.1.17 Test Results—Single
- Requirement 3.1.18 Test Results—Suite

- Requirement 3.1.19 Create Requirements Traceability Matrix
- Requirement 3.1.20 Backup—Test Case
- Requirement 3.1.21 Backup—Test Suite
- Requirement 3.1.22 Backup Results
- Requirement 3.1.23 Restore Test Case
- Requirement 3.1.24 Restore Test Suite
- Requirement 3.1.25 Restore Test Results
- Requirement 3.1.26 Export Test Case
- Requirement 3.1.27 Export—Test Suite
- Requirement 3.1.28 Export—Test Results
- Requirement 3.1.29 Help
- Requirement 3.1.30 Multiuser Functionality

Tests were run on all features with the results described earlier in Section 2.

4   Features Not Tested

The following is a list of functionality and/or system configurations that were not tested.
- The Web Server (Apache or IIS) was not tested directly.
- Expansive client server stress testing was not conducted. Multiuser functionality was tested with five real users, which was specified as a minimal multiuser configuration.

5   Deviations from the Test Plan

There were no deviations from the test plan.

6   Adherence to Schedule

The test effort was completed on schedule, although there were minor deviations in the start and stop dates of the individual test cycles.

7   References

C. Brown, *Test Management Toolkit, Requirements Definition, Release 1.0*. Document TMT-RD-10, which is located under document control at:
   http://www.tmtcointernal.com/usr/www/docstores/design/requirements/TMT-RS-10.doc
C. Brown and J. Barnes, *Test Management Toolkit, Release 1.0, Test Plan*. Document TMT-TP-10, which is located under document control at:
   http://www.tmtcointernal.com/usr/www/docstores/design/plans/TMT-TP-10.doc
C. Brown and J. Barnes, *Test Management Toolkit, Release 1.0, Test Procedure Specification*. Document TMT-TPS-10, which is located under document control at:
   http://www.tmtcointernal.com/usr/www/docstores/design/specs/TMT-TPS-10.doc

Appendix 1—Acronyms

Not applicable.

Appendix 2—Definition of Terms

Not applicable.

Appendix 3—Email Approvals

From: Bret Gater [bgater@tmtco]

Sent: Thurs 9/10/2001 07:30 AM

To: J. Barnes [jbarnes@tmtco]; test@tmtco; development@tmtco

Cc: marketing@tmtco; customersupport@tmtco

Subject: TMT 1.0 Test Summary

Team,

I have reviewed the test summary report TMT-TSR-10, Rev 2, and approve it as accurately representing the test results. The test team recommends that TMT Release 1.0 be approved for release. Congratulations to the development and test teams for a job well done!

Regards,

Bret

Bret Gater

Manager, Software Engineering

TMTCO

Credits

p. 5 From *Verification and Validation of Modern Software-Intensive Systems* by Schulmeyer & MacKenzie. © 2000. Reprinted by permission of Pearson Education, Inc., Upper Saddle River, NJ.

pp. 6–7, 73 From *Rapid Development: Taming Wild Software Schedules* by Steve McConnell. Copyright 1996. Reproduced by permission of Microsoft Press. All rights reserved.

pp. 10, 40 From *Software Engineering: Theory and Practice*, 2nd ed., by S. Pfleeger. © 2001. Material is reprinted by permission of Pearson Education, Inc.

pp. 25, 66, 134, 139 From *Software Engineering Economics* by Boehm, B.W. © 1981. Reprinted by permission of Pearson Education, Inc., Upper Saddle River, NJ.

p. 28 From *Software Engineering: A Practitioner's Approach*, 4th ed., by R. Pressman. © 1997 McGraw-Hill, Inc.

p. 31 Information regarding the content and format of requirements documents is reprinted with permission from IEEE Std. 830-1993: *The IEEE Guide to Software Requirements Specifications*. Copyright 1993 by IEEE.

p. 36 From *Software Testing in the Real World: Improving the Process*, by E. Kit. © 1995 Addison-Wesley, Inc.

p. 55 From *Automated Software Testing* (pp. 32–38) by E. Dustin, J. Rashka, & J. Paul. © 1999 Addison Wesley Longman, Inc. Reprinted by permission of Pearson Education, Inc.

p. 61 Material excerpted from *Managing the Test Process* by permission of the author, Rex Black; second edition in press by John Wiley & Sons, Inc., ISBN 0-471-22398-0.

p. 70 From *The Mythical Man-Month* (p. 18) by F. Brooks, Jr. © 1999 Addison Wesley Longman, Inc. Reprinted by permission of Pearson Education, Inc.

pp. 77, 80 Information regarding the content and format of test documents is reprinted with permission from IEEE Std. 829-1983: *IEEE Standard for Software Test Documentation*. Copyright 1983 by IEEE.

pp. 214–215 Information regarding defect reporting is reprinted with permission from IEEE Std. 1044-1993: *IEEE Standard for Software Anomalies*, Copyright 1993 by IEEE.

Index